Business Essentials

Supporting HNC/HND and Foundation degrees

Company and Commercial Law

Course Book

In this July 2010 edition:

- Full and comprehensive coverage of the key topics within the subject

- Activities, examples and quizzes

- Practical illustrations and case studies

- Index

- Fully up to date as at July 2010

- Coverage mapped to the Edexcel Guidelines for the HNC/HND in Business

BPP
LEARNING MEDIA

First edition September 2007
Second edition July 2010

Published ISBN 9780 7517 6839 8
(previous edition 9780 7517 4485 9)
e-ISBN 9780 7517 7676 8

British Library Cataloguing-in-Publication Data
A catalogue record for this book is available from
the British Library

Published by
BPP Learning Media Ltd
BPP House, Aldine Place
London W12 8AA

www.bpp.com/learningmedia

Printed in the United Kingdom

Your learning materials, published by BPP
Learning Media Ltd, are printed on paper
sourced from sustainable, managed forests.

Contents

Introduction

BPP Learning Media's **Business Essentials** range is the ideal learning solution for all students studying for business-related qualifications and degrees. The range provides concise and comprehensive coverage of the key areas that are essential to the business student.

Qualifications in business are traditionally very demanding. Students therefore need learning resources which go straight to the core of the topics involved, and which build upon students' pre-existing knowledge and experience. The BPP Learning Media Business Essentials range has been designed to meet exactly that need.

Features include:

- In-depth coverage of essential topics within business-related subjects

- Plenty of activities, quizzes and topics for discussion to help retain the interest of students and ensure progress

- Up-to-date practical illustrations and case studies that really bring the material to life

- A glossary of terms and full index

In addition, the contents of the chapters are comprehensively mapped to the **Edexcel Guidelines**, providing full coverage of all topics specified in the HND/HNC qualifications in Business.

Each chapter contains:

- An introduction and a list of specific study objectives
- Summary diagrams and signposts to guide you through the chapter
- A chapter roundup, quick quiz with answers and answers to activities

Other titles in this series:

Generic titles

Economics

Accounts

Business Maths

Mandatory units for the Edexcel HND/HNC in Business qualification

Unit 1	Business Environment
Unit 2	Managing Financial Resources and Decisions
Unit 3	Organisations and Behaviour
Unit 4	Marketing Principles
Unit 5	Business Law
Unit 6	Business Decision Making
Unit 7	Business Strategy
Unit 8	Research Project

Pathways for the Edexcel HND/HNC in Business qualification

Units 9 and 10	Finance: Management Accounting and Financial Reporting
Units 11 and 12	Finance: Auditing and Financial Systems and Taxation
Units 13 and 14	Management: Leading People and Professional Development
Units 15 and 16	Management: Communications and Achieving Results
Units 17 and 19	Marketing and Promotion
Units 18 and 20	Marketing and Sales Strategy
Units 21 and 22	Human Resource Management
Units 23 and 24	Human Resource Development and Employee Relations
Units 25-28	Company and Commercial Law

For more information, or to place an order, please call 0845 0751 100 (for orders within the UK) or +44(0)20 8740 2211 (from overseas), e-mail learningmedia@bpp.com, or visit our website at www.bpp.com/learningmedia.

If you would like to send in your comments on this Course Book, please turn to the review form at the back of this book.

Study Guide

This Course Book includes features designed specifically to make learning effective and efficient.

- Each chapter begins with a summary diagram which maps out the areas covered by the chapter. There are detailed summary diagrams at the start of each main section of the chapter. You can use the diagrams during revision as a basis for your notes.

- After the main summary diagram there is an introduction, which sets the chapter in context. This is followed by learning objectives, which show you what you will learn as you work through the chapter.

- Throughout the Course Book, there are special aids to learning. These are indicated by symbols in the margin:

Signposts guide you through the book, showing how each section connects with the next.

Definitions give the meanings of key terms. The *glossary* at the end of the book summarises these.

Activities help you to test how much you have learned. An indication of the time you should take on each is given. Answers are given at the end of each chapter.

Topics for discussion are for use in seminars. They give you a chance to share your views with your fellow students. They allow you to highlight holes in your knowledge and to see how others understand concepts. If you have time, try 'teaching' someone the concepts you have learned in a session. This helps you to remember key points and answering their questions will consolidate your knowledge.

Examples relate what you have learned to the outside world. Try to think up your own examples as you work through the Course Book.

Chapter roundups present the key information from the chapter in a concise format. Useful for revision.

- The wide **margin** on each page is for your notes. You will get the best out of this book if you interact with it. Write down your thoughts and ideas. Record examples, question theories, add references to other pages in the Course Book and rephrase key points in your own words.

- At the end of each chapter, there is a **chapter roundup** and a **quick quiz** with answers. Use these to revise and consolidate your knowledge. The chapter roundup summarises the chapter. The quick quiz tests what you have learned (the answers often refer you back to the chapter so you can look over subjects again).

- At the end of the Course Book, there is an index.

Part A

The Law of Agency

Chapter 1 :
AGENCY

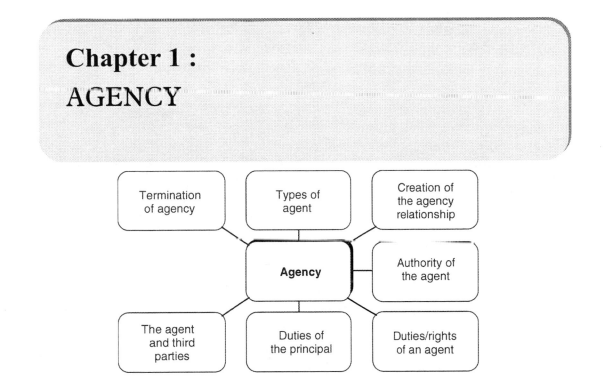

Introduction

Agency has a variety of important business applications, particularly for those acting on behalf of companies or partnerships. In this chapter we examine how the agency relationship arises and how the agent's authority is acquired and defined.

'Agents' are employed by 'principals' to perform tasks which the principals cannot or do not wish to perform themselves, typically because the principal does not have the time or expertise to carry out the task.

If businessmen did not employ the services of factors, brokers, estate agents, *del credere* agents, bankers and auctioneers, they would be weighed down by the need to make contracts with, or dispose of property to, third parties and would probably achieve very little else.

In normal circumstances the agent discloses to the other party that he (the agent) is acting for a principal whose identity is also disclosed. However, this is not necessarily the case. If a person enters into a contract apparently on his own account as principal but in fact as agent on behalf of a principal, the doctrine of the undisclosed principal determines the position of the parties (and this is described below).

We also consider the legal position, rights and duties of the third party with whom the agent has contracted. Finally, we examine termination of agency.

Your objectives

In this chapter you will learn about the following:

    (a)   A definition of agency and some examples of different types of agent

    (b)   The ways in which an agent may have, or appear to have, authority to act on behalf of a principal

    (c)   The rights and duties of agent and principal

    (d)   The liability of the agent to third parties

    (e)   Termination of the agency relationship

NOTES

1   AGENCY

Agency is a very important feature of modern commercial life.

Definition

> **Agency**: a relationship which exists between two legal persons (the principal and the agent) in which the agent has legal authority to deal with a third party on behalf of the principal.

In practice, there are many examples of agency relationships which you are probably accustomed to, although you may be unaware that they are examples of the laws of agency. The following are some examples of agency relationships:

(a)   *Partners.* A **key feature** of partnerships is that the partners are agents of each other.

(b)   *Promoters.* Promoters are **agents of an unincorporated company** (that is, one which has not yet been formed).

(c)   *Factors.* A factor is a type of 'mercantile agent' (or person whose ordinary business is to sell goods, or consign them for sale, or to buy goods, or to raise money on the security of goods: Factors Act 1889). His principal gives him implied authority to enter into such transactions and usually gives him possession of the goods.

(d)   *Brokers.* There are many kinds of broker in different trades. Any broker is essentially a middleman or intermediary who arranges contracts in return for commission or brokerage.

(e)   *Estate agents.* An estate agent is an intermediary who seeks to find a buyer of a house or other property belonging to his principal. This profession is regulated by the Estate Agents Act 1979 which among other things requires an estate agent to give notice of his charges to his principal and to insure against liability for loss of any deposit paid by a buyer to the agent as stakeholder etc pending completion of the sale. There are also regulations governing provision of information, education and professional conduct.

(f)   *Del credere agents.* A *del credere* agent undertakes (in return for extra commission) responsibility for due payment of the contract price by persons whom he introduces to his principal. He undertakes that a buyer will pay for goods delivered to him but not that he will accept the goods. It is a form of financial support which is convenient where the other party and his creditworthiness is unknown to the principal.

(g)   *Bankers.* The duties owed by a bank to its customer are similar to those owed by an agent, but the **banker-customer contract** is **not** one of **agency** in the normal run of things, such as in the operation of a current account. Banks **often do act as agents** for their customers: examples are where they undertake to arrange the buying and selling of shares or where they offer advice on other investments, such as life assurance and pensions.

(h)   *Auctioneers.* An auctioneer is an agent who is authorised to sell property at auction, usually in a room or place to which the public has access. He is the agent of the vendor. But when the sale has been completed he is also the agent of the buyer for the purpose of making a written record of the sale. This serves to provide the written evidence (against both parties) which is required to make enforceable a contract for the sale of land (although obviously auctioneers are involved in many sales other than just those of land).

(i) *Commercial agents.* A commercial agent is an independent self-employed agent who has a continuing authority in connection with the sale or purchase of goods.

- An independent agent is not a partner, director or employee. He or she is self-employed.

- A continuing authority means that one-off transactions, such as a one-off sale at auction or a one-off sale by an estate agent, are excluded.

- An individual or a company can be a commercial agent.

- The business of the principal must be the sale or purchase of goods.

Activity 1   **(10 minutes)**

Explain whether or not an insurance broker is an agent. If so, who is the principal?

2 CREATION OF THE AGENCY RELATIONSHIP

The relationship of principal and agent is usually created by mutual consent. The consent (with one exception, discussed below) need not be formal nor expressed in a written document. **It is usually an 'express' agreement**, even if it is created in an informal manner. Agency may be created in a number of different ways:

- Consent
- Necessity
- Estoppel or 'holding out'
- Ratification

Capacity

The agent does not form contracts with third parties on his own behalf and so it is not necessary that he has full contractual capacity. The principal must have **full contractual capacity**.

2.1 Agency by consent

Consent may be express or implied. When an agent is authorised by his principal to carry out a certain task or act in a certain capacity, he is said to have **actual authority.**

Express agency

Usually an agent is **expressly appointed** by the principal to undertake certain transactions. Very often the appointment is oral, but the informality of the appointment does not make any difference to the fact that agency is created.

NOTES

In **commercial transactions** it is usual to appoint an agent **in writing**, so that the terms and extent of the relationship are set down to avoid misunderstanding. As noted above, this is not essential.

Implied agency

Two persons may by their relationship or their conduct to each other **imply** an agreement between them that one is the agent of the other. For example, an employee's duties may include making contracts for his employer, say by ordering goods on his account, the employee is, by implied agreement, the agent of the employer for this purpose. An agent authorised in this way is said to have **implied authority** (see below).

This implied authority may fall into one of three categories. These will be examined in more detail in the section on authority of the agent below.

2.2 Agency by necessity

Agency may arise by operation of law in situations of pressing need or emergency.

Definition

> '**Agency of necessity** arises by operation of law in certain cases where a person is faced with an emergency in which the property or interests of another person are in imminent jeopardy and it becomes necessary, in order to preserve the property or interests, to act for that person without his authority'.
>
> *(Bowstead on Agency)*

The principle of agency of necessity is of restricted application. Its origins can be found in mercantile law, and in shipping law in particular. A number of conditions must be satisfied for agency of necessity to arise:

(a)   The agent must have **no practical way of contacting** the principal to obtain the principal's instructions.

Springer v Great Western Railway 1921
The facts: A carrier discovered that a consignment of fruit was going bad. He sold it locally instead of delivering it to its destination.

Decision: He was not an agent of necessity as he could have obtained instructions from the owner of the fruit.

(b)   The actions of the agent must be as a result of some **pressing need for action**, usually an emergency of some kind, involving for example perishable goods or starving animals.

Prager v Blatspiel, Stamp and Heacock Ltd 1924
The facts: An agent of a fur merchant bought skins on behalf of his principal, but could not send them to the principal because of the prevailing wartime conditions. Being unable to communicate with the principal, he sold the skins.

Decision: He was not an agent of necessity. He could have stored the skins until after the war since they were not likely to drop in value.

(c)   The agent must have acted ***bona fide*** (in good faith). This means that he must act in the interests of the principal rather than in his own interests.

Sachs v Miklos 1948

The facts: M agreed to store furniture which belonged to S. After a considerable time had elapsed M needed the storage space for his own use. He tried to contact S to get the furniture removed but was unable to trace S. M then sold the furniture. S sued M for conversion and M pleaded agency of necessity in making the sale.

Decision: There was no agency of necessity since no emergency had arisen and M had sold the furniture for his own convenience. If M's house had been destroyed by fire and the furniture left in the open M would then have been justified in selling it.

(d) The **action** taken by the agent must have been **reasonable and prudent in the circumstances**.

Great Northern Railway v Swaffield 1874
The facts: S delivered a horse to a railway for transport to another station but failed to collect it on arrival as agreed. The railway claimed from S the cost of feeding and stabling the horse.

Decision: The railway's claim would be upheld.

It should be noted that cases of necessity have usually involved carriers. Modern **telecommunications mean that agency of necessity is unlikely to arise**.

2.3 Agency by estoppel (or 'holding out')

Agency by estoppel arises when the words or conduct of the principal **give to a third party** the **impression** that the agent's authority is greater than it really is and the third party, as a result, acts upon this. This introduces the concept of ostensible, or **apparent, authority**.

For example, if Paul leads Tina to believe that Adam is Paul's agent, and Tina deals with Adam on that basis, Paul is bound by the contract with Tina which Adam has made on his behalf. This situation may arise in the following circumstances.

- When Adam, who dealt with Tina as Paul's authorised agent, continues to do so after his authority as agent of Paul has been terminated but Tina is unaware of it

- When Adam, to Paul's knowledge, enters into transactions with Tina as if Adam were Paul's agent and Paul fails to inform Tina that Adam is not Paul's agent

- When Adam, who dealt with Tina as Paul's authorised agent, acts beyond the scope of the authority actually conferred upon him by Paul but Tina is unaware of any restriction on his authority.

Agency by estoppel can only arise where the **conduct** of the **apparent principal** creates it. Agency does not arise by estoppel if it is the 'agent' who 'holds himself out' as agent, not the 'principal': *Armagas Ltd v Mundogas SA, The Ocean Frost 1986*.

2.4 Ratification by the principal

In certain circumstances the relationship of principal and agent can be created or extended with **retrospective effect**. If A makes a contract on behalf of P at a time when A has no authority from P, the contract may later be ratified by P and then has retrospective effect to the time when A made the contract.

NOTES

Ratification only validates past acts of the purported agent. It gives no authority for the future: *Irvine v Union Bank of Australia 1877.*

Method of ratification

Ratification may be express or implied. Express ratification is usually fairly clear-cut. Implied ratification must be deduced from the conduct of the 'principal' and from the circumstances of the case. In particular, the principal **may only ratify if the following conditions are satisfied.**

(a)   He does so within a **reasonable time** after the agent has made the contract for him.

(b)   He ratifies the **whole contract** and not merely parts of it. Otherwise the effect would be that a new contract would exist which the third party had not intended to enter into.

(c)   He **communicates a sufficiently clear intention of ratifying**, either by express words or by conduct such as refusing to return goods purchased for him by an agent who lacked authority (mere passive inactivity does not amount to ratification).

(d)   He is either **fully informed** of the terms of the contract **or** is **prepared to ratify whatever** the agent may have **agreed** to on his behalf.

Who may ratify?

Only a principal may ratify the acts of the purported agent. There are **four conditions** of ratification.

(i)   *Existence of principal*

The principal must have been in existence at the time of the agent's act.

(ii)   *Legal capacity of the principal*

In order to be able to ratify a contract, a **principal must have the legal capacity** to make the contract himself, both at the time the act was carried out and at the time of the purported ratification.

Boston Deep Sea Fishing and Ice Co Ltd v Farnham 1957
The facts: The appellants, a company of trawler owners, took control of a French trawler lying in an English port when France fell to the German army. The French company purported to ratify their acts.

Decision: Since, at the time the acts were done, the French company was an alien enemy at common law, it could not have carried out the acts itself. It did not therefore have legal capacity and could not ratify.

(iii)   *Principal capable of being ascertained*

An **unnamed** principal should be **capable of being ascertained**, or identified, at the time that the unauthorised actions occurred.

(iv)   *Agent acting on behalf of principal*

If the agent has not revealed that he was acting as an agent, in other words that there is an **undisclosed** principal, then the **undisclosed principal will not be able to ratify.**

The effects of ratification

Ratification, as we have seen, has retrospective effect. Once ratification has taken place, the following situation arises:

- The principal may sue or be sued by the third party
- The agent no longer has any liability to the third party
- The agent is no longer liable for exceeding his authority
- The principal is liable to pay the agent reasonable remuneration

---

Activity 2   **(15 minutes)**

Anna purports to act as Pat's agent. Tim offers to buy goods from Anna, who accepts this offer. Can Tim revoke his offer before Pat ratifies the acceptance?

3   AUTHORITY OF THE AGENT

The **contract** made by the agent is **binding** on the principal and the other party **only if** the **agent was acting within the limits of his authority** from his principal.

In analysing the limits of an agent's authority, three distinct sources of authority can be identified:

- Actual express authority
- Actual implied authority
- Ostensible or apparent authority

3.1   Actual express authority

This is authority explicitly given by the principal to the agent to make a particular contract.

The extent of the agent's express authority will depend on the construction of the words used on his appointment. If the appointment is in writing, then the document will need to be examined. If it is oral, then the scope of the agent's authority will be a matter of evidence.

If the agent contracts outside the scope of his express (actual) authority, he may be liable to the principal and the third party for breach of warranty of authority.

3.2   Actual implied authority

Where there is no express authority, authority may be **implied** from the nature of the agent's activities or from what is usual in the circumstances, except insofar as such implied authority would be contrary to authority expressly given. **Implied authority** falls into one of three categories.

(a)   The basis of **implied incidental authority** is that the principal, by appointing an agent to act in a particular capacity, gives him authority to make those contracts which are a necessary or normal incident of the agent's activities. Commonly, incidental authority applies to subordinate acts necessary for the execution of express actual authority. It supplements the express authority, and may cover such things as the authority to advertise when given express authority to sell goods.

(b)   **Implied customary authority** is that which an agent operating in a particular market or business usually has.

(c)   **Implied usual authority** is that which an agent who occupies a particular position or engages in a particular trade usually has.

Between principal and agent the latter's express authority is paramount; the agent cannot contravene the principal's express instructions by claiming that he had implied authority for acting in the way he did.

But as far as **third parties** are concerned, they are entitled to assume that the agent has implied usual authority unless they know to the contrary.

Watteau v Fenwick 1893

The facts: The owner of a hotel (F) employed the previous owner H to manage it. F forbade H to buy cigars on credit but H did buy cigars from W. W sued F who argued that he was not bound by the contract, since H had no actual authority to make it, and that W believed that H still owned the hotel.

Decision: It was within the usual authority of a manager of a hotel to buy cigars on credit and F was bound by the contract (although W did not even know that H was the agent of F) since his restriction of usual authority had not been communicated.

Express and implied authority are sometimes referred to together as **actual authority**. This distinguishes them from **ostensible** or **apparent authority** , which is discussed next in this section.

Definition

> **Actual authority** is the authority conferred on an agent which arises from a legal relationship between principal and agent created by a consensual agreement to which they alone are parties.

3.3   Ostensible or apparent authority

The ostensible (or apparent) authority of an agent is that which his principal represents to other persons (with whom the agent deals) that he has given to the agent. As a result an agent with limited **express** or **implied** authority can be held in practice to have a more extensive authority.

Ostensible authority (unlike implied authority) is not restricted to what is usual and incidental. The principal may expressly or by inference from his conduct confer on the agent any amount of ostensible or apparent authority.

For example, a partner has considerable but limited implied authority merely by virtue of being a partner. If, however, the other partners allow him to exercise a greater authority than is implied, they represent that he has it and they are bound by the contracts which he makes within the limits of this ostensible authority.

It is not necessary that the agreement is in the form of a contract.

Freeman & Lockyer v Buckhurst Park Properties (Mangal) Ltd 1964

The facts: K and H carried on business as property developers through a company which they owned in equal shares. Each appointed another director, making four in all, but H lived abroad and the business of the company was left entirely under the control of K. As a director K had no actual or apparent authority to enter into contracts as agent of the company but he did make contracts as if he were a managing director without authority to do so. The other directors were aware of these activities but had not authorised them. The claimants sued the company for work done on K's instructions.

Decision: There had been a representation by the company through its board of directors that K was the authorised agent of the company. The board had authority to make such contracts and also had power to delegate authority to K by appointing him to be Managing Director. Although there had been no actual delegation to K, the company had by its mere acquiescence led the claimants to believe that A was an authorised agent and the claimants had relied on it. The company was bound by the contract made by K under the principle of 'holding out' (or estoppel). The company was estopped from denying (that is, not permitted to deny) that K was its agent although K had no actual authority from the company.

It can be seen that it is the conduct of the 'principal' which creates ostensible authority. It does not matter whether there is a pre-existing agency relationship or not.

This is important – ostensible authority arises in two distinct ways. It may arise where a person makes a representation to third parties that a particular person has the authority to act as their agent without actually appointing them as their agent. Alternatively, it may arise where a principal has previously represented to a third party that an agent has authority to act on his or her behalf.

Representation

The **representation must be made by the principal or an agent acting on his behalf.** It cannot be made by the agent who is claiming apparent authority: *Armagas Ltd v Mundogas SA, The Ocean Frost 1986.*

It must be a **representation of fact, not one of law.** For example, if a third party is shown a power of attorney and misunderstands its effect, he will be unable to recover from the principal. This is because the content and interpretation of such a document is a matter of law.

The representation must be **made to the third party.** This also distinguishes ostensible authority from actual authority, where the third party need know nothing of the agent's authority.

Reliance

It must be shown that the **third party relied on the representation.** If there is no causal link between the third party's loss and the representation, the third party will not be able to hold the principal as liable.

Alteration of position

It is enough that the third party alters his position as a result of reliance on the representation. He does not have to suffer any detriment as a result, but damages would in such an event be minimal.

Where a principal has represented to a third party that an agent has authority to act, and has subsequently revoked the agent's authority, this may be insufficient to escape liability. The principal should inform third parties who have previously dealt with the agent of the change in circumstances: *Willis Faber & Co Ltd v Joyce 1911.* This is particularly relevant to partnerships and the position when a partner leaves a partnership.

Activity 3	(10 minutes)
Categories of ostensible authority were discussed earlier in this chapter. Give three examples of occasions when ostensible authority may arise.	

4 DUTIES AND RIGHTS OF AN AGENT

The courts have always sought to ensure that a person does not abuse the confidence of another for whom he is acting.

> 'The position of principal and agent gives rise to particular and onerous duties on the part of the agent, and the high standard of conduct required from him springs from the fiduciary relationship between his employer and himself. His position is confidential, it readily lends itself to abuse. A strict and salutary rule is required to meet the special situation. '
> *Armstrong v Jackson 1917*

When an agent agrees to perform services for his principal for reward there is a contract between them. However, even if the agent undertakes his duties without reward (but provided there is some consideration to make the contract valid), he has obligations to his principal. Agents' duties arise both in common law and equity and also by statute.

In the case of commercial agents, the **Commercial Agents (Council Directive) Regulations 1993** include the following provisions for the rights and duties of the parties.

Duties of the agent	Duties of the principal
To act dutifully and in good faith	To give notice of termination
To negotiate in a proper manner	To provide indemnity or compensation on termination
To execute contracts that he is obliged to undertake	To provide the agent with necessary information and documentation
To communicate any necessary information	To warn the agent of an anticipated decline in volume of business or if the third party declines to confirm a deal
To comply with the principal's reasonable instructions	To provide remuneration, either as expressly agreed or (in the absence of agreement) an amount in accordance with custom, if applicable, or a reasonable amount.

Even where these regulations do not apply, the law implies the following duties into any contract of agency.

4.1 Duties

Performance

The agent who agrees to act as agent for reward has a contractual obligation to perform his agreed task. An unpaid agent is not bound to carry out his agreed duties (there is no consideration). Any agent may refuse to perform an illegal act.

Obedience

The agent must act strictly in accordance with his principal's instructions insofar as these are lawful and reasonable. Even if he believes disobedience to be in his principal's best interests, he may not disobey instructions. Only if he is asked to commit an illegal act may he disobey instructions.

Skill

A paid agent undertakes to maintain the standard of skill and care to be expected of a person in his profession. For example, a lawyer has a duty to his client to show the skill and care of a competent lawyer. An unpaid agent if he acts as agent (which he need not do) must show the skill and care which people ordinarily use in managing their own affairs.

Personal performance

The agent is usually selected because of his personal qualities and owes a duty to perform the task himself and not to delegate it to another. He may only delegate in limited circumstances where a right to delegate may be implied from the parties' conduct or custom or where there is an unforeseen emergency.

Accountability

An agent must both provide full information to his principal of his agency transactions and account to him for all monies arising from them.

Any benefit must be handed over to the principal unless he agrees that the agent may retain it. Although an agent is entitled to his agreed remuneration, he must account to the principal for any other benefits. If he accepts from the other party any commission or reward as an inducement to make the contract with him, it is considered to be a bribe and the contract is fraudulent.

> *Boston Deep Sea Fishing & Ice Co v Ansell 1888*
>
> *The facts:* A, who was managing director of the claimant company, accepted commissions from suppliers on orders which he placed with them for goods supplied to the company. He was dismissed and the company sued to recover from him the commissions.
>
> *Decision:* The company was justified in dismissing A and he must account to it for the commissions.

No conflict of interest

The agent owes to his principal a duty not to put himself in a situation where his own interests conflict with those of the principal; for example, he must not purchase property which he was entrusted to sell: *Oliver v Court 1820*.

Confidence

The agent must keep in confidence what he knows of his principal's affairs even after the agency relationship has ceased.

4.2 Remedies of the principal regarding agent's bribes

The principal who discovers that his agent has accepted a bribe may do the following.

- **Dismiss** the agent

- **Recover the amount** of the bribe from him (as in *Ansell's* case)

- **Refuse to pay him** his agreed remuneration and recover amounts already paid

- **Repudiate the contract** with the third party

- **Sue** both the agent and the third party who paid the bribe to recover damages for any loss. He may not recover any more than this – so he may not, for instance, recover the bribe from the agent and compensation from the third party so as to make a profit

- **Seek prosecution** of the agent under the Fraud Act 2006

4.3 Rights of the agent

Indemnity

The agent is entitled to be repaid any expenses properly paid and to be indemnified by his principal against losses and liabilities. These rights are limited to acts of the agent done properly within the limits of his authority.

Remuneration

The agent is also entitled to be paid any agreed remuneration for his services by his principal. The amount may have been expressly agreed or be implied, for example by trade or professional practice. If it is agreed that the agent is to be remunerated but the amount has not been fixed, the agent is entitled to a reasonable amount.

Lien

The agent has the right to exercise a lien over property owned by the principal, ie a right to retain and hold goods pending payment of sums owed to him.

5 DUTIES OF A PRINCIPAL

There is a degree of overlap between the *rights* of an agent and the *duties* of a principal. The duties of a principal include the following:

(a) Provided the agent has performed the acts he was employed to do, and has abided by his duties, the principal has a duty to pay him his agreed remuneration, even if he has derived no benefit from his acts.

(b) The principal has a duty not to prevent his agent from performing the acts for which he is to receive remuneration.

(c) If the principal agrees to pay the agent only on the occurrence of a certain event which the agent is to bring about, and then the event happens without the agent's intervention, the principal does not have to pay: *Miller, Son & Co v Radford 1903*.

(d) The principal has a duty to indemnify his agent for expenses legitimately incurred.

6 THE AGENT AND THIRD PARTIES

6.1 Personal liability of the agent

An agent contracting for his principal within his actual and/or apparent authority generally has no liability on the contract and is not entitled to enforce it. However, there are **circumstances** when the **agent will be personally liable** and can enforce it.

(a) When he intended to undertake personal liability – as where he signs a contract as party to it without signifying that he is an agent. In particular, he will be liable on a cheque which he signs without indicating his agency status: s 26 Bills of Exchange Act 1882.

(b) Where the **principal was undisclosed** (see below)

(c) Where it is usual business practice or trade custom for an agent to be liable and entitled. For example, an advertising agent is liable to the media for contracts made on its client's behalf.

(d) Where the agent is acting on his own behalf even though he purports to act for a principal (see *Kelner v Baxter 1866* in Chapter 3, where the agents thought they were acting on behalf of a company principal which was not yet in existence)

(e) Where the agent contracts by deed without having a power of attorney from the principal

Where an agent enters into a collateral contract with the third party with whom he has contracted on the principal's behalf, there is separate liability and entitlement to enforcement on that collateral contract.

It can happen that there is **joint liability** of agent and principal. This is usually the case where an agent did not disclose that he acted for a principal.

Breach of warranty of authority

An agent who **exceeds his ostensible authority** will generally have **no liability to his principal**, since the latter will not be bound by the unauthorised contract made for him unless he chooses to ratify it. The agent **will be liable** in such a case **to the third party** for breach of warranty of authority if he genuinely thought he had authority but was mistaken. If he knew of his lack of authority, made a representation to the contrary and caused loss to the third party, he may be liable for the tort of deceit.

6.2 Disclosed principal

In normal circumstances the agent discloses to the other party that he (the agent) is acting for a principal whose identity is also disclosed. The contract, when made, is between the principal and the other party.

The agent has no liability under the contract and no right to enforce it. An agent may, however, be liable under the contract in some cases.

(a) If the agent **executes a deed** in his own name he should sign 'J Smith by his attorney H Jones' (Smith being the principal and Jones the agent).

(b) If the agent signs a **negotiable instrument** without indicating that he does so in a representative character on behalf of a principal he may be liable. For instance, if a director signs a company cheque 'H Black, Director XYZ Ltd' he merely describes his position as director. To avoid liability, he should sign 'for and on behalf of XYZ Ltd'. The same rules may apply to other written contracts signed by an agent.

NOTES

(c)   Where by **trade custom** the agent is liable, for example, advertising agents are liable to the media for contracts made on behalf of their clients.

(d)   Where the **principal is fictitious or non-existent**, the agent contracts for himself and so is liable as the true principal.

6.3   Unnamed principal

If, in making the contract, the agent discloses that he acts for an **unnamed principal** the position is also as described above. (You should note that an unnamed principal is a disclosed principal.)

6.4   Undisclosed principal

If a person enters into a contract apparently on his own account as principal but in fact as agent on behalf of a principal, the doctrine of the undisclosed principal determines the position of the parties.

Definition

> The doctrine of the **undisclosed principal** states that, provided that the agent acts within the scope of his authority, it is possible to put forward evidence which shows that the undisclosed principal is a party to the transactions. As a result he may sue or be sued on the contract made between agent and third party.

The undisclosed principal will usually intervene and enforce the contract on his own behalf against the other party since it is really his contract, not the agent's. Until such time as the principal takes this action, the agent himself may sue the third party (since he is treated as the other party to the contract).

The undisclosed principal's right to intervene in a contract made by his agent is limited to those contracts which the agent was authorised to make as agent – he cannot ratify an unauthorised act or seek to take over the agent's contract without the third party's consent.

The **undisclosed principal** is also **prevented** from **taking over a contract** in the following circumstances.

(a)   Where the contract terms are such that **agency is implicitly denied**.

Humble v Hunter 1848
The facts: The principal (P) authorised his agent (A) to charter out his ship. A contracted with a third party for the charter of the vessel, describing himself as 'owner' of it.

Decision: The principal could not enforce the contract against the third party because the agent had implied that he was the owner and hence the principal. P's ownership contradicted the contract's terms.

(b)   Where the contract terms are such that **agency is expressly denied**.

United Kingdom Mutual SS Assurance Association v Nevill 1887
The facts: The managing part-owner of a vessel became a member of the claimant mutual association and insured a ship under the rules of the association, which prescribed that only members were liable to pay

BPP
LEARNING MEDIA

premiums. The part-owner became bankrupt and the defendant, a part-owner, was approached for contributions.

Decision: As the defendant was not a member, he could not intervene as an undisclosed principal.

(c) Where the agent, when making the contract, **expressly denied that a principal was involved**.

(d) Where the **identity of the parties is material to the third party** – that is, where the third party wanted to contract with the agent and would not have contracted at all if he had known of the identity of the principal.

Said v Butt 1920
The facts: The claimant, a theatre critic, had a disagreement with the defendant, who was manager of a particular theatre and who had banned him from attending there. He wanted to see the first night of a new play, 'The Whirligig', at the theatre and so asked Pollock, whom the manager did not know to be connected with him, to obtain a ticket for him. The claimant was refused admission on the ticket and sued for breach of contract.

Decision: Said's identity was of great importance to the theatre and it would not have contracted with Pollock if it had known that the claimant was his undisclosed principal. The claimant could not enforce the ticket.

The legal effects of undisclosed agency

If the contract is not performed as agreed the third party may, on discovering the true facts:

(a) Hold the agent personally bound by the contract (as the agent appeared to be contracting on his own account)

(b) Elect to treat the principal as the other party to the contract.

But he must elect for one or the other within a **reasonable time** of discovering the facts, and cannot sue both principal and agent.

The third party who commences legal proceedings against either agent or principal may withdraw (before judgment is given) in order to sue the other. If, however, he obtains judgment on the breach of contract he cannot sue the other even if the judgment is unsatisfied.

Activity 4   **(15 minutes)**

If A purports to enter into a contract with X on behalf of P, A warrants, or guarantees, to X that P exists and has capacity to enter into the contract, and that A has authority from P to make the contract for him.

What remedies are available to X if any of these implied warranties proves to be untrue?

NOTES

7 TERMINATION OF AGENCY

Agency is primarily terminated when the **parties agree** that the relationship should end.

It may also be terminated by **operation of law** in the following situations:

- Principal or agent dies

- Principal or agent becomes insane

- Principal becomes bankrupt, or agent becomes bankrupt and this interferes with his position as agent

Termination brings the **actual authority** of the agent to an end. However, third parties are allowed to enforce contracts made later by the 'agent' until they are actively or constructively informed of the termination of the agency relationship.

Chapter roundup

- Agency can be defined as a relationship which exists between two legal persons, the principal and the agent, in which the function of the agent is to form a contract between his principal and a third party.

- There are a number of specific types of agent. These have either evolved in particular trades or developed in response to specific commercial needs. Among the more frequently encountered types of agent are factors, brokers, estate agents, del credere agents, bankers and auctioneers.

- The relationship between principal and agent is usually created by mutual consent. It may also arise by operation of law.

- An agent's authority may be express, implied or ostensible.

- Consent to agency need not be formal, nor, with one exception, need it be contained in a written document. An agency relationship may also be created by operation of law or by estoppel.

- In certain circumstances the relationship of principal and agent can be created, or extended, with retrospective effect. This is the doctrine of ratification.

- Ostensible, or apparent, authority is that which a principal represents to third parties (with whom the agent deals) that he has given to the agent.

- The principal is usually liable to the third party for contracts formed by his agent within the latter's actual or apparent authority. There are certain circumstances, however, where the agent will be personally liable on the contract and can enforce it.

- In normal circumstances the agent discloses to the third party that he is acting for a principal whose identity is also disclosed. The contract is between the principal and the third party. This is disclosed agency.

- If a person enters into a contract apparently on his own account as principal but in fact as agent on behalf of a principal, the doctrine of the undisclosed principal applies: the undisclosed principal may intervene and enforce the contract on his own behalf. There are certain situations where the undisclosed principal is prevented from taking over a contract.

- Agency is usually terminated by agreement.

NOTES

Quick quiz

1   Give a definition of agency.

2   Define implied incidental authority.

3   Give a definition of ostensible authority.

4   Give three instances of where an undisclosed principal is prevented from taking over a contract.

Answers to quick quiz

1   Agency is the relationship which exists between two legal persons, the principal and the agent, in which the function of the agent is to form a contract between his principal and a third party.

2   Implied incidental authority is the implied authority to do whatever is necessary and incidental to the agent's activities.

3   Ostensible authority is the authority which the principal represents to other persons that he has given to the agent.

4   Any of:

    (1)   Where contract terms are such that agency is implicitly denied
    (2)   Where contract terms are such that agency is expressly denies
    (3)   Where the agent expressly denied the existence of a principal
    (4)   Where the identity of the parties is material to the third party

Answers to activities

1   An insurance broker is an agent of an insurer who arranges contracts of insurance with the other party who wishes to be insured. However, in some contexts (for example, when the broker assists a car owner to complete a proposal form) he is also treated as the agent of the insured. Insurance, especially marine insurance, has complicated rules applicable to the relationship (insurer-broker-insured).

2   Under the law of contract, an offer may be revoked at any time up to acceptance. However, once Pat ratifies her agent's actions, the ratification has retrospective effect. Pat is of course free to decide whether or not to ratify.

This situation may appear strange. the third party is bound as soon as the agent acts, while the principal is not bound unless and until he ratifies.

This rule appears somewhat unjust to the third party, and certain limitations have been developed. Three are given below.

- Ratification must take place within a reasonable time so as to minimise uncertainty.

- The third party's offer may be made expressly subject to ratification.

- If the third party commits a breach of contract after the agent's acceptance but before ratification, he will not be liable to the principal.

3   (a)   Where a person allows another, who is not his agent, to appear as if he is.

(b)   Where a principal allows his agent to give the impression that he has more extensive authority than is really the case.

(c)   Where, following termination of the agency relationship, a principal allows his former agent to continue to appear as his agent.

4   Unless P ratifies the contract, X may claim damages from A for his loss, provided that X was unaware that A had no authority to make the contract. A is liable even though he was himself unaware that he lacked authority, eg because P had died. In *Kelner v Baxter 1866* the promoters of a company were liable since they made a contract for a non-existent principal.

Part B

Company Law

Chapter 2 :
THE CHOICE OF BUSINESS ENTITY

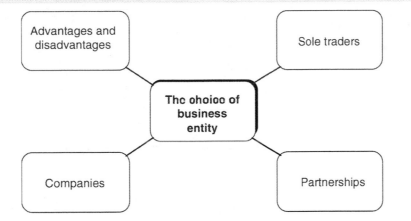

Introduction

There are various forms of business entity. A person or group of people choosing to operate a business must decide how they want to operate and therefore which form of business unit to use. There are various factors that such a person must evaluate in making the choice and these factors will be considered in this chapter. Important factors tend to be the question of liability and therefore risk, the issue of publicity, the source of business finance that is being considered, the size of the operation and the flexibility required.

Three main forms of business unit will be considered in this chapter: sole traders and partnerships (in detail) and companies (at an introductory level).

Your objectives

In this chapter you will learn about the following.

  (a)   Sole tradership: nature, features, administration and dissolution

  (b)   Partnerships: nature, types, formation, administration and dissolution

  (c)   The nature and features of companies

  (d)   Key factors in making a choice between forms of business units

NOTES

1 SOLE TRADER

Definition

> A **sole trader** is a person carrying on business with total legal responsibility for his/her actions, neither as a partnership nor as a company.

A person carrying on business

If a person sets up in business on his own but take no steps to register the business with a regulatory authority, this will, by default, be a sole tradership. If he did it in association with other people, it would be a partnership (see below).

However, this does not mean that to be a sole tradership, a business has to be a one man show. A sole trader can employ other people to work for him. In theory, a sole tradership can be a substantial business enterprise.

Total legal responsibility

The significant feature of a sole tradership is that it has no legal distinction from the sole trader. This means that persons contracting with the business contract directly with the businessman. This is the case even if the business appears to be separate from the person, for example, if it has a trading name.

This means that a sole trader has unlimited business liability. In other words, if his business fails, he personally will legally be required to honour debts to creditors, even if that results in his personal bankruptcy. Despite this risk, many people set up as sole traders every year.

Other factors

On the positive side, a sole trader has absolute control over the management of his business. There are also very few formal procedures involved in setting up as a sole trader, unless the business intends to operate in a regulated industry and the sole trader therefore requires a licence (for example, a publican/retailer of alcohol, or a business offering consumer credit).

On the negative side, the fact that the person and the business have no legal distinction may make it difficult to raise finance. The most obvious way for a sole trader to raise finance is through raising personal loans.

The combination of these factors means that a person wanting to set up in business on a small scale might well find that it is best for him to set up as a sole trader. The key advantages and disadvantages of doing so are as follows.

1.1 Forming a sole tradership

There are no legal requirements associated with setting up as a sole trader (per se, although as mentioned above, there may be legal restrictions associated with the business). The law views a sole trader in the same way the day before he decides to set up in business as the day after he makes that decision. This is because the business of a sole trader has **no separate legal personality** from the proprietor himself.

The sole trader will have to consider various laws which may regulate aspects of his business, for instance health and safety laws and employment law.

Advantages

- **No formal procedures** are required to set up in business

- A sole trader need consult nobody about business decisions and is not required to reveal the state of the business to anyone (other than the tax authorities each year)

- **Personal supervision** of the business by the sole trader should ensure its effective operation. Personal contact with customers may enhance commercial flexibility.

- **All** the **profits** of the business **accrue** to the sole trader. This can be a powerful motivator and satisfying to the individual whose ability/energy results in reward

Disadvantages

- If the business gets into debt, a sole trader's personal wealth might be lost if the debts are called in, as they are the same legal entity

- Expansion of the business is usually only possible by **ploughing back** the **profits** of the business as further capital, although loans or overdraft finance may be available

- The business has a **high dependence** on the **individual**, which can mean long working hours and difficulties during sickness or holidays

- The **death** of the proprietor may make it **necessary** to **sell** the **business** in order to pay the resulting tax liabilities, or family members may not wish to continue the business anyway

- The **individual** may **only have one skill**. A sole trader may be, say, a good technical engineer or craftsman but may lack the skills to market effectively or to maintain accounting records to control the business effectively

- **Disadvantages** associated with small size, lack of diversification, absence of economies of scale, problems of raising finance etc

FOR DISCUSSION

A sole trader has no legal identity beyond the natural person. What implications are there for the sole trader in terms of his rights and the management of his business?

2 PARTNERSHIPS

2.1 Ordinary partnership

Definition

Partnership is the relation that subsists between persons carrying on a business in common with a view of profit.

Between persons

As noted above, partnerships involve more than one person. However, as we shall see later, a company is seen in law to be a legal person, so a partnership can exist between a 'natural' person and a company (a 'legal' person). There is a minimum of two partners. If there were fewer partners than this, the business unit would be a sole trader. There is a statutory maximum of twenty partners, although this limit has been waived for a number of types of partnership, for example, solicitors and accountants.

Carrying on a business with a view to profit

In this context, 'business' means every trade, occupation or profession. A partnership can exist for the purposes of a single transaction (these are often called joint ventures). A partnership must be formed with an intention to make profits. For most people, this is a natural assumption when setting up in business. However, persons setting up in business to achieve charitable aims or just to gain business experience (*Davids v Newman 2000*) and not seeking to make a profit could not operate as a partnership.

In common

Partners are considered in law to be joint proprietors, even if in practice, a partner does not take an active part in the business. Such a partner is often known as a sleeping partner. A sleeping partner shares the risk and responsibility with any other partners.

2.2 Key factors in ordinary partnerships

Partners are jointly and severally liable without limit for the debts of the partnership. In a similar way to sole traders, in the event of business failure, partners are liable for the debts of the partnership to the extent of their personal wealth.

The difference in this case is that the business might fail due to the act of a one partner, but the liability extends to all partners. This may mean that a partner faces personal bankruptcy as a result of a contract, which he was not even aware of, but which was entered into by a fellow partner. In other words, the risk is the same as that faced by a sole trader, but the responsibility may be reduced.

Unless they have agreed otherwise, the death of a partner dissolves an ordinary partnership.

On the positive side, in terms of financing, the fact that more than one person is involved means that there is greater capacity to seek finance. There is also very little regulation of partnerships, and no formal procedures are required to set one up, although there are some requirements relating to retirement from partnership and dissolution of partnerships. There is little requirement to make information publicly available, in contrast to companies which must publish significant amounts of information.

Generally, ordinary partnerships are very similar to sole traders, the key difference, of course, being the number of people involved in the business unit. As partners, the owners operate the business unit.

2.3 Forming an ordinary partnership

There are no legal requirements associated with setting up as an ordinary partnership, *per se*. Again, this is because the general partnership has no separate legal identity from that of the partners, and so there is no need to register a separate entity coming into existence.

As with sole traders, the partners will have to consider the effect of laws which are relevant to their new business. Specifically, they may have legal considerations associated with their choice of name and will have to obey regulations ensuring that the public (or those dealing with the partnership) can be made aware of who all the individual partners are. This will be fairly clear if partners use their own names ('Smith and Jones, Partners') but if there are several partners, a different name might be used ('The Business Partnership').

While there are no legal requirements involved in the formation of a partnership, as more than one person is involved partners often find it expedient to put together a **partnership agreement.** This is allowed for, but not required, by the Partnership Act 1890.

Partnership agreement

The partnership agreement fills in the details which the law would not imply into an agreement between partners. This means a partnership agreement is likely to cover such issues as:

- The nature of the firm's business
- The firm's name
- The bank at which the firm will maintain its bank account

A partnership agreement will also **override** terms implied by the Partnership Act 1890 which the partners **do not want to apply.** For example the Partnership Act 1890 provides that partners will share profits equally: in practice, partners often wish to provide that older, more experienced partners take a larger share than junior ones.

Partnership Act 1890

(a) **Freedom of variation.** Under s 19 Partnership Act 1890, the partnership agreement may be varied with the consent of all the partners. This may be formal or informal.

(b) **Good faith.** There is a duty of utmost good faith once the partnership is established, although the contract of partnership is not itself *uberrimae fidei* ('of the utmost good faith').

(c) **Profits and losses.** These are shared equally in the absence of contrary agreement. However, if the partnership agreement states that profits are to be shared in certain proportions then, prima facie, losses are to be shared in the same proportions.

(d) **Interest on capital.** None is paid on capital except by agreement. However, a partner is entitled to 5% interest on advances beyond his original capital.

(e) **Indemnity.** The firm must indemnify any partner against liabilities incurred in the ordinary and proper conduct of the partnership business or in doing anything necessarily done for the preservation of the partnership property or business.

(f) **Management.** Every partner is entitled to take part in managing the firm's business; ordinary management decisions can be made by a majority of partners.

(g) **Change in business.** Any decision on changing the nature of the partnership's business must be unanimous.

(h) **Remuneration.** No partner is entitled to remuneration such as salary for acting in the partnership business.

(i) **Records and accounts.** These must be kept at the main place of business, and must be open to inspection by all partners.

(j) **New partners.** New partners must only be introduced with the consent of all existing partners.

(k) **Expulsion.** A partner may only be expelled by a majority of votes when the partnership agreement allows; even then, the power must only be used in good faith and for good reason.

(l) **Misrepresentation.** When a partner is induced to enter into a partnership by misrepresentation he remains liable to creditors for obligations incurred whilst a partner, but he has several remedies against the maker of the statement including, for example, rescission and/or damages (reflecting the basic contractual rules on misrepresentation).

(m) **Dissolution.** The authority of the partners after dissolution continues so far as is necessary to wind up the partnership affairs and complete transactions already begun. On dissolution, any partner can insist on realisation of the firm's assets (including goodwill), payment of the firm's debts and distribution of the surplus, subject to any contrary agreement.

(n) **Capital deficiency.** A distinction is made between a loss (including a capital loss such as the sale of a fixed asset for less than its book value) and a capital deficiency. It can happen that as a result of normal losses a partner's capital is exhausted and in addition he becomes (by reason of his share of the losses) a debtor to the firm. If in those circumstances he is unable to pay what he owes to the firm, there is a capital deficiency. If there are two or more solvent partners with credit balances on capital account the assets (less the irrecoverable sum owed by the insolvent partner) will be less than the aggregate of those balances. They share the deficiency not as a loss but in ratio to the amounts of capital which they originally contributed to the firm. This is the rule in *Garner v Murray 1904*.

2.4 Partners authority

The terms implied by the Partnership Act 1890 include an implied term about the management of the partnership. Partners are agents of each other, which means that the act of one partner will generally bind the others.

The Partnership Act 1890 defines the apparent authority of a partner to make contracts as follows. The definition is found in section 5 which is one of the most important sections in the Act.

'Every partner is an agent of the firm and his other partners for the purpose of the business of the partnership; and the acts of every partner who does any act for carrying on in the usual way business of the kind carried on by the firm of which he is a member bind the firm and his partners, unless the partner so acting has in fact no authority to act for the firm in the particular matter, and the person with whom he is dealing either knows that he has no authority, or does not know or believe him to be a partner': s 5.

The Act also states that the partnership is only bound by acts done by a partner in the firm's name and not apparently for the partners personally: ss 6 and 7.

Apparent authority

Sometimes a single partner enters into a transaction which the other partners wish to repudiate on the ground that it is outside the limits of the **business of the kind carried on by the firm**. It is indeed usual to specify in a partnership agreement what is the nature of the firm's business. But unless the person with whom a partner deals is aware of the agreed limits he may hold the firm bound by a transaction which would appear to him (and other outsiders) to be the kind of business which such a firm ordinarily carries on.

Mercantile Credit v Garrod 1962

The facts: P and the defendant entered into partnership to let lock-up garages and repair cars. P ran the business and the defendant was a sleeping partner. Their partnership agreement provided expressly that the firm would not buy and sell cars. But P sold a car which the firm did not own to a finance company (the claimant) so that it might be let on hire purchase to a customer. The claimant sued the defendant to recover the £700 which it had paid P for the car. The defendant denied liability on the ground that P in selling the car had been acting outside the agreed limits of the firm's business and so P had no actual or apparent authority from him. Evidence was given that other garage businesses of the type carried on by P and the defendant did deal in cars.

Decision: The test of what is the firm's business is not what the partners agreed it should be but 'what it appeared to the outside world' to be (established by the practice of 'businesses of a like kind'). By that test P appeared to the claimant to be carrying on business of the kind carried on by such a firm. Buying and selling the firm's goods is within the authority of a single partner.

The 'usual way' of business

The second test of s 5 is that a partner is agent of the firm in carrying on the firm's business **in the usual way**. What is usual in any particular business must always depend partly on the general practice of businesses of a similar type and size. In particular a distinction is made between commercial firms which trade in buying and selling goods and non-commercial firms (including of course professional partnerships) which do not do so. A single partner of a commercial firm (acting on behalf of the firm and within the apparent limits of its kind of business) is deemed to have the authority of the other partners to engage in any of the following transactions.

(a) To buy and sell goods in the course of the firm's business (including the purchase of fixed assets for use in the business such as a typewriter or a delivery van).

(b) To receive payment of debts owed to the firm and to issue receipts.

(c) To engage employees to work in the firm's business.

(d) To sign cheques drawn on the firm's bank account.

(e) To sign bills of exchange as drawer acceptor or endorser.

(f) To borrow money and to give security by pledging the firm's goods or by deposit of title deeds etc relating to the firm's land and buildings.

Transactions outside a partner's apparent authority

The following transactions are not within the apparent authority of a single partner in any kind of partnership.

    (a)   To execute a deed such as a legal mortgage of property; for this he requires a power of attorney executed by all the partners.

    (b)   To give a guarantee of another person's debt unless it is the custom in the firm's trade to do so.

    (c)   To submit a dispute to arbitration.

    (d)   To accept property, eg fully-paid shares of a company, in satisfaction of a debt owed to the firm.

Activity 1 (10 minutes)

Andrew, Brian and Cecil are in partnership as antique dealers and repairers. Cecil entered a contract with Tom to repair a grandfather clock belonging to Tom. Once it was repaired, Cecil sold the clock and has disappeared with the money. Do you think Tom has any course of action against Andrew and Brian?

2.5 Dissolution of an ordinary partnership

Reasons for dissolving a partnership

Dissolution of a partnership occurs in the following situations.

    (a)   By **passing of time**, if the partnership was entered into for a fixed term.

    (b)   By **termination of the venture**, if entered into for a single venture.

    (c)   By the **death or bankruptcy** of a partner, unless the partnership agreement otherwise provides.

    (d)   By **subsequent illegality**, such as an event which makes it unlawful to continue the business.

    (e)   By **notice** given by a partner if it is a partnership of indefinite duration.

    (f)   By **order of the court** granted to a partner, for one or several reasons - for example the permanent incapacity of a partner or because it is just and equitable to order dissolution.

Changes in membership

Changes in the membership will theoretically dissolve the partnership. So, for example, if A and B are in partnership and B retires, but A invites C to join the partnership in B's place, in the eyes of people dealing with the partnership, the partnership still exists. However, in the eyes of the law, a new partnership exists. AB has been dissolved, and AC has been formed. This has practical effects for partners.

Retirement of a partner

The effect of retirement is that the partner who retires:

(a) Is still liable for any outstanding debts incurred while he was a partner unless the creditor has agreed to release him from liability, and

(b) Is also liable for debts of the firm incurred after his retirement if the creditor knew him to be a partner (before retirement) and has not had notice of his retirement. This is due to the principle that a person who was previously known to be a partner continues to be an 'apparent member' of the partnership and liable for all its debts until notice is given that he is no longer a partner: s 36.

Notice of retirement

To avoid being still an 'apparent member' of the firm after his retirement the retiring partner should give notice of his retirement.

(a) To creditors who had dealings with the firm while he was a partner, he should give actual notice of his retirement. This need not be an express notice. If for example the firm reprints its letterhead to omit him from the list of partners and writes a letter on the new letterhead to a creditor that is sufficient notice to the creditor of the change.

(b) To persons who may have known that he is a partner (before his retirement) but who begin to have dealings with the firm for the first time after his retirement, the retired partner cannot easily give actual notice since he does not know (at his retirement) who they may prove to be. But sufficient notice is given to them if he advertises the fact of his retirement in the London Gazette: s 36(2). They are then deemed to have notice even if they have not read the advertisement.

Introducing a new partner

A new partner admitted to an existing firm is liable for debts incurred only after he becomes a partner. He is not liable for debts incurred before he was a partner unless he agrees to become liable.

Partnership agreement

As discussed above, the death of a partner may itself dissolve the partnership (s33 so provides unless otherwise agreed). This is usually avoided by expressly agreeing that so long as there are two or more surviving partners, the partnership shall continue. The estate of a deceased partner is only liable for the debts of the partnership incurred **before** his death.

The partnership agreement may also make provision for other changes in membership such as retirement, so that a partnership may continue despite changes in membership.

However, such provision in the partnership agreement **does not** affect the potential liability of retiring partners. They must still give notice to creditors as discussed above.

Insolvency

Partners are jointly and severally liable for business debts. If a partnership is insolvent, therefore, creditors may sue individual partners for payment.

However, it is also possible for a creditor to present a petition to the court for a winding up of a partnership, in a similar fashion to the winding up of an unregistered company.

(The compulsory liquidation of companies is covered in Chapter 6.) The only ground for such a petition is that the partnership cannot pay its debts. Bankruptcy petitions may be presented against one or more of the partners at the same time.

2.6 Limited partnerships

There are two ways in which partnerships can be formed which entail limited liability for some or all parties: under the Limited Partnership Act 1907 (LPA 1907) and under the Limited Liability Partnerships Act 2000 (LLPA 2000). The latter are described at Section 2.7 below.

Limited partnerships under the 1907 legislation

A limited partnership under the Limited Partnership Act 1907 is very rare today and accounts for fewer than 1% of all partnerships in the UK. A limited partnership is formed when one or more of the partners invest capital into the business but do not participate in running and managing the business. These partners therefore have limited liability as they can only lose the amount of money that they initially invested into the business.

In a limited partnership, the law states that there must be at least one partner that has limited liability and at least one partner that has unlimited liability (a general partner). Consequently, the law further allows this type of partnership to have more than twenty owners.

The general partner has control of the management of the business, but none of the limited partners are permitted to participate in the management of the business. If they do, their limited liability is lost. A limited partner cannot bind the partnership. Only a general partner can do that.

In order to take advantage of the protection afforded by limited liability, an organisation which constitutes itself as a limited partnership must comply with the requirements of the Limited Partnership Act 1907. In particular, the partnership must be registered at Companies House giving details of the partners and the extent of their liability.

Legislative Reform (Limited Partnerships) Order 2009 introduces a revised process of registration, among other things, but does not substantially alter the nature of limited partnerships created under the 1907 Act. The order takes effect in October 2009.

2.7 Limited liability partnerships under the LLPA 2000

Limited liability partnerships (LLPs) are a relatively new form of business structure, following the enactment of the LLPA 2000. An LLP combines the features of a partnership along with the limited liability and creation of a legal personality more usually associated with limited companies. (The separate legal personality of companies and LLPs is described at Section 3.1 below.) An LLP is not dissolved on a change of membership. At the end of the life of a partnership, it is wound up rather like a company.

An LLP can be incorporated wherever 'two or more persons associated with the carrying on of a lawful business with a view to profit ... have subscribed their names to an incorporation document ...'. The rights and duties of the partnership are usually set out in a partnership agreement (failing which the Limited Partnership Regulations 2001 (as amended) govern their legal obligations). Broadly, these apply relevant companies legislation to LLPs. (The Limited Liability Partnerships (Application of Companies Act 2006) Regulations 2009 were fully in force by 1 October 2009.)

An LLP is a body corporate and therefore an artificial legal person with its own property and liabilities, separate from its members. Each member-partner is treated as an agent of the LLP and therefore (usually) has authority to bind the LLP by his actions. However, the LLP will not be bound where the member does not have authority and the third party is either aware of this, or does not believe him to be part of an LLP.

Since the LLP is a separate legal entity the members are not jointly liable for contracts entered into by the LLP, nor are they jointly and severally liable for any wrong doings committed by the LLP (however, members will be liable for their own acts of negligence or wrongdoing much in the same way as company directors are.) In addition each member in an LLP of professionals, such as an accountancy firm, owes a duty of care. The rules on fraudulent and wrongful trading apply to an LLP in much the same way as they do to a limited company, as do the Companies Act provisions regarding the disqualification of directors, insolvency and winding-up procedures.

Activity 2 (1 hour)

Find out what you can about the legal structure of some of the UK's largest law firms and accountancy firms.

2.8 Forming an LLP

An LLP must be incorporated to be recognised in law, if it is not so recognised it becomes an unlimited partnership by default. There is a form which must be filled in, signed by at least two members and sent to the Registrar of Companies. There is a registration fee. The form must state the following:

- The **name** of the LLP
- The location of its **registered office** (England and Wales/Wales)
- The **address** of the registered office
- The **names** and **addresses** of all the **members** of the LLP
- Which of the members are to be **designated members** (see below)

Designated members

LLPs are required to have designated members who are responsible for signing the relevant documents and returning them to the Registrar. Each LLP must have two designated members.

Designated members are required to:

- Sign notices sent to the Registrar
- Appoint auditors if they are required
- Sign the annual accounts of the LLP
- Deliver these accounts to the Registrar

The Registrar will maintain a file containing the publicised documents of an LLP at Companies House.

Activity 3   **(15 minutes)**

Imagine that the two largest firms of solicitors in the UK wanted to merge. The Partners agreed on 1 September 2010 that they would merge and form a new partnership. What practical and legal issues arise?

3 COMPANIES

A company is an extremely common form of business unit in the UK. There is a basic concept of 'corporate personality' but there are several forms of company. This means that a company can be suitable for very small enterprises and also for huge, multi-national enterprises.

Definition

A **company** is an entity registered under the Companies Act 2006 or any earlier Companies Act.

3.1 Legal personality

A person possesses legal rights and is subject to legal obligations. In law the term 'person' is used to denote either a natural person (ie an individual human being) or an artificial person (including companies and LLPs).

The most significant factor about a company is that the law recognises it as a legal person distinct from its owners. This is known as the concept of corporate personality.

Definition

Corporate personality is a common law principle that grants a company a legal entity, separate from the members who comprise it. It follows that the property of a company belongs to that company; debts of the company must be satisfied from the assets of that company; and the company has perpetual succession (until wound up) so it is unaffected by the death of any member.

Whereas it is a key feature of sole traders and partnerships that the owners bear responsibility for business debts, a company bears responsibility for its own debts. However, the other side of this is that the owners have no direct interest in the assets owned by the business, as the company owns those too.

The first case which clearly demonstrated the separate legal personality of companies is of great significance to any study of company law and is therefore set out in some detail below.

Salomon v Salomon & Co Ltd 1897

The facts: The claimant had carried on business as a leather merchant and boot manufacturer for 30 years. He decided to form a limited company to purchase the business, he and six members of his family each subscribing for one share. The company then purchased the business for £38,782, the purchase price being payable to the claimant by way of the issue of 20,000 £1 shares, the issue of debentures for £10,000 (effectively making Salomon a secured creditor) and the payment of £8,782 in cash. The company did not prosper and was wound up a year later, at which point its liabilities exceeded its assets. The liquidator, representing unsecured trade creditors of the company, claimed that the company's business was in effect still the claimant's (he owned 20,001 of 20,007 shares) and that he should bear liability for its debts and that payment of the debenture debt to him should be postponed until the company's trade creditors were paid.

Decision: The Court of Appeal held that since the other shareholders were 'mere puppets' and that the company had been irregularly incorporated, Salomon should indemnify the company against its liabilities. The House of Lords however held that the business was owned by, and its debts were liabilities of, the company. The claimant was under no liability to the company or its creditors, his debentures were validly issued and the security created by them over the company's assets was effective. This was because once the company had been formed in compliance with the Companies Act, it was regarded as a separate legal entity in its own right, notwithstanding Salomon's dominant position in the company.

3.2 Liability

A key feature of corporate personality is therefore that the liability of owners of a company is limited (as Salomon's was in the case outlined above).

Definition

Limited liability is a protection offered to members of limited liability companies. In the event of business failure, the members will only be asked to contribute identifiable amounts to the assets of the business.

The **company** itself is **liable without limit for its own debts.** If the company buys goods from another company, for example, it must pay the purchase price for those goods to the other company.

Protection offered to members

Limited liability is a benefit for the company's members (shareholders). They own the business, so might be the people who the creditors logically asked to pay the debts of the company if the company were unable to pay them itself. Limited liability prevents this by stipulating that the creditors of the company cannot demand the company's debts from members of the company but must demand payment from the company itself.

Not surprisingly, most companies are registered with limited liability.

Business failure

As the company is liable for all its own debts, limited liability only becomes an issue in the event of a business failure when the company is unable to pay its own debts. This may result in the winding-up of the company, which will enable the creditors to be paid from the proceeds of any assets remaining in the company. It is at winding-up that limited liability becomes relevant.

NOTES

Members asked to contribute identifiable amounts

Although the creditors of the company cannot ask the members of the company to pay the debts of the company, there are some amounts that members are required to pay, in the event of a winding-up.

TYPE OF COMPANY	AMOUNT OWED BY MEMBER AT WINDING-UP
Company limited by shares	Any outstanding amount from when the shares they hold were originally purchased.
	If the member's shares are fully paid, they do not have to contribute anything in the event of a winding-up.
Company limited by guarantee	The amount they guaranteed to pay in the event of a winding-up

3.3 Regulation

To balance the benefit of limited liability, there is significant regulation and requirement associated with companies. Companies are not just formed; they must be registered. If a company is not registered, it does not exist, and the people who formed contracts in the name of the company will be found personally liable with regard to those contracts.

A company is subject to regulation throughout the course of its life. It must file information to be made publicly available with the Registrar of Companies. It may be limited in the actions that it can take, for example, with regard to raising finance or the nature of the business it undertakes.

The owners of a company may also manage it, but this is not necessarily the case. In large companies, shareholders may invest in a company but have nothing to do with the management whatsoever. They may not even attend shareholder meetings (investors are not required to do so). This means that there are legal rules in place that govern the relationship between the management of a company and the owners. All these things will be looked at in greater detail in later chapters.

Lastly, as a company is a legal entity in its own right, in the event that the shareholders decide to cease the business which the company operates, the company itself does not cease to exist. It must be dissolved. There are legal rules attaching to this too, which are discussed in Chapter 6.

3.4 Veil of incorporation

As a result of the law stated in Salomon's case, a '**veil of incorporation**' is said to be drawn between the members and the company, separating them for the purposes of liability and identification. This often results in protecting the members from the consequences of the company's actions, as you will see below. Occasionally the separate legal personality symbolised by the veil can be problematic as where, for example, an individual incorporated his business but insured the company's property in his own name rather than that of the company. When the property was destroyed by fire, it was held that he had no insurable interest (either as creditor or member) and that the company, as a separate legal entity, should have insured its own assets (*Macaura v Northern Assurance Co Ltd 1925*).

A rigid application of the principle of separate legal personality can sometimes produce harsh or inequitable results and so the law sometimes 'lifts the veil' in order to expose the commercial reality of the situation.

Generally speaking, this may be done by the courts in order to defeat fraud, sharp practices or illegality although it is difficult to define a set of consistent principles underlying the cases. Examples of where the veil has been lifted by the courts are below.

COURTS	
Situation where the veil might be lifted	**Examples**
Groups of companies – where the subsidiary can be regarded as the agent of the holding company	
• To produce tax liability	*Firestone Tyre & Rubber Co Ltd v Lewellin 1957:* English subsidiary (S) deemed to be agent of American holding company (H) (thus rendering H liable to UK tax) where H entered into agreement with distributors under which the distributors should place orders with H, to be carried out by S. In fact, S received orders direct, handled business completely (free from control of H) and forwarded money (less a percentage) to it.
• To give entitlement to compensation	*Smith, Stone & Knight Ltd v Birmingham Corporation 1939:* Compensation for compulsorily-acquired premises was payable to an owner-occupier (H in this case) but not a tenant-occupier (S). Held that S occupied the premises as an agent of H since it was wholly-owned and the directors of H and S were the same.
• To prevent evasion of excise duty	*Re H and others 1996:* Where evasions were alleged to have been committed by H, the court also allowed restraint of S's assets, refusing to recognise the companies as separate.

It is important to note, however, that cases such as these do not mean that groups of companies will generally be regarded as a single entity. There are numerous examples of where the courts have refused to lift the veil between companies within a group, including cases where creditors of an insolvent subsidiary are not paid in full even though the holding company remains solvent or where a claimant proceeds against a subsidiary company that is not as asset-rich as its holding company.

To reveal true national identity and expose illegality	*Daimler Co Ltd v Continental Tyre & Rubber Co (GB) Ltd 1916:* A company was registered and had its registered office in England. However, since all of its member with control of the company (except one) were German, the veil could be lifted to expose the company as an enemy alien. Therefore trading with this company was against the law (in wartime). (See too Re FG Films below.)

COURTS	
Situation where the veil might be lifted	**Examples**
Quasi-partnership	*Ebrahimi v Westbourne Galleries 1972:* In this case, the courts lifted the veil to reveal a company so completely in the nature of a partnership, that a winding-up of the company could be ordered on the grounds of it being just and equitable, because one of the directors being excluded from the management of the company represented a complete breakdown in the management of the company, just as it would be unlawful in a partnership.
Where a company is a sham	
• To prevent an evasion of obligations	*Gilford Motor Co Ltd v Horne 1933:* An employee was contractually bound not to solicit customers form his ex-employer after leaving its service. In order to get round this, he formed a company and carried on his work, soliciting his ex-employer's customers in the process. The veil was lifted to reveal his company as a 'mere cloak or sham' and an injunction was granted against it and the employee.
• To reveal national identity	*Re F G Films Ltd 1953:* An English company was formed to make an English film. In fact the staff and finance were American, the film was produced in India and there were neither premises nor employees in England. The veil was lifted to expose a 'sham' company with the result that the marketing and other advantages available to British films were not available in this case.

In addition to the courts sometimes exercising their discretion to lift the veil, **legislation** can also provide for the veil to be lifted, usually in order to confer a personal liability on those who run a company for breach of obligations imposed on the company. You should note that the following examples are only legitimate illustrations of the veil being lifted if the directors or others (upon whom liability is imposed) are also members of the company.

STATUTE	
Situation where the veil might be lifted	**Explanation**
Where a director is disqualified	Directors who participate in the management of a company in contravention of an order under the Companies Disqualification Act 1986 will be **jointly** or **severally liable** along with the company for the company's debts.

STATUTE

Situation where the veil might be lifted	Explanation
Fraudulent and wrongful trading (ss 213, 214 Insolvency Act 1986)	Where a company is being wound up • All persons who are knowingly parties to carrying on business with the intent of defrauding creditors or for some other fraudulent purpose (fraudulent trading) and • Directors who carry on business when they knew or should have known that the company would not avoid insolvent liquidation (wrongful trading) can be held **personally liable** to make such contribution to the company's assets as the court thinks fit.
Trading without a trading certificate (s 767)	A public company must obtain a certificate from the Registrar before it commences to trade. (We shall come back to this in Chapter 3.) Failure to do so leads to **personal liability** for the directors for any loss or damage suffered by a third party to a transaction entered into by the company in contravention of this section.

Activity 4   **(10 minutes)**

Following the collapse of Forest Ferns Ltd, Sandy is disqualified from being a director for five years. However, after three years, he sets up a company, Beach Holidays Ltd, of which he is a director and 95% shareholder. As a result of a terrorist attack on a passenger jet from Heathrow, the overseas holiday market collapses and Beach Holidays Ltd goes into insolvent liquidation. Which of the following best describes the legal position?

A   Beach Holidays Ltd is a separate legal personality and is therefore solely responsible for its debts.

B   Sandy is liable for Beach Holidays Ltd's debts as a 95% shareholder and the veil will be lifted to reveal the company as a sham, designed to conceal a sole proprietor's business.

C   The veil will be lifted on a statutory basis because Sandy is disqualified and he will be solely liable for the debts of Beach Holidays Ltd.

D   The veil will be lifted because Sandy was acting whilst disqualified and both he and Beach Holidays Ltd will be liable for the debts on a joint and several basis.

41

3.5 Types of company

As mentioned above, there are various types of company. The three main types are unlimited companies, companies limited by shares and companies limited by guarantee. Companies limited by shares fall into two further categories, **private** limited companies (as signified by 'Ltd' in the name) and **public** limited companies (as signified by 'plc'). An unlimited company is always a private company.

Definitions

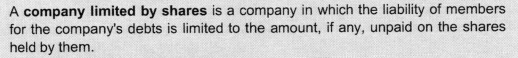

A **company limited by shares** is a company in which the liability of members for the company's debts is limited to the amount, if any, unpaid on the shares held by them.

A **company limited by guarantee** is a company in which each member undertakes to contribute (to the limit of his guarantee) on a winding-up towards the payment of the liabilities of the company.

An **unlimited liability company** is a company in which the members have no limited liability, so in the event of winding-up the members will be required to contribute to the debts of the company to any extent required.

Companies limited by shares are the most common form of company. Unlimited companies (always private) are similar to sole trader/ordinary partnerships in terms of liability for owners and publicity (they are not required to file information for public viewing unless the company is a subsidiary or a parent of a limited company) but the company still has a separate legal identity to the owners, so third parties trade with the company, not directly with the owners. This way the owners can remain 'hidden', if they so choose, while the company continues in operation.

There is some flexibility when choosing a type of company as there is limited provision in the law to entitle companies to re-register once from limited to unlimited and vice versa.

Definitions

A **public company** is a company limited by shares and registered as a public company under the Act.

A **private company** is a company which has not been registered as a public company under the Companies Act. The major practical distinctions between a private and public company are that the former may not offer its securities to the public and it is less heavily regulated as a result.

Because private companies cannot offer shares to the public they tend to be used for smaller family businesses, with plcs often being larger. This is a generalisation, however, and it is not automatically the case. Private companies can re-register once as public companies and vice versa, if circumstances change.

The principal differences between a public and a private company are that a public company is subject to more stringent rules and regulation than private companies and only a public company can offer its securities to the public. The principal features of public and private companies can be summarised as follows (at the same time illustrating the differences between them):

Feature	Public	Private
Liability	Must be limited	May be limited or unlimited
Share capital	Subject to authorised minimum (currently £50,000)	No minimum
Ability to commence trading	Must have trading certificate before it can commence trading (s 761)	May commence trading once incorporated
Public offers	Can offer its securities to the public (and may obtain a listing from the Stock Exchange or other investment exchange)	Prohibited from offering its securities to the public (s 755)
Name	Must end with 'public limited company' or 'plc' (or Welsh equivalent) (s 58)	Must end with 'limited' or 'ltd' (or Welsh equivalent) although certain companies (including charities) may be exempt from this requirement (ss 59–62)
Loans etc	Loans to persons connected with directors and quasi-loans and credit transactions to directors or connected persons need members' approval (ss 198–202)	These rules do not apply (unless the company is associated with a public company)
Directors	Must have at least two directors (s 154)	Must have at least one
Company Secretary	Must have one (s 271)	Need not have one (s 270)
Written resolutions	Not applicable	May pass written resolutions instead of calling meetings (s 288)
Annual general meetings (AGMs)	Must hold AGM (s 336)	Need not hold AGM
Accounts and reports	Must lay these before general meeting. Must file within 6 months (s 442)	Need not do so. Must file within 9 months (s 442)
Small-and medium-sized companies	Not applicable	May qualify as small or medium-sized, and take advantage of audit exemptions (small companies) and less stringent regime for filing
Appointment of auditors	Must appoint auditors each year if necessary (s 489)	Existing auditors may be deemed to be re-appointed, subject to conditions (s 487)
Pre-emption rights	May not be excluded	May be excluded

NOTES

Feature	Public	Private
Payment for shares	Additional rules apply to public companies, including that shares must be at least ¼ paid up (s 586) and concerning valuations for non-cash consideration (s 593)	Not applicable
Reduction of capital	Needs special resolution confirmed by the court (s 641)	Needs only special resolution and directors' solvency statement (s 642)
Power to redeem or purchase shares out of capital	Not applicable	May do so, subject to conditions (s 709)

In addition, special rules apply to **quoted companies** with regard to publication of details on the company website and directors' remuneration reports.

A private company may apply to the Registrar of Companies to be re-registered as a public company (or a public company as a private company) provided certain conditions and procedures are satisfied (ss 90–101).

Some of the differences between private and public companies will be looked at in more detail in the rest of this part of the book.

Activity 5 (30 minutes)

Look at one of the broadsheet newspapers on a Monday. Turn to the business pages and find out what information is given about public limited companies in the UK.

4 CHOICE OF ENTITY – ADVANTAGES AND DISADVANTAGES

The choice of which kind of business entity to adopt is often as follows:

Company	or	Partnership/Sole trader

The choice between operating as a partnership or sole trader is determined by the number of people intending to be involved in the business. The key considerations in terms of risk and reward are similar.

The key factors, often highlighted when making the choice between partnerships and companies, are:

- Ability to raise finance
- Liability of the owners

- Publicity requirements
- Flexibility

Flexibility

Flexibility is an important issue to consider when setting up a business, as it may not be possible to predict accurately the future of the business. A sole trader can easily make the decision to incorporate his business, that is, register a company through which to trade in the future. A person who has incorporated a company will be subject to regulations to dissolve that business should he wish to return to being a sole trader. The same can be said for ordinary and limited partnerships. A small business forming a private limited company has the option to convert to a public company, should it wish to raise finance from the public later on.

4.1 Table of factors

The details of some of these factors will be considered in the following chapters. However, the table below summarises all the factors that should be considered when making a choice between business entities.

Factor	Company	Ordinary partnership
Entity	Is a legal entity separate from its members.	Has no existence outside of its members.
Liability	Members' liability can be limited	Partner's liability is unlimited
Size	May have any number of members (at least two for a public company)	Some partnerships are limited to twenty members (professional partnerships excluded)
Succession	Perpetual succession – change in ownership of a company does not affect its existence	Partnership is dissolved when any of the partners leaves it, subject to any agreement to the contrary
Owners' interests	Members own transferable shares (that is, they can sell them)	Partners cannot assign their interests in a partnership
Assets	Company owns the assets	Partners own assets jointly
Management	Company must have at least one director; plc must have at least two	All partners can participate in management
Constitution	Company must have a written constitution (memorandum)	A partnership may have a written partnership agreement
Accounts	A company must usually deliver accounts to the Registrar	Partners do not have to send their accounts to a registrar
Withdrawal of capital	Strict rules concerning repayment of subscribed capital	More straightforward for a partner to withdraw capital

NOTES

Activity 6 (20 mins)

Alex, Barry and Catherine have traded as a partnership for several years. The business has been successful and has expanded rapidly. They believe it could expand further, but require additional capital to continue to expand in the way that they want to. They are considering registering their business, as they believe that this will enable them to seek the capital they need.

What options do they have, and what factors should they consider in making this decision about their business entity?

Chapter roundup

- An individual trading alone is a sole trader, while two or more people trading together may constitute a partnership.

- Both sole traders and ordinary partners incur personal liability for the debts of the business.

- The two main features of corporate personality are limited liability, in that the liability of the shareholders is limited to any amount unpaid on their shares, and separate legal personality, which means that the company is separate in the eyes of the law from its shareholders.

- A public company (plc) must be registered as such and is subject to more stringent regulations in many cases than a private company.

- A public company can issue its shares to the public, while a private company cannot.

Quick quiz

1 What sort of liability does a sole trader have?

2 Why do people like to trade in ordinary partnerships?

3 What is meant by limited liability?

4 Write down two advantages and two disadvantages of forming a limited company.

Answers to quick quiz

1 Unlimited personal liability

2 Privacy (no need to publish accounts)
Informality (no need to follow Companies Act)
Participation by partners
Freedom of action

3 That the liability is the shareholders is limited to the amount (if any) unpaid on their shares

4 Separate legal personality
Limited liability
Detailed accounts
Subject to company law

Answers to activities

1 Yes, as Cecil was acting in the normal course of the firm's business and he had apparent authority to bind the firm.

2 Law firms to investigate might include Linklaters and Slaughter & May. Accountancy firms might include KPMG and PwC.

3 The partners will not have to register the new partnership, unless they wish it to have LLP status. As they are the two largest firms in the UK, their merger might need to be considered in the light of competition law (see chapter 9). They will also need to draft a partnership agreement to cover the new partnership as there is likely to be a high number of partners. This would need to cover (for example) profit shares, partnership property, future partners policy, recruitment.

4 D. Directors who participate in a company's management while disqualified can be liable for its debts on a joint and several basis. If the director is also a member, as here, this is an example of the veil being lifted.

5 From Tuesday to Saturday, the Stock Exchange listings include the volume of trading on the previous day and the closing share price. On a Monday, following the weekend, information given includes the company's market capitalisation.

6 Alex, Barry and Catherine could register their business as a limited liability partnership or as a company. If they choose to register as a company, they must also consider whether they want to register it as a private company or as a public company.

There are various factors to consider. The key issue appears to be the requirement for additional finance. They would probably find it easier to raise finance for their business if it was a limited company. They further need to consider where they want the additional finance to come from. If they wanted to raise finance from the public, they could form a public company. However, this would add a burden of responsibility to those public investors in their business and could significantly reduce their control over the business, even if they established themselves as directors at the outset.

If they form a private company, they are still entitled to sell shares to friends and family and raise finance from them. Alternatively, they could issue loan capital. As the loan is made to the company and not to the partners individually, investors might consider this a better option than lending to a partnership. This would mean that the company was committed to paying interest on the borrowing, but that Alex, Barry and Catherine as shareholders and directors would retain control of their business.

Chapter 3 :
COMPANY FORMATION

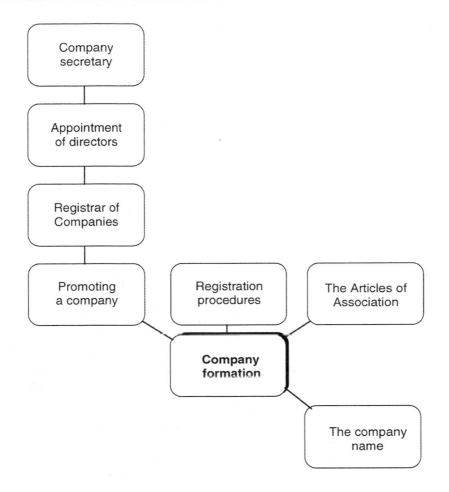

Introduction

Factors mentioned when considering what sort of business entity to form were the formalities and procedure connected with so doing. It is more complex to set up in business as a company than as a sole trader or partnership.

What you should bear in mind at this stage is that we are talking about **legal** complexity. In terms of the practical issues of setting up a business, they may well be similar. The parties involved will have to seek premises, buy or lease equipment, possibly employ people and also set up separate bank accounts for the business. Setting up a business may be similar whichever entity is preferred, but the legal requirements to follow (which will impinge on the practical issues) are very different.

Your objectives

In this chapter you will learn about the following:

(a) The legal requirements associated with forming limited companies

(b) Some of the legal documents associated with companies

(c) The rules regarding appointment of directors and the company secretary

Statutory references in this chapter are to the Companies Act 2006 unless otherwise indicated.

1   PROMOTING A COMPANY

There is substantial regulation involved in forming a company and trading as one. Forming a company is the subject of the rest of this chapter.

1.1   Promoters

A company cannot form itself. It needs a promoter to undertake the task.

Definition

> A **promoter** is 'one who undertakes to form a company with reference to a given project and to set it going and who takes the necessary steps to accomplish that purpose (Cockburn CJ in *Twycross v Grant 1877*).

Often, therefore, the promoter is the businessman. Whereas when a sole trader took the decision to go into business, the law did not change its view of him, when a businessman takes steps to form a company to conduct his business, he becomes a promoter. This is because he is seeking to form a new legal entity.

However, the promoter does not have to be the person behind a business project. Someone else can undertake to form a company with reference to the project. It is important to note at this stage, however, that professional people (for example, accountants or solicitors) helping to form a company in their professional capacity are **not** promoters on that account.

If the promoter is to be the owner of the company, it does not matter if he obtains some personal advantage from the process of forming a company. If, however, anyone else buys some or all of the shares, the promoter **owes certain duties** to the company:

- A general duty to exercise **reasonable care and skill**

- A **fiduciary duty** to disclose any personal interest in a transaction and, sometimes, to account for monies received. Generally speaking, any profits which he makes from promoting the company and fails to disclose must be surrendered to the company. However, if he discloses them and the company gives consent, he may retain any legitimate profits.

  In the case of a public company, disclosure is made through the listing particulars or prospectus. Disclosure in a private company should be to existing and prospective members or to the board of directors provided it is independent of him.

1.2 Promoters and pre-incorporation contracts

Since a company has no capacity to enter into contracts prior to its coming into existence, if a promoter makes a contact on the company's behalf prior to incorporating (a '**pre-incorporation contract**'), the following will apply:

- The **company cannot ratify** the contract since it did not exist when the contract was made *(Kelner v Baxter 1866)*

- The **company is not bound by it** even after incorporation and even if it has derived some benefit from it *(Re National Motor Mail Coach Ltd, Clinton's Claim 1908)*

- The **company cannot enforce the contract** against the third party unless the promoter and third party have given rights of action to the company under the Contracts (Rights of Third Parties) Act 1999

- The contract takes effect (subject to any agreement to the contrary) in the same way as one made with the **promoter** and he is **personally liable** on it (s 51)

A promoter can **avoid potential liability**, most usually by

- not making contracts until the company has been incorporated, or

- using an off-the-shelf company (see below)

- agreeing a draft only with the third party on the basis that the company, once formed, will enter into the agreed form with the third party.

Where a promoter is already liable on a pre-incorporation contract, he may be able to arrange for the company to **novate** the contract (ie enter into a new contract on identical terms), in which case he should also secure the third party's consent to the promoter thereupon being released from personal liability.

Note that giving rights to the company under the Contracts (Rights of Third Parties) Act 1999 does not also remove a promoter's liability since the Act provides that the original parties remain liable on the contract.

A promoter usually incurs **expenses** in preparations, such as drafting legal documents, made before the company is formed. He cannot legally claim any remuneration or indemnity for his services or expenses but, in practice, will generally arrange that the first directors, of whom he may be one, agree that the company shall make such payment to him.

Part B: Company Law

Activity 1 (10 minutes)

Imran is in the process of setting up a new company, Silver Stumps Ltd. Before submitting the application for registration, he enters into a contract on behalf of the company with Greenfields plc for the purchase of a cricket ground on the banks of the River Avon. Shortly after the company is registered and a certificate of incorporation issued, Silver Stumps Ltd finds that it is unable to raise sufficient funds and so fails to complete on the purchase on the due date. Which of the following best describes the legal position?

A   Greenfields plc may enforce the contract against Silver Stumps Ltd because Silver Stumps Ltd automatically assumes responsibility for contracts entered into on its behalf upon incorporation.

B   Provided Silver Stumps Ltd ratifies the contract with Greenfields plc, Greenfields plc may enforce the contract against Silver Stumps Ltd.

C   Greenfields plc may enforce the contract against Imran personally because Silver Stumps Ltd cannot ratify the contract

D   Imran's liability on the contract ceased because he has transferred all rights to Silver Stumps Ltd in accordance with the Contracts (Rights of Third Parties) Act 1999

2   REGISTERING A COMPANY

In most cases, when it is decided to incorporate a business, those responsible will apply to register a brand new tailor-made company. In some cases it may be appropriate to purchase a company that has already been registered.

2.1   'Off-the-shelf' companies

Because the registration of a new company can be a lengthy business, it is often easiest for people wishing to operate as a company to purchase one 'off-the-shelf'. This is possible by contacting enterprises specialising in registering a stock of companies ready for sale when a person comes along who needs the advantages of incorporation.

It is possible to buy a company that has already been incorporated. There are two principal advantages of such 'off-the-shelf' companies.

*   It is obviously a quicker way of achieving the result of having a company 'ready to go'.

*   It avoids any potential liability arising from pre-incorporation contracts as the company already exists.

There are disadvantages, however, since the following changes may need to be made.

*   Change of name
*   Transfer of subscribers' shares
*   Change of directors and possibly company secretary
*   Alteration of articles

2.2 Application for registration

A company is **formed by the issue of a certificate of incorporation** by the Registrar. The certificate names and describes the company and gives its registered incorporation number at the registry and date of incorporation.

To obtain the certificate of incorporation it is necessary to deliver to the Registrar certain prescribed documents (see below).

Document	Description
Memorandum of Association	A memorandum in the prescribed form stating that the subscribers (a) wish to form a company and (b) agree to become members of the company and, in the case of a company with a share capital, agree to take at least one share each. It must be authenticated by each subscriber.
Application	This must state • The company's proposed name (which is subject to certain rules designed to prevent the company misleading the public regarding its identity and/or activities (see below). • Whether the liability of the members is to be limited and, if so, whether by shares or guarantee • Whether the company is to be private or public • Whether the registered office is to be in England or Wales or Scotland or Northern Ireland • The intended address of the registered office (the registered office is the address for delivery of legal documents which may need to be served on a company and also where company registers must or may be kept (see below)).
Articles of Association (copy)	If none is supplied, the default articles will apply (see below).
Statement of capital and initial shareholdings (applicable to a company with a share capital)	It must state • the total number of shares • their aggregate nominal value • details of individual classes of shares • the amount to be paid and unpaid on each share This is essentially a snapshot of the company's share capital at the time of registration.
Statement of guarantee (applicable to a company limited by guarantee)	It must state the maximum amount which each member undertakes to contribute to the net assets of the company if the company is wound up while he is a member or within one year thereafter.

Document	Description
Statement of proposed officers	This must give particulars of and the consent of • the first director(s) of the company • the first company secretary (optional in the case of a private company).
Statement of compliance	This is a statement that the requirements of the Act have been complied with.

If the Registrar is satisfied that the registration requirements of the Act have been complied with, he will register the documents and issue the **certificate of incorporation**.

This certificate is conclusive evidence that the company is registered in accordance with the Act and is a body corporate. If irregularities in formation procedure or an error on the certificate are later discovered, it is nonetheless valid and conclusive (*Jubilee Cotton Mills Ltd v Lewis 1924*).

Note that a **public company** also needs to obtain a **trading certificate** before it can commence trading. It must submit

- an application stating (amongst other things) that the nominal value of the company's allotted share capital is not less than the 'authorised minimum' and

- a statement of compliance (s 762).

Any transaction in **contravention** of this provision will render any company officer in default liable to a fine but the transaction will remain valid. Failure to obtain a trading certificate within a year of incorporation may result in a compulsory winding-up (s 122 Insolvency Act 1986).

Activity 2 (10 minutes)

'Off the shelf' companies cannot exist on the shelf, waiting to be bought, unless all the usual formalities of registration have already been complied with. What changes are the buyers of an off the shelf company likely to make immediately on purchase?

---

3 THE ARTICLES OF ASSOCIATION

A company's articles form part of its constitution, along with all special resolutions and other relevant resolutions and agreements (s 17). Sometimes a power conferred on a company by the Act is subject to the authority to exercise that power being contained in the company's articles (for example, the power to reduce capital provided power to do so is given in the articles). Where the Act prohibits something permitted by the articles, the Act will prevail.

3.1 Model articles

'**Model articles**' prescribed by the Secretary of State in respect of different types of companies, will apply wherever a company is formed without registering articles or insofar as it registers articles that do not exclude or modify the model articles. The prescribed articles thus operate as **default** articles. Thus **Table A** refers to the model articles for a company limited by shares. Listed companies must have their own full-length articles containing a number of special provisions as required by Stock Exchange rules.

3.2 The contractual effect of a company's constitution

Under s 33 CA06, the provisions of a company's constitution (ie articles and relevant resolutions and agreement) bind the company and its members as if each had covenanted to the other to observe those provisions. They do not bind the company to third parties.

This principle applies only to rights and obligations which affect members **in their capacity as members** and applies when an outsider who is also a member seeks to rely on the articles in support of a claim made **as an outsider**. This point can be illustrated by the following case:

> *Eley v Positive Government Security Life Assurance Co 1876*
> *The facts:* Eley, a solicitor, drafted the original articles and included a provision that the company must always employ him as its solicitor. Eley became a member of the company some months after its incorporation. He later sued the company for breach of contract in not employing him as a solicitor.
>
> *Decision:* Eley could not rely on the article since it was a contract between the company and its members and he was not asserting any claim **as a member**.

Section 33 gives to the constitution the effect of a contract made between (a) the company and (b) its members individually. It also acts as a contract on the members **in their dealings with each other**.

In certain cases, if a contract contains no specific term on a particular point but the articles do, then the **contract may be deemed to incorporate the articles** to that extent. In one case, for example, a director's contract with the company was silent as to remuneration but the articles provided that directors would be paid £1,000 per annum. The court held that although the articles did not constitute a contract between the company and the director (in his capacity as director) they could be used to imply the term as to remuneration into his contract (*Re New British Iron Co, ex parte Beckwith 1898*).

Generally speaking, if a contract incorporates terms of the articles, it is subject to the company's **right** to **alter** its articles. However, where rights have already accrued under a contract, say for services rendered **prior** to the alteration, those rights will be unaffected by any alteration of the articles.

3.3 Alteration of articles

A company may normally alter its articles by passing a special resolution to that effect (s 21). However, where the articles contain '**provision for entrenchment**' (on first registration or later by unanimous agreement) such provisions can only be altered with the agreement of all company members or by court order (ss 21, 22). Such a provision for entrenchment might, for example, require that certain articles can only be changed if particular conditions are met or procedures followed that are more restrictive than the usual requirement for a special resolution. A company cannot provide that a provision for entrenchment can never be replaced or amended and must give notice to the Registrar whenever one is included or removed.

A copy of any amended article must be sent to the Registrar within fifteen days.

A member will not be bound by any alteration made after he became a member insofar as the alteration requires him to take more shares or increases his liability in any way to pay money to or contribute to the company (s 25).

4   THE COMPANY NAME

The name of the company serves to identify it and to distinguish it from any other company. For this reason, and to control the use of company names which might mislead the public, the registrar has statutory powers of control over the choice of names.

4.1   Choice of name

The choice of name of a limited company must conform to the following rules.

- (a)   The name must **end** with the word(s):

    - (i)   Public limited company (or plc) if it is a public company, or
    - (ii)   Limited (or Ltd) if it is a private limited company.

- (b)   No company may have a name which is the same as that of any existing company appearing in the statutory index at the registry. For this purpose two names are treated as 'the same' in spite of minor or non-essential differences; for instance the word 'the' as the first word in the name is ignored. 'John Smith Limited' is treated the same as 'John Smith & Company Ltd'.

- (c)   No company may have a name the use of which would in the registrar's opinion be a criminal offence or which he considers offensive.

- (d)   The approval of the Secretary of State is required if the name is sensitive in some way or likely to suggest some connection with the government or a local public authority. Words such as 'International' or 'British' are only likely to be sanctioned if the size of the company matches its pretensions.

Disclosure of company name

The name of the company must be displayed in certain locations and on certain documents in accordance with regulations made by the Secretary of State (s 82). The name must also be engraved legibly on the company seal (s 45). Breach of either provision may result in a fine.

4.2   Change of name

A company may change its name by passing a special resolution (which requires a 75% majority of the shareholders who vote) or otherwise as provided for in the articles, and obtaining the registrar's certificate of incorporation that he has registered the company under a new name: s 77. The certificate makes the change effective from when it is issued, though the company is still the same legal entity as before.

The Secretary of State can compel a company to change its name (within such time as he may allow) if:

- (a)   The name is the same as or virtually the same as that of an existing company, or

- (b)   The company's name may mislead the public.

Business names

Most companies trade under their own registered names. But a company may prefer to use some other 'business name', which need not be registered but which otherwise are regulated as for company names.

5 REGISTRAR OF COMPANIES

Under company law the privileges of trading through a separate corporate body is matched by the duty to provide information which is available to the public about the company. The prime sources of information on a UK registered company are as follows:

- Its **file at the Companies Registry** in which the Registrar holds all documents delivered to him by the company for filing. Any member of the public, for example someone who intends to do business with the company, may inspect the file.

- The **registers and other documents** which the company is required to hold at its registered office (or in some cases at a different address).

- The **London Gazette** in which the company itself or the Registrar is required to publish certain notices or publicise the receipt of certain documents.

- The **company's letterheads** and other forms which must give particulars of the company's place of registration, its identifying number and the address of its office: s 82.

5.1 The role of the Registrar

The Registrar's full title is the Registrar of Companies and Companies House is an agency of the Department for Business, Innovation and Skills (BIS).

In its application to Companies House for registration a company must state whether its registered office is to be situated in **England** (which includes Wales) **or** Wales, or Northern Ireland, or **Scotland**. The main headquarters of Companies House is in Cardiff and there are two regional offices in Edinburgh and London.

Throughout its existence the company deals only with Companies House, which holds its 'register' of details.

The company is identified by its **name** and **serial number** which must be stated on every document sent to Companies House for filing.

5.2 Contents of the company's register

On first incorporation the company's register, held at Companies House, includes a copy of its certificate of incorporation and the original documents presented to secure its incorporation.

If a company has been in existence for some time the register is likely to include the following:

- Certificate of incorporation
- Public company trading certificate
- Each year's annual accounts and return
- Copies of special and some ordinary resolutions
- Notices of change of directors

The Registrar is required to keep certain information in electronic form (including the articles, annual accounts and reports, annual return, statements of capital and statement of directors), but otherwise may keep the register in such form as he thinks fit.

Subject to exceptions listed in the Act (s 1087), any person has the right to inspect the register and, with payment of a fee, to require a copy of any material on the register. The exceptions to this right to inspect include the following:

- Protected information on directors' residential addresses
- The contents of any charges

Any person also has the right to a copy of any certificate of incorporation and the right to inspect the Registrar's index of company names.

6 COMPANY RECORDS, ACCOUNTS AND REPORTS

6.1 Company records

The term 'company records' refers to any register, agreement, minutes, accounting records or other documents required to be kept by the Act. They may be kept in hard copy or electronic form. In each case, the company record is to be kept at the company's registered office or at any other place specified in regulations made by the Secretary of State. The Act sets out rules relating to rights of inspection (and sometimes rights to receive copies) for members and others. Generally speaking, any contravention of any of these provisions renders the company and every company officer in default guilty of an offence and liable to a fine.

In particular, a company is required to keep the following company records:

- A register of members

- A register of directors and (if applicable) company secretaries

- A register of directors' residential addresses (this information is 'protected information' and must not be made available for public inspection)

- Copies of directors' service contracts and indemnity provisions restricting directors' liabilities

- Records of resolutions and minutes (for a period of ten years)

- Directors' statement and auditor's report

- A register of charges and copies of charges

In addition, a company is required to give copies of the company's articles, and certain other documents of constitutional importance, free of charge upon request (s 32). A company is not required to keep a register of debenture holders but, if it does, it must comply with the provisions concerned with its availability for inspections (s 743).

6.2 Accounts, reports and returns

Generally speaking, every company must keep accounting records and must produce annual accounts which normally require to be audited. In addition, the directors are responsible for producing a report. These accounts and reports need then to be circulated to members and filed at the registry. You should be familiar with the following framework, although be aware that there are many exceptions and points of detail which may be relevant in practice.

Document	Notes
Accounting records (s 386)	'Adequate accounting records' that are sufficient to show the company's financial position at any time with reasonable accuracy, including: • Daily entries of income and expenditure • Record of assets and liabilities • (If applicable) statements of stock and stocktakings
Annual accounts (s 393)	ie a balance sheet and profit and loss account. Consolidated group accounts are normally required where the company is a parent company. The accounts must give a 'true and fair view' of the company's financial position in respect of its financial year. Notes to the accounts must deal with employee numbers and costs and directors' benefits. The accounts must be approved by and signed on behalf of the board of directors.
Directors' report (s 415)	In respect of the financial year, the • Names of directors • Principal activities of the company • Statement that the auditor is not unaware of any relevant audit information A recommended dividend and business review, (including principal risks and uncertainties facing the company) are usually included although not always (for example small companies). (A consolidated report should be produced where group accounts are prepared). The directors' report must be approved by and signed on behalf of the board of directors.
Directors' remuneration report (s 420)	This applies to **quoted companies only** and is subject to the members' approval.
Auditor's report (s 495)	Where accounts are audited (see section 6.4 below) the report must • Identify the accounts audited and the financial reporting framework applied in their preparation • Describe the scope of the audit • State that, in the auditor's opinion, the accounts give a true and fair view of the company's financial affairs • State that the directors' report is consistent with the accounts

Document	Notes
Annual return (s 885)	The return must state the date to which it is made up and contain information including • The address of the company's registered office • Prescribed particulars of the directors and any company secretary • The type of company and its principal business activities • The address(es) of where the register of members and any register of debenture holders may be inspected (if not kept at the registered office) • A statement of capital and prescribed particulars concerning the members and the shares in the company The return must be signed by a director or secretary and delivered to the Registrar within 28 days of the return date (usually the anniversary of the date of incorporation).

Non-compliance with these provisions may render the company and any relevant officer liable to a fine and, in some cases, imprisonment.

A company's accounts and reports must be publicised in compliance with the Act, including filing them at the Registry within **nine months** (**private** company) or **six months** (**public** company) after the end of the relevant accounting reference period.

You should be aware that a less stringent regime applies to **small- and medium-sized companies** (for example, they may file 'abbreviated accounts'). Broadly, these are private companies which comply with two or more of the following requirements (s 382):

	Small	**Medium**
Turnover	≤ £6.5m	≤ £25.9m
Balance sheet	≤ £3.26m	≤ £12.9m
Employees	≤ 50	≤ 250

6.3 Audit requirements

Generally speaking, a company is required to appoint auditors to carry out an audit of its annual accounts. Some companies are exempt, namely:

• Small companies (that satisfy the small companies requirements as to turnover and balance sheet) } but not certain companies, including insurance or banking companies

• Dormant companies

• Non-profit-making companies subject to public sector audit

Even where an exemption applies, an audit can be required by 10% or more of the members or by members representing at least 10% of the nominal value of the company's issued share capital.

An auditor or auditors must be **appointed** for each financial year and can be appointed by the directors or by the members passing an ordinary resolution or, in the event of default, by the Secretary of State. The auditor's remuneration should be fixed by those appointing him. An auditor of a private company is deemed to be re-appointed unless the company decides otherwise (s 487).

The auditor has a **right of access** at all times to the company's books and accounts. He has a **duty** to carry out a proper investigation in preparing his report. He may be **removed** by ordinary resolution, subject to **special notice** being given and the auditor having the right to make representations.

Any person who knowingly or recklessly causes an auditor's report to include any matter that is misleading, false or deceptive commits an **offence** punishable by a fine.

6.4 Company secretary

Every **public company** must appoint a company secretary who satisfies the qualification requirements contained in the Act (s 273). Private companies may choose to have a company secretary but are not obliged to do so. The company secretary is usually appointed by the directors.

A company secretary is an employee of the company. He is also an 'officer' of the company and therefore faces potential civil and criminal liability where the Act so provides in the event of contravention by the company of legislative requirements.

The Act does not define the role of the company secretary and it will vary according to the size and nature of each company. However, typically, a company secretary will convene the meetings of the board of directors, issue the agenda and draft the minutes. He will also be responsible for the various statutory registers and for filing documents with the Registrar. In a smaller company, he is also likely to act as general administrator and compliance manager and might even be responsible for the accounts and taxation aspects of the company's business.

The company secretary is recognised as having the power to contract on behalf of the company in respect of its administrative operations, including the employment of office staff and management of the office generally. Thus he may bind the company by his actions on the basis of implied actual authority as well as any express or ostensible authority. However, a company secretary's implied authority is limited and does not extend to buying land, for example, nor to borrowing money, nor to doing other acts usually undertaken by the directors.

7   DIRECTORS: APPOINTMENT AND VACATION OF OFFICE

Definition

> Any person who occupies the position or fulfils the role of a **director** (ie to conduct the company's affairs) is treated as such, whatever he is called: s 250.

7.1 Directors and their appointment

Every company is required to have at least one director who is a natural person and a public company must have at least two directors (s 154). Generally speaking, a director should be aged sixteen or more (although there are exceptions) and he does not need to hold any particular qualifications. However, certain persons may be **disqualified** from acting, either by the Company Directors Disqualification Act 1986 or by the articles of association. A sole director cannot also hold the position of auditor of the company. You should be familiar with the following types of director:

Director	How such a director comes to be in office
Director (on incorporation or subsequently)	As provided by the articles, usually appointed • By existing directors or • By ordinary resolution (directors of public companies should be voted on individually (s 160))
De facto director (literally 'director in fact')	ie anyone who acts as a director, although not validly appointed as one. He becomes a director (and subject to all provisions concerning directors) by virtue of his conduct, rather than by formal appointment. He has the same powers as a properly appointed director.
Shadow director	ie someone 'in accordance with whose directions or instructions the directors are accustomed to act' save where that person is merely giving advice in a professional capacity, for example lawyers and accountants. Whether someone is a shadow director is a question of fact.
Alternate director	The articles usually provide that a director may appoint an alternate director to attend and vote at board meetings which he himself is unable to attend. The alternate director may be another director or an outsider. Some articles provide for such an appointment to be subject to the approval of the board.
Executive director	ie a director who is also charged with performing a specific role, eg a finance director, usually as an employee of the company. The articles usually provide for the directors to appoint one or more of their number to any executive function and on such terms as to remuneration and powers as they see fit. If an executive director ceases to be a director, his office will also terminate, but without prejudice to any claim he may have for breach of any service contract.
Non-executive director	ie a director (appointed or otherwise as above) who does not have a particular function but generally just attends board meetings. Directors' duties apply to non-executive directors in the same way as to executive directors. Many directors of public companies are non-executive and it is generally regarded as a great strength for a company to have a board consisting of both executive and non-executive directors. They are seen as helpful in contributing an independent view to the board's deliberations and ensuring the continuing effectiveness of the executive directors and their management of the company's affairs. A company normally appoints a **chairman** of the board of directors who also acts as chairman at general meetings. He is usually regarded as a non-executive director.
Managing director (MD)	The articles usually provide for the directors to appoint one or more of their number to be managing director(s), charged with carrying out day-to-day management functions.

A director's actions are valid even if his appointment is subsequently found to have been defective or void (s 161).

Any **change in the directors** of a company should be recorded in the company's register of directors and notified to the registrar within fourteen days.

7.2 Directors' vacation of office

A director might leave office in any one of the following ways:

- Death of the director or winding-up of the company

- Removal (see below)

- Disqualification (see 7.3 below)

- Resignation

- Not offering himself for re-election, where the articles provide for retirement and re-election of directors. (In the case of public companies, for example, Table A provides that one-third of all non-executive directors (those who have been in office the longest) shall retire each year and be eligible for re-election.)

In addition to any provision in the articles for removal, a company may **remove a director** from office by passing an **ordinary resolution** to that effect (s 168). **Special notice** (of 28 days) must be given of the intended resolution and the director then has the right to address the meeting and to request that any written representations that he makes be circulated to members or read out at the meeting.

Note that **removal** of a director may entitle the director to sue for **breach of contract** if he also has a contract of service with the company. Note too that this power of removal may be limited in the following ways:

- A director who is also a member may have weighted voting rights given to him under the constitution for such an eventuality, so that he can automatically defeat any motion to remove him as a director (*Bushell v Faith 1970*).

- It is possible to draft a shareholders' agreement stating that a member holding each class of share must be present at a general meeting to constitute a quorum. If so, a member holding shares of a certain class could prevent a director from being removed by not attending the meeting.

Activity 3   **(10 minutes)**

(1) Which of the following terms describes a person in accordance with whose directions or instructions the directors are accustomed to act?

    A   Alternate director
    B   Shadow director
    C   *De facto* director
    D   Non-executive director   **(cont'd)**

> (2) Which of the following accurately states the requirements for the removal of a director?
>
> A   Special resolution with ordinary notice
> B   Ordinary resolution with special notice
> C   Ordinary resolution with ordinary notice
> D   Special resolution with special notice

The Company Directors Disqualification Act 1986 provides that a court may formally **disqualify** any person from being (without leave of the court) a director (including a shadow director), liquidator, administrator, receiver or manager of a company's property or in any way directly or indirectly being concerned or taking part in the promotion, formation or management of a company. Disqualification is considered below.

In addition, the **articles** may provide that a director must vacate office if he becomes bankrupt or of unsound mind, or if he is absent from board meetings for, say, 6 consecutive months and the directors resolve that he should vacate office on that account.

Activity 4   **(10 minutes)**

A company has three members who are also directors. Each holds 100 shares. Normally the shares carry one vote each, but the articles state that on a resolution for a director's removal, the director to be removed should have three votes per share. On a resolution for the removal of Jeremy, a director, Jeremy casts 300 votes against the resolution and the other members cast 200 votes for the resolution. Has Jeremy validly defeated the resolution?

A   No, the articles are invalid insofar as they purport to confer extra votes.

B   Yes, the proceedings and articles are valid.

C   Yes. Whilst the articles are invalid and the voting is therefore 200 to 100 in favour, a special resolution is required and the necessary 75% majority has not been obtained.

D   No. A director is not entitled to vote on a resolution for his own removal.

7.3   Disqualification of directors

The Company Directors Disqualification Act 1986 (CDDA) was introduced in response to public disquiet with directors of failed companies being able to walk away from the wreckage of a company with no personal liability, regardless of the reasons for which the company failed. In many cases they would then go on to start new, very similar companies (so-called 'phoenix' companies) which had no liability to the previous creditors, who usually ended up with nothing.

The CDDA provides that a court may disqualify a person from being a director, liquidator, administrator, receiver or manager of a company and from being concerned in the promotion or management of any company. In some circumstances an order is in the courts' discretion; in others, it is mandatory:

	Grounds
A disqualification order for up to **fifteen years may** be made:	Where a person is **convicted** of a **serious offence** (usually in connection with the promotion, formation, management or liquidation of a company).
	Where it appears in the course of the **winding up** of a company that a person has been guilty of **fraudulent trading** (though not necessarily convicted of the offence).
	Where the **Secretary of State** considers it to be **in the public interest**.
	Where a director is guilty of certain **breaches of competition law**.
	Where a director has participated in **wrongful trading**.
A disqualification order for up to **five years may** be made:	Where a person has been **persistently in default** in relation to provisions of **company legislation** (and three convictions for default in five years are conclusive evidence of persistent default).
A disqualification order **must** be made, for a minimum of two years and a maximum of fifteen years:	Where a person has been a director of a company which has at any time become insolvent (whether while he was a director or subsequently) and his conduct as a director of that company makes him **unfit to be concerned in the management of a company**. (The courts may also take into account his conduct as a director of other companies, whether or not these other companies became insolvent. Directors can be disqualified under this section even if they take no active part in the running of the business.)

Note that a **bankruptcy order** made against a person **automatically disqualifies** him from acting as a director of a company or being concerned in the management or promotion of a company (s 11).

Offences for which directors have been disqualified include the following:

- Insider dealing
- Failure to keep proper accounting records
- Failure to read the company's accounts
- Loans to associated companies on uncommercial terms to the detriment of creditors

The courts' approach has been to view 'ordinary commercial misjudgement' as insufficient to justify disqualification.

> *Re Uno, Secretary of State for Trade and Industry v Gill 2004*
> *The facts:* A group consisting of two furniture companies carried on trading while in serious financial difficulties, while the directors tried to find a way out of the situation. Uno continued to take deposits from customers for furniture to fund its working capital requirements.
>
> *Decision:* The directors were not disqualified for acting in this way as their behaviour was not dishonest or lacking in commercial probity and did not make them unfit to manage a company. They had been trying to explore realistic opportunities to save the businesses, and were not to blame for the eventual collapse of the businesses and the subsequent loss of customers.

On the other hand, disqualification might be appropriate in cases of gross negligence or total incompetence. For example in *Secretary of State for Trade and Industry v Thornbury 2008*, a director was declared unfit to be concerned in the management of a company and disqualified for two years after failing to take steps to appraise himself of the company's financial position. It was considered wrong to rely totally on other directors' verbal assurances when, in fact, the company was in breach of its obligations to HMRC.

Breach of a disqualification order can result in a fine and/or imprisonment.

The following circumstances may result in the court imposing a lower period of disqualification **in mitigation.**

- Lack of dishonesty
- Loss of director's own money in the company
- Absence of personal gain (such as excessive remuneration)
- Efforts to mitigate the situation
- Low likelihood of re-offending

Administrators, receivers and liquidators all have **a statutory duty to report** to BIS on directors of companies in whose affairs they have become involved, where they believe the conditions for a disqualification order have been satisfied. The Secretary of State then decides whether to apply to the court for an order, but if he does decide to apply, he must do so within **two years** of the date on which the company became insolvent.

Activity 5	(10 minutes)

In *Bushell v Faith 1969*, the company had three members who were also the directors and each held 100 shares. On a resolution to remove a director, that director was to have three votes per share while other members were to have one vote per share. Could a director prevent a resolution to remove him from being put forward? Could he prevent it from being passed?

Activity 6	(10 minutes)

S was a director of a company which, a month after her resignation, became insolvent. She was also responsible for wrongful trading while a director of another company.

Consider whether she would be disqualified from being a director, if a court considered the matter.

Chapter roundup

- A company is formed by its promoters. They have a fiduciary duty to the company.

- A company cannot be a party to a pre-incorporation contract, but such a contract can be replaced by a new contract to which the company is a party.

- Several documents must be submitted in order to obtain a registration certificate for a new company.

- A private company may commence business without further formality, but a public company must obtain a trading certificate.

- A director is a person who runs the company, whether or not he is called a director. Directors may also be employees of their company, with contracts of employment. A private (but not a public) company may have only one director.

- Directors are generally elected by the existing directors and members.

- A director may resign. He may also be removed from office, either in accordance with the articles or by an ordinary resolution of the members.

- A director may be required by the articles to vacate office in certain circumstances. Any person may be disqualified from being a director under the Company Directors Disqualification Act 1986.

- Every public company must have a company secretary who must be appropriately qualified. The secretary is effectively the company's chief administrative officer and has apparent authority to bind the company in administrative contracts. A private company is not required to have a company secretary.

Quick quiz

1   What is a promoter?

2   What documents must be sent to the Registrar to form a private company limited by shares?

3   What additional step must a public company take before it commences business?

4   What are the rules about the number of directors?

5   What are the practical limitations on the members' statutory powers to remove a director from office?

6   Name the usual ways in which a director might vacate office.

7   Upon what grounds may a director be disqualified by a court order from holding office? When must the court disqualify him?

Answers to quick quiz

1 The person who establishes the company in law.

2 Memorandum
Articles (optional – if none set, default articles will apply)
Application
Statement of capital
Statement of proposed officers
Statement of compliance

3 Fee (2.2) Obtain a trading certificate.

4 All companies must have at least one
Plcs must have at least two

5 The members must form the appropriate minority to table a resolution. The director might have weighted voting rights.

6 Disqualification
Removal by the shareholders
Death or company liquidation
Resignation
Under the articles (eg bankruptcy or becoming of unsound mind or being absent from board meetings for 6 months without consent

7 Conviction for an indictable offence

Persistent default over company documents

Fraudulent trading

Wrongful trading

Public interest

Breaches of competition law

Must disqualify: conduct as a director of an insolvent company makes him unfit to be a director.

Answers to activities

1 C There is no automatic assumption of responsibility for promoters' contracts on incorporation. A company cannot ratify a contract entered into by a promoter before the company is formed because a principal must have been in existence at the time the contract was made in order to be capable of ratifying it. The reference to Imran's rights being transferred by the Act in D is inappropriate.

2 The buyers are likely to change the company's name and its directors.

3 (1) B

   (2) B

4 B See **Shirlaw v Southern Foundries Ltd**.

5 A resolution to remove a director could be put forward against his wishes, but he could prevent it from being passed (by 300 votes to 200).

6   S might be disqualified, but she need not be (unless her conduct while a director of the insolvent company makes her unfit to be concerned in the management of a company).

NOTES

Chapter 4 :
COMPANY ADMINISTRATION

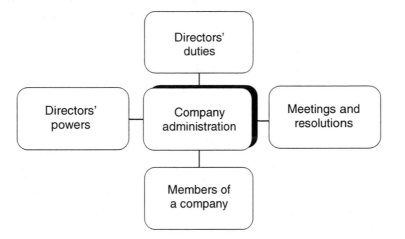

Introduction

In this chapter, we will look at company members and directors and see what rights and duties they have in law.

As an 'abstract' person, a company cannot manage itself. Company law therefore requires that every company must have one or more directors. Directors may also be shareholders although they are not required to own shares in the company. In smaller companies the shareholders and directors are quite likely to be the same people.

As a company is a separate legal entity from its owners, and people who are not its owners may manage it, there are more significant layers of rights attached to being a member of a company. These rights are generally derived from law and from the articles of association of a company. The two sources complement each other, although a company's constitution cannot give members rights that are illegal. The rights of members are considered in detail in the last sections of this part, especially in relation to general meetings and the passing of resolutions.

Your objectives

In this chapter you will learn about the following:

    (a)   The powers of directors

    (b)   Directors' duties

    (c)   The legal position of the members of a company

    (d)   General meetings of members and passing resolutions

Statutory references are to the Companies Act 2006 unless otherwise stated.

1 DIRECTORS' POWERS

The powers of the directors are defined by the company's articles. Normally directors are authorised, in general terms, to manage the business of the company and to exercise all the powers of the company. The old requirement for companies to specify their objects (which restricted the scope of their powers) no longer applies and companies now have **unrestricted objects** unless the articles specifically restrict them (as charitable companies are required to do under charities legislation and community interest companies might choose to do) (s 31). The directors' powers are to be exercised properly and within the company's constitution, but the directors are **not** agents of the members and subject to their instruction as to how to act. There are, however, some restrictions on these powers which result in powers being placed in the hands of the members rather than the directors.

Restriction	Explanation
Statutory (general)	The directors are statutorily bound to exercise powers only 'for the purpose for which they are conferred' (see section 2 below).
Statutory (specific)	For example alteration of the articles and reduction of capital need a special resolution, which the directors must secure from the shareholders in general meeting before they can act. Directors' actions which expressly require members' approval are detailed in section 3.3 below.
Articles	For example the articles may set a maximum amount that the directors are entitled to borrow, any greater amount needing approval of the company in general meeting. (As to whether such a restriction will be effective against a third party, see section 1.1 below.)
Members	The members can exercise control over the directors' powers • By passing a special resolution to alter the articles, thereby re-allocating the powers between the board and the general meeting • Ultimately by removing directors from office

The directors' powers are vested in them as a **collective body** and are exercised by the directors in board meetings. Generally speaking, it is considered sufficient if the directors are in communication with each other, usually by telephone, rather than necessarily being in one place at the same time and articles may make such provision. Equally, even if the directors are assembled together, there can be no board meeting if any of the directors object to a meeting being held in those circumstances.

1.1 Directors' authority and managing directors

If the board acting collectively or one director acting on his own has **authority** to enter into a contract on behalf of the company, then the contract will be binding on the company. A director's authority may be express or implied (actual authority) or it may be ostensible or apparent authority. The position is as follows:

Authority	Explanation
Express	Binding
Implied	Binding. **Managing directors**, and to some extent other executive directors (such as sales directors or finance directors), are much more likely to bind the company by their actions, since greater powers are usually delegated to them. There is little guidance from statute or case law, on the other hand, on what authority might be deemed to attach to non-executive directors or directors in lower or middle management, but it will not be as wide ranging as that attaching to a managing director. Thus a managing director has implied usual authority to make general business contracts on behalf of the company (in addition to any actual authority given to him by the board).
Ostensible	Binding. If the board permits a director to behave as if he were a managing director or give the impression that he is one, that director will have the **apparent or ostensible** authority to enter into all commercial contracts relating to the business as a managing director would have and to bind the company in respect of them.

See *Freeman & Lockyer v Buckhurst Park Properties (Mangal) Ltd 1964* in Chapter 1 in respect of managing directors.

1.2 s 40 Companies Act 2006

Where a director acts beyond any restriction placed on his authority, the position is governed by s 40. This provides that 'in favour of a person dealing with a company in good faith, the power of the directors to bind the company or authorise others to do so, is deemed to be free of any limitation under the company's constitution (s 40).

Note in particular:

- The section relates to **any transaction or dealing** between the company and a third party (ie not just to contracts)

- The other party is **deemed to be acting in good faith** unless the contrary is proved (and will not be deemed to be acting in bad faith just because he knows of the limitation)

- The **limitations to be disregarded** include any imposed on the directors by resolution or agreement of the members.

Section 41 provides that s 40 will not apply where the person dealing with the company is a director or person connected with a director. In such cases, the transaction becomes voidable at the instance of the company and that party is liable to account for any gain and to indemnify the party against any loss.

NOTES

Activity 1 (20 minutes)

Under the articles of association of Farming Ltd the directors of the company need the consent of the general meeting by ordinary resolution to borrow sums of money in excess of £50,000.

Mary has been appointed managing director of the company and she holds 1% of the issued shares of the company. Mary has recently entered into two transactions for the benefit of Farming Ltd. First, she arranged to borrow £100,000 from Conifer Bank Ltd, secured by a floating charge on the company's assets. However she failed to seek the approval of the members as required by the articles. Second, she placed a contract worth £10,000 with Saw Ltd to buy some agricultural machinery.

Advise the directors of Farming Ltd whether they are bound by the agreements with Conifer Bank Ltd and Saw Ltd.

A   The company is not bound by either contract
B   The company is bound by both contracts
C   The company is only bound by the contract with Conifer Bank Ltd
D   The company is only bound by the contract with Saw Ltd

---

2   DIRECTORS' DUTIES

For the first time, the Companies Act 2006 provides a **statutory code** of most **directors' duties** which take effect 'in place of' the common law rules and equitable principles which used to make up the law on directors' duties, but which will depend on those rules and principles for their interpretation and application (s 170).

There are, of course, **specific statutory duties** owed by directors, such as the obligation to prepare the directors' report, and other common law duties may remain that have not been codified, such as a duty to consider creditors' interests when insolvency is inevitable. However, the duties listed below are of more general application (indeed the Act refers to them as '**general duties**') and they are expressly stated to apply to shadow directors also.

2.1   General duties of directors

Duty	Explanation
To act within powers (s 171)	A director must • Act in accordance with the company's **constitution** • Exercise powers only for the **purpose for which they were conferred** If the directors infringe this rule by exercising their powers for a collateral purpose, the transaction will be invalid **unless** it is approved or ratified by the **company** in **general meeting**. If the irregular use of directors' powers is the allotment of shares, the votes attached to the new shares may not be used in reaching a decision in general meeting to sanction it.

Duty	Explanation
	Howard Smith Ltd v Ampol Petroleum Ltd 1974
	The facts: Shareholders who held 55% of the issued shares intended to reject a take-over bid for the company. The directors honestly believed that the bid's success was in the company's interest and so allotted new shares to the prospective bidder so that the shareholders opposed to the bid would then have less than 50% of the enlarged capital and the bid would succeed.
	Decision: The allotment was invalid. 'It must be unconstitutional for directors to use their fiduciary powers over the shares in the company purely for the purpose of destroying an existing majority or creating a new majority which did not previously exist'.
	If the majority approve what has been done (or have authorised it in advance) however, that decision is treated as a proper case of majority control to which the minority must normally submit.
	Bamford v Bamford 1969
	The facts: The directors of Bamford Ltd allotted 500,000 unissued shares to a third party to thwart a take-over bid. A month after the allotment, an ordinary resolution was passed ratifying the allotment, the holders of the newly-issued shares not voting. The claimants (minority shareholders) alleged that the allotment was not made for a proper purpose.
	Decision: The ratification was valid and the allotment was good. There had been a breach of fiduciary duty but the act had been validated by an ordinary resolution passed in general meeting.
To promote the success of the company (s 172)	A director must act in the way he considers, in **good faith,** would be most likely to **promote the success** of the company **for the benefit of its members** as a whole.
	He should have regard to the:
	• Likely **long-term consequences** of any decision
	• Interests of the company's **employees**
	• Need to foster the company's **businesses relationships** with suppliers, customers and others
	• Impact of the company's operations on the community and the **environment**
	• Desirability of the company maintaining a **reputation** for high standards of business conduct
	• Need to act **fairly** as **between members** of the company
	The duty is expressed to be subject to any legal rule or provision which requires directors, in certain circumstances, to have regard to the interests of creditors.
	What will promote the success of the company is a matter for the directors' good faith judgment.

Duty	Explanation
To exercise independent judgment (s 173)	It does not mean that he is **not** exercising independent judgment where he acts in accordance with • an agreement duly entered into by the company that restricts the future exercise of discretion by its directors, or • the company's constitution
To exercise reasonable care, skill and diligence (s 174)	ie the care, skill and diligence that would be exercised by a **reasonably diligent person** with • the general knowledge, skill and experience that may **reasonably be expected** of a person performing **his functions** as director • his **actual** general knowledge, skill and experience Thus it is no excuse for a director to say that he lacked expertise if a reasonable director in his position would have that expertise. Further more, his **actual** expertise may result in a **higher** standard than that of the reasonable director. The courts have held, for example, that a director who signs an insurance proposal without reading it may be liable in negligence. An executive director with expertise in a particular area, or even a non-executive director who is qualified or experienced in a relevant discipline, will be expected to show a higher standard of care than simply attending board meetings. Even someone with no commercial or business experience or qualification is required (by the Act) to demonstrate the care that may be expected of a person fulfilling his director's role. Simply attending board meetings and not attending to the company's interests in between meetings is unlikely to be sufficient in modern times.
To avoid conflict of interest (s 175)	A director must avoid a situation in which he **has or can have** a **direct or indirect interest** that **conflicts or possibly may conflict** with the **interests of the company** or **another duty**. This duty is particularly applicable to the exploitation of any property, information or opportunity, (regardless of whether the company could actually take advantage of it) but is expressly stated not to apply to any conflict arising in relation to a transaction or arrangement with the company (where ss 177 and 182 apply, see below). The **duty is not infringed** if the matter has been **authorised by the directors**. This may happen in a • **private** company, provided the company's constitution does not invalidate such authorisation • **public** company, provided the company's constitution expressly allows such authorisation In each case, the relevant director cannot be counted towards a quorum and his votes will not be included in determining whether the authorisation is given.

Duty	Explanation
To avoid conflict of interest (s 175) (cont)	If such authorisation is given there is no need for further approval by the members unless the company's constitution so provides. If the case falls within the statutory provisions for matters requiring members' approval (and these provisions are satisfied), then the director does not also need to comply with this duty.
Not to accept benefits from third parties (s 176)	A director must not accept a benefit from a third party by reason of his • being a director or • doing (or not doing) anything as director unless the acceptance of the benefit cannot reasonably be regarded as likely to give rise to a conflict of interest. If the case falls within the statutory provisions for matters requiring members' approval (and these provisions are satisfied), then the director does not also need to comply with this duty.
To declare interest in proposed transaction or arrangement (s 177)	Provided the director is, or ought reasonably to be, aware of the situation, he must **declare the nature and extent of any such interest** (direct or indirect) **to the other directors,** unless it cannot reasonably be regarded as likely to give rise to a conflict of interest. The notice may be made • at a board meeting • by notice in writing or • by a general notice, ie that he has an interest in the third party and is therefore to be regarded as interested in any transaction or arrangement with that third party (in which case he should take reasonable steps to ensure that such general notice is brought up at the next board meeting). Provided such declaration is made, there is no need for approval by the members or the board, unless the company's constitution so provides or unless it is an arrangement between a director and the company for the transfer of a 'substantial non-cash asset' (see section 3.3 below). (Note that a specific duty exists likewise in relation to **existing** transactions or arrangements as soon as is reasonably practicable (s 182). This duty applies also to shadow directors (s 187). Breach of this specific duty is punishable by fine.)

A person may continue to be subject to the duties in ss 175 and 176 even after he ceases to be a director, in certain circumstances (s 170 (2)).

One or more of the general duties may overlap, in which case each will apply. For example, taking a bribe from a third party would contravene the duty not to accept benefits from third parties (s 176). It might also amount to a failure to promote the success of the company for the benefit of its members (s 172) and/or a failure to exercise independent judgment (s 173).

EXAMPLE: DIRECTORS' DUTIES

Xray Ltd intends to enter into a contract for the supply of medical supplies from a firm in which Xavier, a director of Xray Ltd, is a partner. The terms of the contract are no less onerous than those of contracts between the company and other suppliers, but nonetheless Xavier is concerned that he may commit an offence if the contract goes ahead due to his interest in the firm. Advise Xavier.

Solution

Xavier is under a duty to avoid any situation in which he has an interest that, even potentially, conflicts with the company's interests, even if the company is not actually prejudiced as a result (it may even fair better as a result). However, this duty does not apply to a conflict of interest arising in relation to a transaction with the company, as is the case here. The relevant duty, with which Xavier must comply, is a duty to disclose his interest to the other directors pursuant to s 177. He should make such disclosure at a board meeting or in writing. He could provide a general disclosure of the nature and extent of his interest in the firm, so that he is to be regarded as interested in any transaction with it. Such general notice should be given at a board meeting or brought up at the next meeting following it. If he fails to do so, the contract will be voidable at the instance of the company and he could be liable to indemnify the company against any loss.

2.2   Breach of directors' duties

A director in breach of any of the duties imposed on him may be required to make good any loss suffered by the company, including accounting for any secret profits. Any contract entered into between the company and a director may be rendered voidable by the director's breach of duty. Any property taken by the director from the company can be recovered if it is still in his possession. It may be recoverable from a third party unless that third party required it for value and in good faith.

Where the breach has not yet occurred or is continuing, an injunction might be an appropriate remedy.

If another director, or directors, is or are also in breach then their liability will be joint and several. In the absence of any breach, however, a director will not be jointly liable with another who is in breach.

The articles of a company may impose **more onerous** requirements on its directors. They cannot, however, **dilute** the duties except to the extent that is permitted by certain provisions. For example:

- s 173: that a director will not be in breach of the duty to exercise independent judgement if he has acted in a way authorised by the constitution

- s 175: some conflicts of interest by independent directors may be permitted, subject to the constitution

- s 180 preserves any rule of law that would otherwise be a breach of duty.

Any **ratification** of conduct amounting to negligence or other breach of duty by a director (or former director or shadow director) must be made by an ordinary resolution of the members, disregarding the votes of that director and any member connected with him (s 239).

Note that any provision to exempt a director from or indemnify him against liability for breach of duty or negligence (or default or breach of trust) is **void** (s 232), save that a company may provide insurance and qualifying indemnity in respect of third parties.

2.3 Wrongful and fraudulent trading

In addition, a director faces personal civil and criminal liability and possible disqualification where he engages in wrongful or fraudulent trading.

Wrongful trading applies only where a company goes into insolvent liquidation and the liquidator can show that, at sometime before the commencement of the winding up, the director(s) knew or should have known that there was no reasonable prospect that the company could have avoided going into insolvent liquidation. However, no declaration of wrongful trading will be made where the court is satisfied that the director(s) took every step that he or they ought to have taken to minimise the potential loss to creditors (s 214 Insolvency Act 1986).

The standard applied is that of a **reasonably diligent person** with the general knowledge, skill and experience that might reasonably be expected of a person carrying out that particular director's duties (ie a reasonable occupant of a similar post). Where a director has greater skill and experience than a 'normal' director, he is also judged by reference to his own capacity. Thus the standard expected of a listed company director would be higher than for the director of a small owner-managed private company.

Where a director is liable under s 214 the court can order him to 'make such contribution to the assets of the company as the court thinks proper'. The fact that wrongful trading is not based on fraud is not a reason for giving a nominal or low figure of contribution, although the figure should be assessed in the light of all the circumstances of the case.

Fraudulent trading occurs where any business of a company is carried on with intent to defraud creditors of the company (or of another person) or for any fraudulent purpose. The offence is committed by any person who is knowingly a party to the business being carried in that manner. Note that only persons who **take the decision** to carry on the company's business in this way or play some active part are liable. '**Carrying on business**' can include a single transaction and also the mere payment of debts as distinct from making trading contracts. The criminal offence (s 993) may be committed whether or not the company has been or is in the course of being wound up and is punishable by a fine and/or imprisonment for up to ten years. It also gives rise to a civil liability for the company's debts on a winding-up (s 213 Insolvency Act 1986). Thus, as in the case of wrongful trading, a director may be ordered to make such contribution to the assets of the company as the court thinks fit.

The assets available for distribution in a winding-up will (potentially) be much increased by a large directors' contribution. It serves as a warning to directors to take professional advice sooner rather than later, as the prospect of making a personal contribution may prove much more expensive than winding-up at the appropriate stage.

3 MEMBERS OF A COMPANY

Any subscriber of a company's memorandum and any person entered on the company's register of members is a member of the company. A single member limited company must include a statement on its register that there is only one member. Subject to limited exceptions, a company cannot be a member of its holding company. Where a member owns shares in a company, he is called a 'shareholder'.

3.1 Regulation of the members

The members are regulated internally by the **articles of association**. These may be supplemented by a **shareholders' agreement** which deals with members rights and duties and which often offers more protection to the individual or minority shareholders, for example by requiring unanimous consent to an alteration to the articles, rather than the usual 75% majority. One advantage of a shareholders' agreement is that it is a private document not requiring registration. Thus it might cover the following matters in a wish to keep them off the public record:

- Confidentiality undertakings and non-competition restrictions, the right of certain shareholders to appoint directors and dispute resolution.

- Choice of bankers, cheque signatories and the company's policy on loans and borrowing.

A shareholders' agreement is of course, a binding contract and therefore enforceable in and subject to the courts' jurisdiction. It is particularly common in the case of companies which were formerly, or are in the nature of, a partnership.

3.2 Members' rights and communication

Members have a number of rights including the right

- to be sent a copy of annual accounts and reports
- to require directors to call a general meeting
- to appoint a proxy

A member may be entitled, under the company's articles, to nominate another person to exercise all or any of those rights in place of him.

Subject to any contrary provision in the company's articles, a company may send communications in electronic form, provided the member has agreed (generally or specifically).

A member of a **listed company** who holds shares on behalf of another person may nominate that other person to enjoy **information rights,** ie the right to receive a copy of all communications required to be sent to members, including accounting reports (s 146). Such information can be provided electronically unless a request is made for hard copies.

A member may take action to **enforce personal rights of membership** for example the right to vote *(Pender v Lushington 1877)* or receive a due dividend. Note that this is not a derivative action, on behalf of the company, but a personal action.

3.3 Approval of directors' actions

As mentioned in section 1, the Act provides for certain matters concerning directors (and shadow directors) to require the approval of the members in general meeting in order to be valid. These are:

Matter requiring approval	Notes	Consequences of breach
Service contracts (s 188)	Approval is required if the service contract provides for a director's employment to be a **guaranteed term of two years or more** (ie not terminable by the company in a lesser period or only in specified circumstances). A written memorandum setting out the proposed contract must be provided to the members prior to the resolution being passed.	The provision is void and the contract is thereafter deemed to include a term entitling the company to terminate it at any time on giving reasonable notice.
Substantial property transactions (s 190)	Approval is required for any arrangement where a director is to acquire from the company (or the company from the director) a **substantial non-cash asset**, ie one (or more) whose (aggregate) value • Exceeds 10% of the company's asset value and is more than £5,000 or • Exceeds £100,000 The section does not apply to transactions permitted under a relevant service contract or to payments for loss of office. There are other exceptions applicable to group companies, companies in winding up or administration and to transactions on recognised investment exchanges.	The company faces no liability for failure to obtain approval. The transaction is **voidable** at the instance of the company except in specified circumstances, unless the members give approval within a reasonable period. The director (and possibly others) is liable to account to the company for any gain and to indemnify the company against any loss or damage.
Loans to directors etc (s 197)	Approval is required for **any loan** by a company to a director or for any **guarantee** or **security** by a company in connection with a loan made by another party to a director. A written memorandum setting out the details of the transaction proposed must be given to the members	The transaction is **voidable** at the instance of the company, except in specified circumstances, unless it is approved by the company within a reasonable period. The director (and possibly others) is liable to account to the company for any gain and to indemnify the company against any loss or damage.

Matter requiring approval	Notes	Consequences of breach
There are similar provisions dealing with quasi-loans to directors and loans and quasi-loans to persons connected with directors, credit transactions (public companies only) and transactions related to any of the above	There are exceptions for • Expenditure on company business, defending proceedings or regulatory action or investigation • Minor transactions or ones in the ordinary course of business • Intra-group transaction • Money-lending companies	
Payments for loss of office (s 217)	Approval is required for **payments or benefits** to be made on **loss of office or retirement**. A written memorandum of the proposed payment (or other benefit) must be sent to all members. There are exceptions for small payments and payments in discharge of legal obligations.	The payment is held **on trust** for the company. Any director who authorised the payment is liable to indemnify the company for any loss.

Note that the general duties still apply even if one of these provisions applies (s 180) so that, for example, the directors should only approve a loan to a director if they are confident that it will not offend the duty to promote the success of the company. On the other hand, if members' approval is obtained under one of these provisions (or an exception applies so that approval is not needed) then the duties to avoid conflicts of interest and not to accept benefits from third parties (ss 175 and 176) will not apply (s 180), (but the other duties will still apply). For example, if a director fails to obtain authorisation from the directors or members for a loan in respect of legal defence costs, he will not be acting in breach of his duty to avoid conflicts of interest.

4 MEETINGS AND RESOLUTIONS

4.1 General meetings

Although a company's management is in the hands of its directors, decisions affecting the company's existence, structure and scope are reserved for members in general meeting.

A general meeting of the company **may** be called by

- The directors

- 10% of the members (broadly speaking, see below)

- The court (of its own motion or on the application of a director or member)

- An auditor who gives notice of his resignation accompanied by a statement of the circumstances connected with his resignation and requesting a meeting (s 518).

A general meeting of a **public** company **must** be called where the net assets fall to half or less of its called up share capital.

A meeting may be required and may specify any proposed resolution by members representing at least 10% of the paid up capital of the company that carries voting rights or (where there is no share capital) at least 10% of the voting rights (5% if more than twelve months has elapsed since the last general meeting and it is a private company) (s 303).

Within 21 days of any such requirement, the directors must call a meeting to take place within a 28-day notice period. If they fail to do so, the members (who requested the meeting or any of them representing over 50% of the total voting rights) may call a meeting to take place within three months of the initial request to the directors. A lesser number may require the company to circulate a statement of up to 1,000 words in respect of any resolution or other business to be dealt with at the meeting (s 314)

Notice of at least fourteen days (or longer if required by the articles) must be given unless **shorter notice** is agreed to by at least 90% (or up to 95% if so required by the articles) of the nominal value of the shares with voting rights or (where there is no share capital) at least 90% of the voting rights (95% in the case of public companies). A listed company, in addition, must pass an enabling resolution at its annual general meeting to allow a notice period of 14 days and must also offer electronic voting (under the Companies (Shareholders' Rights) Regulations 2009).

Notice must be given to **every member** and **every director** (s 310). The notice must state the **time, date and place** of the meeting and the **general nature of the business** to be dealt with. Note that in particular cases, special notice may be required (see 4.5 below).

Activity 2   **(10 minutes)**

Bonanza Ltd is a company limited by shares which last held a general meeting six months ago. Which of the following cannot now call a further general meeting?

A   The directors
B   Members representing at least 5% of the paid-up capital with voting rights
C   An auditor
D   A company secretary

4.2   Annual general meetings

Every **public company** must hold an annual general meeting ('AGM') once a year, during the six months following its accounting reference date (s 336). Failure to do so renders every officer of the company who is in default liable to a fine.

Notice of at least 21 days must be given unless **all the members** entitled to attend and vote agree to **shorter notice**. The notice must state that the meeting is an AGM.

The members of a public company may require the company to give notice of a resolution to be moved at the meeting, provided they represent at least 5% of the total voting rights or number at least 100 with shares on which there is paid up an average of £100 or more per member (s 338).

NOTES

The directors of a public company must lay its annual accounts and reports before the company in general meeting (s 437). This is normally done at the AGM. Typically other business will include the declaration of a dividend and the appointment of directors and auditors.

A private company is not required to hold an AGM.

Activity 3   **(10 minutes)**

In a public company, what percentage of the voting rights or nominal value of shares with voting rights must consent to a notice period of less than fourteen days?

	A For a general meeting	B For an AGM
51%	☐	☐
75%	☐	☐
90%	☐	☐
95%	☐	☐
100%	☐	☐

4.3 Resolutions at general meeting

Section 281 provides that resolutions can only be passed in accordance with the Act, namely:

- **Private** companies: as a written resolution or at a general meeting
- **Public** companies: at a general meeting
- Where a resolution is required but not specified, an **ordinary resolution** will be required (unless a higher majority is required by the articles).

These are two types of resolution which might be passed by the company in general meeting:

Type of resolution	Required majority of the votes cast	Business	Rules
Ordinary	>50%	Any business for which a special resolution is not specifically required by enactment or the articles	
Special	≥75%	Where special resolution is specifically required by enactment or the articles, for example: • Change of name • Alteration of the articles • Reduction of share capital • Winding-up the company	The notice of the meeting must include the text of the resolution and specify that it is to be moved as a special resolution. All special resolutions must be filed with the Registrar within fifteen days.

4.4 Written resolutions

The members or directors of a private company (but **not** a public company) may propose a **written resolution** without the need to hold a meeting in respect of any matter **except**

- Removal of a director
- Removal of an auditor

before the expiration of his period of office

The same majority of votes is required for any written resolution as would be required if the resolution were passed in general meeting. The expression 'written resolution' does not mean that there is a requirement for writing in the sense of hard copy. The members or directors (as the case may be) must comply with the procedural steps for resolutions laid down by the Act.

A written resolution must be passed within **28 days** from its circulation (or any other period specified in the articles). Once signified, a member's agreement to a written resolution cannot be revoked. A written resolution is passed once the necessary majority has signified agreement to it. Articles cannot override a private company's power to pass written resolutions (s 300).

4.5 Notice and special notice

As has been mentioned, fourteen days' notice is required for general meetings except

- For AGMs of a public company, which require 21 days
- Where special notice (of 28 days) is required to be given

The number of days always refers to **clear days**, that is excluding the day of the meeting and the day on which notice is given or a request is received. Thus, for an AGM of a public company on Thursday 25th, notice must be given on Wednesday 3rd.

Special notice of at least **28 days** needs to be given where a resolution is proposed

- To remove an auditor (s 510) or
- To remove a director or to appoint a substitute upon his removal (s 168)

The relevant director or auditor may submit written representations and require that they be circulated to members with notice of the meeting or read out at the meeting. They are also entitled to be heard at the meeting at which the resolution is proposed and/or the ensuing vacancy is filled.

4.6 Proceedings at meetings

Quorum A quorum is the minimum number of persons required to be present at a general meeting. Generally speaking (and subject to the company's articles) a company must have a quorum of two members or proxies or corporate representatives save that a single member company may have a quorum of one.

If the required number is not present, the meeting is said to be inquorate. Normally the articles provide for an automatic and compulsory adjournment in such cases.

Voting The rights of members to vote and the number of votes to which they are entitled in respect of their shares are fixed by the articles. One vote per share is normal but some shares, for instance preference shares, may carry no voting rights in normal circumstances. Voting may be:

- By a **show of hands**, ie where each member (or his proxy) has one vote irrespective of the number of shares held and exercises that vote by raising hands, or

- (More commonly) **by poll**, ie where each member and **proxies** representing absent members, may use as many votes as his shareholding grants him. If a poll is taken, the result of the previous show of hands is disregarded. (The Act provides that a poll may be demanded by a certain contingent of members (s 321).)

In voting, either by show of hands or on a poll, the number of votes cast determines the result. Votes which are not cast, whether the member who does not use them is present or absent, are simply disregarded. Hence the majority vote may be much less than half (or three quarters) of the total votes which could be cast.

Proxies Every member of a company has a statutory right (s 324) to appoint one or more persons as his 'proxy', to exercise all or any of his rights to attend, speak and vote at a meeting of the company and any more extensive rights conferred by the articles.

Records As noted earlier, every company must keep the following records for ten years (s 355) and available for inspection by members.

- Copies of all resolutions passed otherwise than at general meeting
- Minutes of all general meetings
- Details of decisions by sole member companies

Quoted companies must also publish on a website the results of polls at general meetings (s 341).

4.7   Class meetings

Class meetings may be held in respect of individual classes of shareholders or debenture holders and the rules for these are usually found in the articles or the debenture trust deed respectively.

Generally speaking, most statutory provisions relating to meetings and resolutions also apply to class meetings.

4.8   Single member private companies

Similarly, any enactment or rule of law applicable to companies with two or more members applies equally to sole member companies (with any necessary modifications) (s 38). A single member may conduct business informally without notice or minutes. However, he must still provide a written record of any decision that should have been taken in general meeting (or written resolution) and must comply with filing requirements in the normal way.

Chapter roundup

- Directors are empowered by the articles collectively to manage the company's business. They are requested to exercise their powers properly and within its constitution but are NOT the members' agents, so they are not subject to their instruction as to how to act.

- However, directors' powers may be restricted: under statute they may be exercised only for the purpose for which they were conferred: certain actions require specific approval from members; the articles may restrict directors' powers; members may alter the articles and thereby re-allocate powers; members may remove directors.

- A director may have express authority to bind the company, or usual authority may be implied in the case of managing and some other executive directors. A director may also bind the company if he acts within the apparent or ostensible authority that the company allows him.

- In favour of an unconnected party acting in good faith, under contract or otherwise, the directors' power to bind the company is deemed to be free of any limitation in the company's constitution.

- Directors have a minimum general duty under the Companies Act 2006 to: act within their powers; promote the success of the company; exercise independent judgment; exercise reasonable care, skill and diligence; avoid a conflict of interest; not accept benefits from third parties; declare interests in proposed transactions or arrangements. The articles may impose more onerous duties.

- A director in breach of his general duties must make good any loss suffered by the company and account to the company for any secret profit made.

- Directors may face liability and/or criminal sanction if they are involved in the wrongful trading of a company that later becomes insolvent, or if they engage in fraudulent trading at any time.

- Any person entered on the company's register of members is a member (or shareholder). Members are regulated by the articles and by any shareholders' agreement. They have various rights, including rights to information, and may enforce these in a personal action.

- To be valid, the following matters concerning directors must be approved in general meeting of members: service contracts; substantial property transactions; certain loans and guarantees; payments for loss of office.

- Although directors manage the company, members make certain key decisions in general meeting. Every public company must have an annual general meeting (AGM) before which the annual accounts and reports are laid.

- Public companies may only pass resolutions at general meetings; private companies may use written resolutions without the need to meet, unless the resolution is to remove a director or an auditor. These resolutions may be ordinary (simple majority of votes cast) or special (at least 75% majority of votes cast).

NOTES

Chapter roundup continued

- Usually only 14 days' notice is required for a general meeting, but an AGM requires 21 days' notice, and a resolution to remove a director, or to remove or substitute an auditor, requires 28 days' special notice

Quick quiz

1   Name TWO ways which indicate that the power of the directors is subject to the will of the members in general meeting.

   - ....
   - ....

2   List SIX of the general duties imposed on directors by statute.

   - ....
   - ....
   - ....
   - ....
   - ....
   - ....

3   The test of whether a director exercised reasonable care, skill and diligence is partly objective, ie the standard reasonably to be expected of someone performing his role as director, but also partly subjective if having regard to his actual general knowledge, skill and experience would require a higher standard.

   ☐   True

   ☐   False

4   The offences of wrongful trading and fraudulent trading only apply when a company goes into insolvent liquidation and may give rise to a personal liability on the part of a director.

   ☐   True

   ☐   False

5   What is the principal advantage of a shareholders' agreement?

6   Name THREE matters which concern directors but require approval of the members in general meeting and state briefly the consequences of breach.

Matter	Consequence of breach

7   Under what TWO circumstances is a public company required to call a general meeting?

    •   ....

    •   ....

8   Name THREE instances when a written resolution cannot be used.

    •   ....

    •   ....

    •   ....

9   Where special notice is required, how many days' notice must be given?

    ☐   7 days

    ☐   14 days

    ☐   21 days

    ☐   28 days

10   If the voting on a show of hands results in 58% in favour of a resolution and voting on a poll results in 61% in favour, which result counts?

Answers to quick quiz

1   •   Alteration of the articles requires special resolution

      •   Reduction of capital requires special resolution

      •   Borrowing power may need ordinary resolution

      •   Directors' office is subject to members' power to remove by ordinary resolution

2   •   To act within the company constitution and to exercise their powers only for the purposes for which they were conferred

      •   To promote the success of the company

      •   To exercise independent judgement

      •   To exercise reasonable care, skill and diligence

      •   To avoid conflicts of interest

      •   Not to accept benefits from third parties

      •   To declare any interest in a proposed transaction or arrangement

3   True

4   False. Fraudulent trading applies whether or not a company has been or is in the course of being wound up. It is true, however, that the commission of both offences can lead to a personal liability to contribute to the company's debts.

5   It does not need to be registered or open to public inspection.

6

Matter	Consequence of breach
Service contracts	Provision is void and contracts deemed to include provision for termination on reasonable notice
Substantial property transactions	Contract is voidable, director liable to account for any gain and indemnify against any loss
Loans to directors etc	Contract is voidable, director liable to account for any gain and indemnify against any loss
Payments for loss of office	Payment is held on trust for the company, director liable to indemnify for any loss

7   An AGM every year

Wherever its net assets are half or less of its called-up share capital

8   • In a public company
   • To remove an auditor
   • To remove a director

9   28 days

10   The vote on a poll. If a poll is taken, the result of the previous show of hands is disregarded.

Answers to activities

1   B   The company is bound by both agreements (assuming there is no lack of good faith on the bank's part). The transaction is beyond the authority of the managing director, Mary, in that she failed to obtain an ordinary resolution of the company as required by its articles of association. However s 40 provides that, in favour of a person dealing in good faith with a company, the power of the board of directors to bind the company or (importantly in this case) to authorise others to do so, shall be deemed to be free of any limitation under the company's constitution. Therefore the restriction placed on her actual authority (by the article requiring an ordinary resolution) shall be deemed not to exist in favour of the third party, Conifer Bank Ltd.

Farming Ltd will also be bound by the contract with Saw Ltd, as this was within her implied usual authority as managing director.

2   B   10% is required (5% is sufficient if the last meeting was over twelve months previously)

   D   The company secretary has no power to call a meeting

3   A   For a general meeting 95%
   B   For an AGM 100%

Chapter 5 :
COMPANY FINANCING

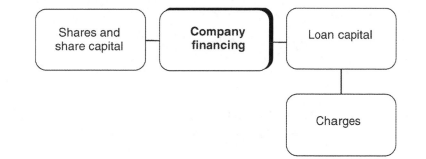

Introduction

In this chapter we shall look in detail at the two main ways in which companies are financed in the long term – by members in **share capital** and by creditors in **loan capital**.

Equity share capital is most usually found in the form of ordinary shares and preference shares. While holders of the latter are entitled usually to receive a priority dividend, that dividend is fixed and they do not always have voting rights. If they carry a preferential right to return of capital, they do not share in any surplus of assets in a liquidation after payment of capital. Ordinary and/or preference shares can be further split into different classes of share, each class having different rights.

We shall see that the power to allot shares is that of the directors, though the members can amend this authority by ordinary resolution. Shares are said to be issued once the shareholder receives either his allotment letter or his share certificate. A company does not have to call up from its shareholders the full amount due from them, but it is usually required to offer shares first to holders of similar shares in proportion to their holdings, under what is called the shareholders' pre-emption rights. This means that the current owners of shares have the choice as to whether a capital-raising exercise ends with their interest in the company being diluted. Shares need not always be paid for in cash and they can be issued at a price which exceeds the face value.

Loan capital is provided by the company's creditors and represents a series of contractual obligations by which the company is obliged to pay interest and to repay capital. Loan capital is often issued in the form of secured debentures, which are written acknowledgements of debt that are secured by means of a charge (such as a mortgage) over the company's assets. There are detailed rules about the creation and registration of different types of charge which affect what would happen in the event of the company being wound up.

Your objectives

In this chapter you will learn about:

(a) types of share and capital

(b) allotting, paying for and transferring shares

(c) paying dividends

(d) maintenance of capital provisions

(e) the features of debentures and the rights of their holders

(f) fixed and floating charges

1 SHARES AND SHARE CAPITAL

A **share** is a transferable form of personal property, carrying rights and obligations, by which the interest of a member of a company limited by shares is measured. A member of a company who holds one or more shares is a **shareholder**.

1.1 Types of shares

If the constitution of a company states no differences between shares, it is assumed that they are all ordinary shares. However, often a company will choose to confer different rights on different classes of share. You will remember from Chapter 3 that the statement of capital submitted on formation (or on subsequent actions of the company that have an effect on share capital) includes the prescribed particulars of the rights attached to each type of the company's shares. Details are also likely to be included in the company's articles.

The most common types of share are ordinary shares and preference shares. They (and redeemable shares) are described below:

Share	Feature
Ordinary	Ordinary shareholders have an automatic right to have their capital repaid and to participate in the distribution of profit, when the company is wound up, provided the company has surplus assets once creditors have been satisfied.
	Dividends are payable to ordinary shareholders only according to declarations made by the directors and they are not cumulative (whereas dividends payable on preference shares are normally cumulative).
	It is the ordinary shareholders who are normally offered the benefit of rights issues and bonus issues.
	All ordinary shareholders have statutory pre-emption rights (see section 1.5 below).

BPP LEARNING MEDIA

Share	Feature
Preference	Preference shareholders also have a right to have their capital repaid on a winding-up (unless the articles provide otherwise). If there is a surplus after repayment of capital, ordinary and preference shareholders will share equally. Where preference shares are expressed to carry a priority or preferential right to return of capital, the amount paid up on each preference share is to be repaid before anything is repaid to ordinary shareholders. In these circumstances, however, if there is a surplus after repayment of capital, the preference shareholders will have no right to share in that surplus.
	Typically preference shares will carry a prior right to a fixed dividend, in which case
	• it is not a right to compel payment of a dividend, simply to receive a dividend at the specified rate before any other dividend is paid or declared.
	• the right to receive a preference dividend is deemed to be cumulative unless the contrary is stated.
	• on liquidation, the preference shareholders cease to be entitled to any unpaid preference dividends unless
	– A dividend has been declared though not yet paid when liquidation commences and
	– The articles (or other terms of issue) expressly provide that in a liquidation arrears are to be paid in priority to return of capital to members
	• holders of preference shares have **no entitlement** to participate in any **additional dividend** over and above their specified rate unless that is expressly provided.
	Preference shares are usually expressed **not to carry a right to vote** (or only in specified circumstances, such as failure to pay the preference dividend, variation of their rights or a resolution to wind-up). If there is no express provision, they carry the same voting rights as ordinary shares.
	Preference shareholders do not have rights of pre-emption unless they are specifically conferred by the company's articles of association or terms of issue of the shares.
Redeemable	A redeemable share is one which is issued on terms that it can be bought back by the company at the option of the company or the shareholder. (Redemption of shares is dealt with at 1.13 below)

1.2 Class rights

Any share which has different rights from others is grouped with the other shares carrying **identical** rights to form a class. The rights that attach to shares in that class which are different from the rights enjoyed by all shareholders are called 'class rights'.

The rights attached to a class of shares (or members' rights generally in a company without a share capital) can be **varied** only in accordance with the articles or (if they contain no such provision) according to the procedure set out in the Act (s 630), namely

- A special resolution of the relevant class or written consent from at least 75% in nominal value of the issued shares of that class

- The holders of at least 15% of the issued shares of the class in question (who have not themselves consented to or voted in favour of the variation) may apply to the court, within 21 days of the consent being given by the class, to have the variation cancelled.

    The court can either confirm the variation as made or cancel it as 'unfairly prejudicial'. It cannot, however, modify the terms of the variation. A variation will be 'unfairly prejudicial' where it is shown that the majority who voted in favour was seeking some advantage to themselves as members of a different class instead of considering the interests of the class in which they were then voting (*Re Holders Investment Trust, 1971*). A copy of the court order must be forwarded to the Registrar within fifteen days.

- A notice giving particulars of any variation, or creation of a new class, must be delivered to the Registrar within one month of the variation.

Note that the fact that the value of existing rights may be affected will not concern the court if the **rights themselves** are unchanged. A class right is varied only if the right itself is altered. An alteration which affects how the right 'operates', but which leaves the right unchanged is not a variation.

For example, where shares of one class are subdivided with the incidental effect of increasing the voting strength of that class, the class rights of another class are not varied as a result, even though the rights of the non-altered shares are, in practice, less valuable.

Greenhalgh v Arderne Cinemas Ltd 1946

The facts: The company had two classes of ordinary shares, 50p shares and 10p shares. Every share carried one vote. A resolution was passed to subdivide each 50p share into five 10p shares, thus multiplying the votes of that class by five.

Decision: The rights of the original 10p shares had not been varied since they still had one vote per share as before.

1.3 Types of capital

The word 'capital' is used in different ways in relation to companies. You should be familiar with the following terms:

Term	Meaning
A company having a share capital	A company that has power under its constitution to issue shares (s 545)
Issued or allotted share capital	Shares that have been issued or allotted as the case may be (s 546) (including shares taken by the subscribers on the formation of the company).
	A company need not issue all its share capital. Any part of it not issued is called **unissued share capital**.

Term	Meaning
Called-up share capital	So much of the share capital as equals the aggregate amount of the calls made on its shares plus share capital that is paid up without being called and share capital to be paid at a specified future date under the articles or terms of allotment of the relevant shares (s 547)
Equity share capital	The issued share capital excluding any part of it that, neither as respects dividends nor as respects capital, carries any right to participate beyond a specified amount in a distribution (ie usually a company's ordinary share capital, since preference shares normally carry a right to a fixed return).
Loan capital	Loan capital describes the company's borrowed money. We will come back to this.

EXAMPLE: TYPES OF CAPITAL

Portions Ltd has 100 £1 (nominal shares) of which it has issued 80. It has received 25p per share on application and has called on the holders for a further 15p per share.

Its share capital is £100. Its issued share capital is £80. Its called-up share capital is £32 and its paid-up share capital is £20.

Activity 1   **(10 minutes)**

For each of A to D, indicate whether the statement applies to ordinary shares, or preference shares, or both.

		Ordinary	Preference
A	Shares carry statutory rights of pre-emption in the absence of any express provision	☐	☐
B	Shares carry a right to a dividend at a specified rate which is deemed to be cumulative in the absence of any express or implied provision to the contrary	☐	☐
C	Shares carry an automatic right to have capital repaid in the event of the company being wound up	☐	☐
D	Shares carry a right to vote in the absence of any express provision	☐	☐

1.4 Allotment of shares

Shares are **allotted** when a person acquires the unconditional right to be included in the company's register of members in respect of those shares (s 558). Shares are generally said to be **issued** once the allottee receives a letter of allotment or share certificate as evidence of his title. Once his name is entered on the register of members, he is then a member of the company.

The general rule is that the directors of any company may allot shares on the following basis (s 551)

    (1)   There must be authority given either by

- The articles or
- Ordinary resolution

        It can be general or specific, conditional or unconditional.

    (2)   The authority must state the

- Maximum number of shares to be allotted

- Expiry date for the authority, which must be not more than five years after the authority (ie after the incorporation or resolution)

The authority may be given, varied, renewed or removed by an **ordinary resolution**, even if this constitutes an alteration of the articles (which would normally require a special resolution).

The rule does not apply to the allotment of shares in pursuance of an employees' share scheme.

In addition, the directors of a **private** company **with only one class of shares** may allot shares of that class **unless** (and to the extent that) it is prohibited by the company's articles (s 550).

Any director who knowingly contravenes or allows a contravention commits an offence punishable by a fine.

A rights issue is an allotment of additional shares made to existing members, usually *pro rata* to their existing holding in the company's shares. If the members do not wish to subscribe for additional shares under a rights issue they may be able to sell their rights and so obtain the value of the option.

A **bonus issue** is the capitalisation of the reserves of a company by the issue of additional shares to existing shareholders, in proportion to their holdings. Such shares are normally fully paid-up with no cash called for from the shareholders.

1.5 Pre-emption rights

Whenever a company proposes to allot 'equity securities' (usually ordinary shares for cash), it is required to offer those shares first to holders of similar shares **in proportion to their holdings** (s 561) and on the same or more favourable terms. These rights of existing company shareholders to be offered new equity shares issued by the company *pro rata* to their existing holding of that class of shares are called **pre-emption rights**.

The offer must be made in writing or in electronic form and must specify a period of not less than **21 days** during which the offer may be accepted. Equity securities which have been offered to members in this way but are not accepted may then be allotted on the same (or less favourable) terms to non-members.

If equity securities are allotted in breach of these rules the members to whom the offer should have been made may, within two years from delivery of the return of allotment, recover compensation for their loss, if any, from those in default (s 563). The allotment will generally be valid.

These pre-emption provisions **do not apply** in the following cases:

Reason	Explanation
Exceptions	The Act provided that the provisions do not apply to allotments of • Bonus shares • Securities to be wholly or partly paid up otherwise than in cash • Securities relating to an employees' share scheme
Exclusions	A private company may exclude all or any of the provisions in its **articles**, either generally or in relation to allotments of a particular description
Disapplication	Directors of a private company **with only one class of shares** may be authorised to allot equity securities as if s 561 did not apply by either • The articles or • Special resolution Where directors are given **authority** by the company to allot shares, they may also be given the **power** to allot equity securities as if s 561 did not apply by either • The articles (where a general authority is given) or • Special resolution

Activity 2 **(10 minutes)**

The directors of Starwake plc propose to allot 1,000 shares at a nominal value of £5 each for cash.

		Yes	No
A	Can the company amend its articles of association to incorporate a provision excluding statutory pre-emption rights?	☐	☐
B	Is an authority to allot shares given by ordinary resolution sufficient?	☐	☐

1.6 Payment for shares

A company is prohibited from allotting shares at a **discount** to (or for a price which is less than) the nominal value (although it is permitted to pay a commission to someone who agrees to subscribe or to procure subscriptions for shares in the company, in accordance with its articles of association).

Shares must be paid up in **money or money's worth** (including goodwill and know how). Thus payment may be cash or a '**non-cash' consideration** of sufficient value. For instance, a company may issue shares in payment of the price agreed in the purchase of a property. Whilst a blatant and unjustified overvaluation will be declared invalid, the courts generally will not wish to intervene in a directors' valuation of an asset acquired for shares if it appears reasonable and honest. To issue shares '**at par**' is to obtain consideration equal to the nominal value. The prohibition on offering of shares at a discount on **nominal** value does not prevent a company from issuing shares at a price which is **below market value**.

The no-discount rule only requires that, in allotting its shares, a company shall not fix a price which is less than the nominal value of the shares. It may leave part of that price to be paid at some later time. Thus £1 shares may be issued at a price of £1 but only partly paid – 75p on allotment and 25p when called for or by instalment. The unpaid capital passes with the shares, if they are transferred, as a debt payable by the holder at the time when payment is demanded.

Shares are deemed to be allotted or paid up in **cash** where the company receives

- cash

- an undertaking to pay cash to the company (but not to another person) at a later date

- a cheque

- a release of its liability for a liquidated sum

There are additional rules which apply to **public companies**, as follows:

Rule	Explanation
Subscribers (s 584)	Shares taken by subscribers must be paid up in cash.
Services (s 585)	Shares cannot be paid for by an undertaking by someone to do work or perform services for the company or any other person.
1/4 paid up (s 586)	Shares must be paid up at least as to one-quarter of the nominal value plus the whole of any premium payable (except for shares allotted in pursuance of an employees' share scheme).
Long-term undertaking (s 587)	Shares cannot be allotted as fully or partly paid up otherwise than in cash if the payment is or includes an undertaking which may be performed more than five years after the allotment.
Valuation of non-cash consideration (s 593)	Any payment otherwise than in cash must be independently valued (subject to certain exceptions concerning mergers or an arrangement with another company).

Generally speaking, where an allotment is made in contravention of these provisions, the allottee is liable to pay an amount equal to the nominal value of the allotted shares together with interest. He may apply to the court for relief from such liability and the court may grant relief where it considers it just and equitable to do so.

1.7 Shares issued at a premium

Shares may be issued at **a premium**, for cash or otherwise. In such events, a sum equal to the premium on each share must be transferred to a **share premium account**. If a company allots 100 of its £1 (nominal) shares for £1.50 in cash, £1 per share is credited to the share capital account, and 50p to the share premium account. The allotment would be shown in the balance sheet as follows:

	Before share issue £	*After share issue* £
Cash	100	250
Share capital	100	200
Share premium	–	50
	100	250

That amount so transferred may be used to **write off the expenses** of the issue of those shares and any commission lawfully paid on the issue. The account may also be used to pay up new shares to be allotted to members as **fully paid bonus shares**. There are also special rules for group reconstruction relief and merger relief, which relieve companies from the requirement to transfer any premium to a share premium account. Thus if an acquiring company secures at least 90% of the equity capital of another company as consideration for an allotment of its shares, any premium obtained from the excess of the other company's assets over the nominal value of its shares need not be transferred to the share premium account.

Otherwise, the share premium account is treated as part of the company's paid up share capital and is subject to rules on the reduction of capital set out in the Act. For example, a company cannot distribute part of its share premium account

- as a dividend

- to write-off expenses incurred in connection with the formation of the company, nor

- to write-off expenses incurred in connection with an issue of debentures.

1.8 Transfer of shares

Shares are generally freely transferable in accordance with and subject to any restrictions contained in the company's articles (s 544).

Unlisted shares

Once the member-transferor and the transferee have reached agreement, the transferor holds the shares as trustee for the transferee until registration but remains a member of the company with the right to vote as he chooses. Once the transferee pays for the shares, the transferor must vote as directed by the transferee. Once the transferee's name is entered on the register of members, the transferor ceases to be a member and the transferee acquires all the member's rights.

The transferor executes a stock transfer form in favour of the transferee and gives it to him with the share certificate. Both are sent to the company for registration. Once the company receives a proper instrument of transfer, it must either register the transfer and prepare a share certificate or give notice of refusal to the proposed transferee, with reasons for the refusal, **within two months**. Where notice of refusal is given, the transferee's beneficial interest is not affected (that is, he is still entitled to any dividend or return of capital on winding up), but he cannot exercise all members' rights, including voting rights, until the transfer is registered and his name is entered on the register of members. He is also entitled to such information as he may reasonably require as to the reasons for the refusal (but he is not entitled to minutes of directors' meetings). Where the company fails to comply with these provisions, it and its officers are guilty of an offence punishable by a fine.

There is no requirement for certification where shares are transmitted by operation of law, for example where a bankrupt member's trustee in bankruptcy or a deceased member's personal representative becomes entitled to the member's shares.

Listed shares

Securities may be transferred without a written instrument.

CREST Co Ltd is a private company owned by a number of firms connected with all sections of the equities market. The company is currently the approved operator of an electronic system which enables shareholders to hold and transfer their securities without the need for written instruments of transfer. Under the CREST system, a member appoints a custodian broker to hold his shares under a customer agreement, which provides for the broker to deal with the shares only in accordance with the shareholder's directions. Any transfer of shares is normally completed in three days.

Regulations under the Act (made by either the Treasury or the Secretary of State) may provide that companies may be **required** (rather than just permitted) to adopt such a paperless holding and transfer of shares (s 785). Such regulations might impose such a requirement in relation to particular types of company or security or provide for the company to pass an ordinary resolution to that effect.

You should be aware that there are very detailed rules for the disclosure of substantial interests in the relevant share capital (essentially voting shares) of public companies. For example, in the case of companies listed on the Official List or Alternative Investment Market (AIM), issuers are obliged to publish their total share capital and voting rights at the end of each calendar month in which a change has occurred. A shareholder must notify the issuer (by completing a notification form) where his percentage of voting rights reaches 3% of the total voting rights of the company, and each 1% thereafter. It follows that this threshold may be reached even where a shareholder does not actually deal in the shares. He is therefore obliged to make the notification within two trading days of when he became or should have become aware of the notifiable change. These provisions are set out in the Disclosure and Transparency Rules.

1.9 Dividends

A dividend is one type of distribution of a company's assets to members of the company. The general rule is that any distribution can only be made **out of profits** that are available for the purpose and not out of capital.

Profits available for distribution are accumulated realised profits (which have not been distributed or capitalised) less accumulated realised losses (which have not been previously written off in a reduction or reorganisation of capital).

A dividend is a debt only when it is declared and due for payment. A shareholder (ordinary or preference) is not entitled to a dividend unless it is declared in accordance with the procedure prescribed by the articles and the declared date for payment has arrived. The directors may decide to withhold profits and cannot be compelled to recommend a dividend.

A **public company** may only make a distribution if its **net assets are**, at the time, not less than the aggregate of its called-up share capital and undistributable reserves. The dividend which it may pay is limited to such amount as will leave its net assets at not less than that aggregate amount (s 831).

Undistributable reserves are defined as

- Share premium account

- Capital redemption reserve

- Any surplus of accumulated unrealised profits over accumulated unrealised losses (known as a revaluation reserve)

- Any reserve which the company is prohibited from distributing by statute or by its articles.

If a distribution is made in contravention of the Act and the receiving member knows or has reasonable grounds for believing that the distribution is made unlawfully, that member will be liable to repay it (or a sum equal to its value where the distribution is made otherwise than in cash (s 847)). The directors may also be liable to repay the amount of the dividend as a result of the breach of directors' duties which will have occurred.

1.10 Maintenance of share capital

Generally speaking, a company cannot reduce its share capital. The **maintenance of capital** is a fundamental principle of company law that limited companies should not be allowed to make payments out of capital to the detriment of company creditors. In support of this principle, the Act contains provisions restricting dividend payments, financial assistance to aid share purchases, the uses to which share premiums may be put, the freedom of a company to purchase its own shares, and capital reduction schemes.

1.11 Permitted reductions of capital

There are circumstances where a company may be permitted to reduce its share capital which it may wish to do where, for example, its capital exceeds the company's needs or where the company's net assets have fallen in value to below the amount of its capital (as recorded in the accounts) and that position is likely to be permanent. A reduction in share capital may be achieved by various means, including reducing the liability on partly paid shares or by reducing the amount of paid up share capital and either returning it to shareholders or applying it to another purpose.

Companies are only permitted to reduce their share capital in accordance with the two methods prescribed by the Act (s.641). These are designed to reassure creditors with regard to capital invested in the company but also to give directors sufficient flexibility in managing the business effectively and to return unused capital in an appropriate manner. Both methods are subject to any restriction or prohibition contained in the company's articles of association.

Any limited company may reduce its capital by special resolution confirmed by the court. In most cases, any such confirmation is subject to creditors' rights to object to the reduction and to the court being satisfied that all creditors so entitled have either consented to the reduction or had their subsisting debts or claims discharged or secured. If a reduction is confirmed for a public company that results in the nominal value of the allotted share capital falling below the authorised minimum, the company must be re-registered as a private company unless the court directs otherwise.

A private company may reduce its capital by special resolution supported by a solvency statement given by all of the directors in a prescribed form (within 15 days prior to the resolution being passed) confirming the company's ability to pay its debts over a period of twelve months (s.643). This method is only permissible where there is at least one member remaining who holds a non-redeemable share.

A copy of the resolution and a statement of capital, together with a copy of the solvency statement or court order must be filed with the Registrar.

If the net assets of a public company are (or fall to) half or less of the company's called up share capital, the directors must call a general meeting in order to consider whether any steps need to be taken to deal with the situation.

Following a permitted reduction in capital the members' liability is reduced accordingly and any reserve arising from a reduction of capital may be treated as a realised profit for the purposes of distributions.

1.12 Other alterations of share capital

Although reductions are subject to strict controls, a company may alter its share capital as follows and in each case must give notice to the Registrar of such alteration, accompanied by a statement of capital, within one month:

Alteration	Rule
Increase (s 617)	By allotting more shares (see 1.4 above).
Subdivision or consolidation (s 618)	A limited company may pass on ordinary resolution to • subdivide its shares into shares of a smaller nominal amount than its existing shares or • consolidate and divide its share capital into shares of a larger nominal amount than its existing shares The proportion between the amount paid and amount unpaid on the original shares must remain the same. For example, if £1 is unpaid on a £10 share that is subsequently subdivided into ten £1 shares, there will then be 10p unpaid on each of those ten shares.

Alteration	Rule
Redenomination (s 622)	A company's share capital may be altered by a redenomination from one currency to another.
	Any resulting reduction of capital (as a result of rounding up or down nominal values in the new currency) must not exceed 10% of the nominal value of the reduced allotted share capital and a special resolution is required.

1.13 Redemption of shares

A public limited company must contain authority in its articles to issue redeemable shares and a private company may exclude or restrict the issue of redeemable shares in its articles (s 684). The directors' authority to determine the terms, conditions and manner of redemption may also be given by an ordinary resolution (even if it has the effect of amending the company's articles). Redeemable shares can only be issued when there are other shares issued that are not redeemable.

Redeemable shares may not be redeemed unless they are fully paid and, unless the terms of redemption provide otherwise, the shares must be paid for on redemption.

Redeemable shares may only be redeemed out of

(a) distributable profits of the company or

(b) the proceeds of a fresh issue of shares made for the purposes of the redemption *save that* a **private limited company** may redeem shares **out of capital** subject to certain conditions (which apply also to a purchase of shares described in section 1.14 below).

These provide that the company may make a 'permissible capital payment' in such amount as is required for the redemption or purchase after applying for that purpose

any available profits and the proceeds of any fresh issue of shares made for the purpose of the redemption or purchase.

A payment out of capital can only be made where the directors' statement and auditor's report support the payment and it is approved by a special resolution (disregarding the voting rights of shares to which the resolution relates). Any proposed payment out of capital must be publicised appropriately and creditors must be given an opportunity to apply to court for the cancellation of the resolution. The payment must be made within five and seven weeks after the resolution is passed.

When shares in a limited company are redeemed, the shares are treated as cancelled and the amount of the company's issued share capital is diminished by the nominal value of the shares redeemed. Notice of redemption, together with a statement of capital, must be given to the Registrar within one month.

1.14 Purchase of own shares

Generally speaking a company is prohibited from acquiring its own shares save in limited circumstances (s 658), namely:

- the redemption or purchase of shares in accordance with the Act

- the acquisition of shares in a permitted reduction of capital

- the purchase of shares in complying with a court order (eg buying out an unfairly prejudiced minority)

- the forfeiture or surrender of shares in accordance with a company's articles where there is failure to pay for them

A company's ability to purchase its own shares may reassure individual investors who might otherwise be concerned that shareholders do not have sufficient resources to buy them out. It may also enable difficulties to be resolved where one member wishes to retire or resign and the remaining shareholders do not wish to (or cannot) purchase his shares and do not want an outsider brought in.

A limited company may purchase its own shares in accordance with the provisions of the Act, subject to any restriction or prohibition contained in its articles and subject to there being issued shares of the company other than redeemable shares or treasury shares. It can only purchase its own shares where the shares are fully paid and the shares must be paid for on purchase.

A limited company may only purchase its own shares out of

(a) distributable profits of the company or

(b) the proceeds of a fresh issue of shares made for the purpose of financing the purchase *save that* a **private company** may use capital to purchase its own shares provided the conditions described in 1.13 above with regard to redemption of shares out of capital are satisfied.)

A market purchase, ie one made on a recognised investment exchange, must be authorised by a resolution of the company which specifies the maximum number of shares that can be acquired and states a maximum and minimum price that can be paid for them. An off-market purchase, ie one that is not conducted through a recognised investment exchange, must be authorised by a contract approved by (or conditional upon approval by) a special resolution (disregarding the voting rights of the shares to which the resolution relates).

A return giving details of the purchase must be sent to the Registrar of Companies within 28 days. Purchased shares are usually cancelled, although in some cases (generally speaking where the shares are listed or traded on the AIM or regulated market) the company may elect to hold them 'in treasury'. Treasury shares may be sold at a later date without obtaining prior authority from the company's members for the sale.

Where shares are redeemed or purchased out of a company's profits, the amount by which the company's issued share capital is diminished when shares are cancelled must be transferred to the capital redemption reserve. That reserve is treated as part of the company's paid up share capital, except that it may be used to pay up new shares to be allotted to members as fully paid bonus shares.

1.15 Financial assistance for the purchase of shares

- Under the Act, private companies are no longer (since October 2008) prohibited from giving financial assistance for the acquisition of their shares. However, public companies remain subject to restrictions.

Financial assistance may be given in various ways, including by way of gift or a gift of money to buy them or by guaranteeing or providing security for a loan given by a third party for the purposes of purchasing shares. (Lawful dividends and distributions on liquidation, permitted reductions of capital or redemption of shares, allotments of bonus shares and anything done in pursuance of a court order or arrangement with creditors are not prohibited by the rules on financial assistance (s 681).)

A **public company** (or its subsidiary) is prohibited from giving financial assistance at or before the time of an acquisition of shares in the public company, unless the principal purpose of the assistance is something other than the proposed acquisition (s.678) or the giving of assistance is only an incidental part of some larger purpose and (in either case) it is given in good faith in the interests of the company. The same prohibition applies to any financial assistance to be given by a public company for the acquisition of shares in its private holding company.

However, financial assistance *may* be given for the purpose of certain transactions (outlined below) by

- private companies

- public companies where the assistance does not reduce the company's net assets or, to the extent that they are reduced, the assistance is given out of distributable profits

The permitted transactions include:

- where the lending of money is in the company's ordinary course of business

- where the financial assistance is given in good faith in the interests of the company for the purposes of an employees' share scheme

- the making of loans to employees (not directors) in good faith to enable them to acquire fully paid shares in the company

Breach of the financial assistance rules is a criminal offence (s 680), punishable by fine and/or imprisonment, and is also likely to affect the contracts concerned and result in civil liability for breach of directors' duties.

Activity 3 (10 mins)

Scrunchies plc and Duffels Ltd are both companies operating in the retail sector. Which of the following might each of these companies be permitted to do under the Companies Act 2006?

		Scrunchies plc	Duffels Ltd
A	To buy-back redeemable shares out of capital	☐	☐
B	To purchase its own shares out of capital	☐	☐
C	To provide a loan to one of its directors for the purpose of acquiring shares in the company	☐	☐
D	To seek the court's approval to a reduction of capital	☐	☐

2   LOAN CAPITAL

A **debenture** is the written acknowledgement of a debt by a company, which normally contains provisions as to repayment of capital and interest. A debenture may be secured on some or all of the assets of the company by the creation of a **charge** over the company's assets. However a document relating to an unsecured loan is also a debenture in company law. A debenture is usually a formal legal document.

Like shareholders, debentureholders own transferable company securities which are usually long-term investments in the company and the procedure for issue and transfer of shares and debentures is very similar.

There are however important differences:

Factor	Shareholder	Debentureholder
Role	Is a member or owner of the company	Is a creditor of the company
Voting rights	May vote at general meetings	May not vote
Cost of investment	Shares may not be issued at a discount	Debentures may be offered at a discount
Return	Dividends are only paid out of distributable profits and when directors declare them	Interest must be paid when it is due
Redemption	Statutory restrictions on redeeming shares	No restriction on redeeming debentures
Liquidation	Shareholders are the last people to be paid in a winding up	Debentures must be paid back before shareholders are paid

From the investor's standpoint, debenture stock is often preferable to preference shares since the former offers greater security and yields a fixed income.

From the company's standpoint, raising capital by borrowing has obvious advantages but it has to bear in mind also the disadvantages of the rate of interest payable and, in particular, the liability imposed by any charge which is created in order to secure the loan.

3 CHARGES

Definition

> A **charge** is an encumbrance upon real or personal property granting the holder certain rights over that property, usually as security for a debt owed to the chargeholder.

The most common form of charge is by way of legal mortgage, used to secure the indebtedness of borrowers in house purchase transactions. In the case of companies, charges over assets are most frequently granted to persons who provide loan capital to the business. A charge **secured** over a company's assets gives to the creditor (called the 'chargee') a prior claim over unsecured creditors (and may give him priority over other secured creditors) to payment of his debt out of those assets. Charges are of two kinds, fixed and floating.

3.1 Fixed charges

A **fixed charge** is a form of protection given to secured creditors relating to specific assets of a company. It attaches to the relevant asset as soon as the charge is created. By its nature a fixed charge is best suited to fixed assets which the company is likely to retain for a long period.

A company is not permitted to deal with, or dispose of, assets that are subject to a fixed charge without the consent of the chargeholder. If the company does dispose of the asset it will either repay the secured debt out of the proceeds of sale so that the charge is discharged at the time of sale, or transfer the asset to the purchaser still subject to the charge.

The charge grants the holder the right of enforcement against the identified asset in the event of default in repayment so that the creditor may realise the asset to meet the debt owed. Fixed charges rank first in order of priority in liquidation.

When he comes to enforce the charge, the chargee may find that the value of the asset does not fully discharge the debt. In a liquidation, the unpaid balance then falls to be an unsecured debt.

Note that if a fixed charge is created to secure a debt within six months before a company becomes insolvent, then it **may** be invalid as a preference in an insolvency (see Chapter 6).

3.2 Floating charges

Unlike a fixed charge, a floating charge permits a company to deal with the charged assets without the permission of the chargeholder until such time as the charge crystallises (thereby becoming a fixed charge). The nature of a floating charge can be described as

- A charge on a class of assets of a company, present and future

- Which class is, in the ordinary course of the company's business, changing from time to time and

- Until the holders enforce the charge, the company may carry on business and deal with the assets charged.

A floating charge is often created by express words but no special form of words is essential. If a company gives to a chargee rights over its assets while retaining freedom to deal with them in the ordinary course of business, that will be a charge which 'floats'. The particular assets subject to a floating charge cannot be identified until the charge attaches by **crystallisation**, at which point the floating charge is converted into a fixed charge on the company's assets. A floating charge is not restricted however to current assets such as book debts or stock in trade. A floating charge over 'the undertaking and assets' of a company (the most common type) applies to future as well as to current assets. For this reason it is not possible to identify the assets to which a floating charge relates (until crystallisation).

Events causing crystallisation are as follows.

- The **liquidation** of the company

- **Cessation** of the company's **business** (which may occur on the crystallisation of another floating charge)

- **Active intervention** by the chargee, generally by way of appointing a receiver

- Any **event specified** in the charge, such as non-payment of interest on the due date or notice given by the chargee that the charge is converted into a fixed charge (on whatever assets of the relevant class are owned by the company at the time of the giving of notice)

A charge may provide for automatic crystallisation when a **specified event** – such as a breach of some term by the company – occurs, whether or not the chargee learns of the event and whether or not the chargee wants to enforce the charge as a result of the event. If the relevant clause specifies that, on the event happening, the floating charge is converted to a fixed one, then it is likely to be valid. However, if the clause provides only that a company is to cease to deal with charged assets on the occurrence of a particular event, it may not be valid.

3.3 Identification of charges as fixed or floating

It is not always immediately apparent whether a charge is fixed or floating and whatever **label** is given to it by the parties is **not conclusive**. Chargees often do not wish to identify a charge as being floating when it was created since this means that, if a receiver is appointed, preferential creditors must first be paid out of the charged assets (s 40 Insolvency Act (IA) 1986).

The general rule is that a charge over assets will not be registered as fixed if it envisages that the company will still be able to deal with the charged assets without reference to the chargee.

Charges expressed to be fixed but which cover present and future book debts are particularly problematic. In the recent landmark case of *National Westminster Bank plc v Spectrum Plus Limited 2005*, the House of Lords made it clear that, although a fixed charge over book debts is conceptually possible, if the chargor retains the right to deal with the book debts in the ordinary course of business in any way (including being able to withdraw amounts from a designated account into which collected book debts have had to be paid), then the charge (whatever it is called) will be a floating charge. In order to be a fixed charge, it is likely that the chargor must be prevented from dealing with the book debts altogether, perhaps by assigning them to the chargee or having to pay collected debts into a 'blocked account' with the chargee (essentially requiring the chargee's consent to any withdrawals).

Additionally a floating charge, if created within **twelve months** before liquidation, may become **void** automatically on liquidation (s 245 IA 1986).

3.4 Comparison of fixed and floating charges

A fixed charge is normally the more satisfactory form of security since it confers immediate rights over identified assets. However, a floating charge has some advantage in being applicable to current assets which may be easier to realise than fixed assets subject to a fixed charge. If for example a company becomes insolvent, it may be easier to sell its stock than its empty factory.

The principal **disadvantages** of floating charges are as follows.

- The holder of a floating charge cannot be certain until the charge crystallises (often through the company failing) which assets will form his security.

- Even when a floating charge has crystallised over an identified pool of assets the chargee may find himself **postponed** to the claim of other creditors as follows.

    - A **judgment creditor** or landlord who has seized goods and sold them may retain the proceeds if received before the appointment of the debentureholder's receiver (s 183 IA).

    - **Preferential debts** (for example remuneration and holiday pay owed to employees) may be paid out of assets subject to a floating charge unless there are other uncharged assets available for this purpose (ss 40 and 175 IA).

    - The holder of a **fixed charge** over the same assets will usually have priority over a floating charge on those assets even if that charge was created before the fixed charge (see below).

    - A creditor may have sold goods and delivered them to the company on condition that he is to retain legal ownership until he has been paid (a **Romalpa** clause).

    - The Enterprise Act 2002 also introduced a clause into the Insolvency Act 1986 stating that a '**prescribed part**' of the company's net property will be **available to unsecured creditors**, regardless of any charges over that property. This introduces an element of 'proportionality' for unsecured creditors. The amount of money that is to be so prescribed, or '**ring-fenced**', is set by the Secretary of State.

- As noted above, **a floating charge** may become invalid automatically if the company creates the charge to secure an existing debt and goes into liquidation within a year thereafter (s 245 IA); the period is only six months with a fixed charge.

Activity 4   **(10 minutes)**

A   What is the term used to describe the point at which a floating charge is converted into a fixed charge?

B   What is meant by 'ring-fencing'?

3.5 Priority of charges

Where different charges over the **same** property are given to different creditors, their priority must be determined. Thus, if charges are created over the same property to secure a debt of £5,000 to X and £7,000 to Y and the property is sold yielding only £10,000 then either X or Y is paid in full and the other receives only the balance remaining out of £10,000 realised from the security (unless they rank equally).

Leaving aside the question of registration (discussed below), the main points to remember in connection with the priority of any charges are as follows.

- Legal charges rank according to the order of creation (ie the one created first takes priority).

- Equitable charges also take priority according to the order of creation.

- A legal charge created before an equitable one has priority.

- An equitable charge created before a legal charge will only take priority over the latter if, when the latter was created, the legal chargee had notice of the equitable charge.

A creditor to whom a floating charge is given may seek to protect himself against losing his priority, by including in the terms of his floating charge a prohibition against the company creating a fixed charge over the same property, which would otherwise take priority (sometimes called a 'negative pledge clause'). In the absence of such a clause, however, the fixed charge will rank first since, although created later, it attaches to the property at the time of creation (whereas the floating charge attaches at the time of crystallisation). Once a floating charge has crystallised it becomes a fixed charge and a fixed charge created subsequently ranks after it.

3.6 Registration of charges

A company must keep available for inspection

- A copy of every instrument creating a charge which is required to be registered and

- A register of charges, listing all fixed and floating charges and giving the names of the chargees, the amount of the charge and a short description of the property charged either at the company's registered office or at another place specified in regulations and notified to the Registrar. They must be available for inspection by any creditor or member free of charge and by any other person on payment of a fee.

When a company creates a charge specified in the Act, it must also deliver prescribed particulars, together with the instrument by which the charge is created or evidenced, to the Registrar (s 860) within 21 days, beginning on the day after the charge is created (s 870). Registration may, alternatively, be effected by a person interested in the charge, rather than the company.

The Registrar enters details of the charge in the register (including its date, the name of the chargee, the amount secured and short particulars of the property charged). He then issues a **certificate of registration** of the charge, which is conclusive evidence that the registration requirements have been satisfied. The company must then endorse a copy of that certificate on any debenture issued by the company thereafter, the payment of which is secured by the registered charge (s 865).

Failure to register is an offence punishable by fine, although the court may extend the period for registration where it is satisfied that the failure (or mistake) was inadvertent or not likely to prejudice the company's creditors or shareholders, or otherwise just and equitable (s 873).

Failure to register will also affect the validity of the charge. Non-compliance with s 860 renders the charge **void** against any

- liquidator
- administrator and
- creditor

of the company. The money secured by the (void) charge is then immediately payable.

3.7 Lender's remedies

An unsecured creditor may sue the company for the debt or apply to the court for the appointment of an administrator or petition for a compulsory winding-up. A secured creditor may, in addition, appoint a receiver in respect of the property charged.

Liquidation, administration and receivership are addressed in Chapter 6.

NOTES

Chapter roundup

- The most common types of share are ordinary shares and preference shares.

- Shares which have certain rights not enjoyed by other shares in the company are grouped in a class and are said to have class rights.

- Generally speaking, shares may be allotted provided authority is given in the articles or by ordinary resolution and they must first be offered to existing shareholders in proportion to their existing holdings.

- Shares must be paid for in money or money's worth. They can be issued at a premium but not, as a general rule, at a discount.

- Shares are generally freely transferable and may be transferred in a paper or paperless format.

- A company may choose to raise loan capital rather than share capital. A debenture is the document that records the terms of any loan.

- A company may enter into a fixed or floating charge by way of providing security for its borrowing.

- The lender or debentureholder is then a secured creditor and will rank in priority to unsecured creditors in any liquidation of the company.

- Charges need to be registered.

Quick quiz

1   If a company fails to pay preference shareholders their dividend, they can bring a court action to compel the company to pay the dividend. True or false?

2   Which of the following are rights of preference shareholders (unless excluded by the articles)?

    A   The right to receive a dividend is cumulative.

    B   If the company goes into liquidation, preference shareholders are entitled to claim all arrears of dividend from the liquidator.

    C   As well as rights to their preference dividends, preference shareholders can share equally in dividends payable to ordinary shareholders.

    D   Preference shareholders have a priority right over ordinary shares for the return of their capital.

    E   Preference shareholders have equal voting rights to ordinary shareholders.

3   What is meant by 'called-up share capital'?

4   What is the majority of the relevant class required to consent to a variation of class rights?

5   What minimum percentage of shareholders in a class may apply to the court for a variation of class rights to be cancelled?

6   Where authority to allot shares is given to directors in the company's articles, what type of resolution is required to vary or renew that authority given that it results in an alteration of the articles?

7   **Fill in the blanks** in the statements below.

    A .... issue is an allotment of additional shares to existing members in exchange for consideration payable by the members.

    A .... issue is an allotment of additional shares to existing members where the consideration is effectively paid by using the company's reserves.

8   Do rights of pre-emption apply in the following cases?

A	A bonus issue	☐ Yes	☐ No
B	An allotment of ordinary shares for cash	☐ Yes	☐ No
C	An allotment of shares to be partly paid up otherwise than in cash	☐ Yes	☐ No
D	An allotment of shares pursuant to an employees' share scheme	☐ Yes	☐ No

9   Can a company issue shares

A	At a discount?	☐ Yes	☐ No
B	For a premium?	☐ Yes	☐ No
C	Otherwise than for cash?	☐ Yes	☐ No

10 A share premium account can be used for bonus issues of shares or discounts on the issue of debentures. True or false?

11 When a company receives an instrument of transfer, it must register the transfer or give notice of refusal within what time period?

12 Name THREE ways in which a company's share capital can be altered.

- ....

- ....

- ....

13 **Fill in the blanks** in the statement below.

A public company cannot make a distribution if it would reduce the company's net assets to below the aggregate of its .... and ....

14 Which of the following are correct statements about the relationship between a company's ordinary shares and its debentures?

A Debentures do not confer voting rights, while ordinary shares do.

B The company must pay interest on debentures and dividends on ordinary shares.

C A debentureholder takes priority over a member in liquidation.

15 What are the principal characteristics of a floating charge?

16 Company law requires a company to maintain a register of charges and to make it available for inspection by the public, not just members and creditors. True or false?

17 In which of the following situations will crystallisation of a floating charge occur?

A Liquidation of the company
B Disposal by the company of the charged asset
C Cessation of the company's business
D After the giving of notice by the chargee if the contract so provides

18 Within how many days of creation do most charges need to be registered?

19 What particulars of a charge must the Registrar be sent when the charge is registered?

20 What main remedies are available to a secured debentureholder to enforce his security?

Answers to quick quiz

1   False. The company may decide not to pay any dividend, or may be unable to because it does not have any distributable profits. What the preference shareholders have is a right to receive their dividends before other dividends are paid or declared.

2   A and E are implied rights; the others have to be stated explicitly.

3   A company's called-up share capital is so much of the share capital as equals the aggregate amount of the calls made on its shares plus share capital that is paid up without being called and share capital that is to be paid at a specified future date.

4   75%. A special resolution of the relevant class or written consent from at least 75% in nominal value of the issued shares of that class.

5   The holders of at least 15% of the issued shares of the class in question (who have not themselves consented to the variation)

6   An ordinary resolution, even though an alteration in the articles takes place (which would normally require a special resolution). Remember that authority to allot need not be given in the articles, it can be given by ordinary resolution.

7   A **rights** issue is an allotment of additional shares to existing members in exchange for consideration payable by the members.

    A **bonus** issue is an allotment of additional shares to existing members where the consideration is effectively paid by using the company's reserves.

8   A   No
    B   Yes
    C   No
    D   No

9   A   At a discount, no

    B   At a premium, yes

    C   Otherwise than for cash, yes. However note that the non-cash consideration must be independently valued in the case of a public company

10 True

11 Two months

12 • Allotment of more shares
    • Subdivision
    • Consolidation

13 Called-up share capital and undistributable reserves

14 A and C are correct. While the company has a contractual duty to pay interest on debentures, there is no necessity for it to pay dividends on shares. B is therefore incorrect.

15　A floating charge can be described as:

- A charge on a class of assets, present and future

- Which class is in the ordinary course of the company's business changing from time to time

- Until the holders enforce the charge, the company may carry on business and deal with the assets charged

16　True

17　A, C and D are true. As the charge does not attach to the asset until crystallisation, B is untrue.

18　21 days

19
- A copy of the charge
- The date that the charge was created
- The amount of the debt which it secures
- The property to which the charge applies
- The person entitled to it

20
- Take possession of the asset subject to the charge and sell it
- Appoint a receiver of it

Answers to activities

1　A　Ordinary shares
　　B　Preference shares
　　C　Ordinary and preference shares
　　D　Ordinary and preference shares

2　A　No.　Only a private company may do so.

　　B　Yes.　Authority may be given either in the articles or by ordinary resolution.

3

	Scrunchies plc	Duffels Ltd
A	No	Yes
B	No	Yes
C	No	Yes
D	Yes	Yes

4　A　Crystallisation

　　B　A certain percentage (prescribed by the Secretary of State) of a company's net property is 'ring-fenced' and made available for unsecured creditors, notwithstanding any charges over that property.

Chapter 6 :
COMPANY DISSOLUTION

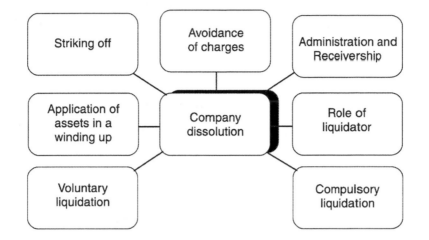

Introduction

Most company dissolutions follow liquidation or 'winding-up' (the terms are used synonymously). The assets are realised, debts are paid out of the proceeds and any surplus amounts are returned to members.

Liquidation begins with a formal decision to liquidate. If the members in general meeting resolve to wind-up the company, that is a voluntary liquidation. This may be either a members' or a creditors' voluntary liquidation, depending on whether the directors believe that the company will or will not be able to pay its debts in full.

A company may also be obliged to wind-up by a compulsory liquidation, ordered by the court on a petition usually presented by a creditor or a member.

Whether liquidation is voluntary or compulsory it is in the hands of the liquidator (or joint liquidators), who takes over control of the company from its directors. No further share dealings or changes in membership will be permitted (unless the court sanctions a rectification or other change) and all invoices, orders, letters and other company documents must state prominently that the company is in liquidation.

Very rarely, a company may be dissolved by the Registrar striking it off the register of companies. There are also provisions for the court to order the dissolution of a company as part of a merger, or a reconstruction of a group.

Your objectives

In this chapter you will learn about the following.

    (a)   How a company may come to be dissolved

    (b)   The effects of a decision to liquidate a company

    (c)   The grounds for compulsory liquidation

    (d)   The difference between a members' and a creditors' voluntary liquidation

    (e)   How each type of liquidation proceeds

    (f)   The role of a liquidation committee

    (g)   The position of contributories

    (h)   The powers and duties of liquidators

Statutory references in this chapter are to the Insolvency Act 1986 unless otherwise stated.

1 COMPULSORY LIQUIDATION

In a compulsory liquidation, a petition is presented to the court specifying the ground for compulsory winding up and is presented (usually) either by a creditor or by a member (called a 'contributory' in the context of liquidation). The standard grounds for compulsory liquidation are listed in s 122:

    (a)   The company has by special resolution resolved that it should be wound up by the court.

    (b)   The company, incorporated as a public company, has failed within a year to obtain a trading certificate.

    (c)   The number of members of a public company has been reduced to below two.

    (d)   The company has not commenced its business within a year of incorporation or has suspended its business for a year.

    (e)   The company is unable to pay its debts: s 122(1)(f). **This is the most common ground.**

    (f)   The court considers that it is **just and equitable** to wind up the company: s 122(1)(g). This ground may be used by a dissatisfied member.

1.1 Company unable to pay its debts

A creditor who petitions on the grounds of the company's insolvency may rely on any of three situations to show that the company is unable to pay its debts: s 123.

    (a)   A creditor (or creditors) to whom the company owes more than £750 serves on the company at its registered office a written demand for payment and the company neglects, within the ensuing 21 clear days, either to pay the debt or to offer reasonable security for it.

    (b)   A creditor obtains judgment against the company for debt and attempts to enforce the judgment but is unable to obtain payment because no or insufficient assets of the company have been found and seized.

(c) A creditor satisfies the court that, taking into account the contingent and prospective liabilities of the company, it is unable to pay its debts. The creditor may be able to show this:

- By proof that the company is not able to pay its debts as they fall due: the **commercial insolvency test**, or

- By proof that the company's assets are less than its liabilities: the **balance sheet test**.

At the hearing other creditors of the company may oppose the petition. If so, the court is likely to decide in favour of those to whom the larger amount is owing. But the court may also consider the reasons for the differences between the creditors.

1.2 The just and equitable ground

Orders have been made for liquidation on the just and equitable ground in the following situations.

(a) The company was formed for an illegal or fraudulent purpose or there is a complete deadlock in the management of its affairs.

(b) The understandings between members or directors which were the basis of the association have been unfairly breached by lawful action.

(c) The directors deliberately withheld information so that the shareholders have no confidence in the company's management.

(d) The main object of the company can no longer be achieved. (This is far less likely now that a company can have very broad purposes.)

Activity 1   **(10 minutes)**

In *Re a Company (No 003729 of 1982) 1984*, the petitioner for compulsory liquidation had demanded a sum due under a contract from the company. The company had disputed the amount due and had only paid part of the sum demanded. The petitioner therefore claimed that the company was unable to pay its debts. Why do you think the petitioner failed?

A member's petition to wind up the company on the grounds that it is just and equitable to do so, will only be considered if the company is solvent (otherwise he has nothing to gain from it) and he has been a registered shareholder for at least six of the last eighteen months prior to the petition (subject to some exceptions).

BIS may petition for the compulsory winding up of a company

- If a public company has not obtained a trading certificate within one year of incorporation

- Following a report by BIS inspectors that it is in the public interest and just and equitable for the company to be wound-up.

1.3 Proceedings for compulsory liquidation

When a petition is presented to the court a copy is delivered to the company in case it objects. It is advertised so that other creditors may intervene if they wish.

Once the court has received a petition, it may appoint a provisional liquidator: s 135. The Official Receiver (an officer of the court) is usually appointed, and his powers are conferred by the court. These usually extend to taking control of the company's property and applying for a special manager to be appointed (ss 144 and 177). He must investigate (s 132) the causes of the company's failure, and generally its promotion, formation, business dealings and affairs.

1.4 Effects of an order for compulsory liquidation

The effects of the order, which may be made some time after a provisional liquidator is appointed, are as follows.

(a)   The Official Receiver becomes liquidator though he may be replaced by an insolvency practitioner at a later date: s 136

(b)   The liquidation is deemed to have commenced at the time (possibly several months earlier) when the petition was first presented. If compulsory liquidation follows voluntary liquidation already in progress, liquidation runs from the commencement of the voluntary liquidation: s 129.

(c)   Any disposition of the company's property and any transfer of its shares subsequent to the commencement of liquidation is void unless the court orders otherwise: s 127. The court will decide whether to validate a disposition made under s 127.

(d)   Any legal proceedings in progress against the company are halted (and none may thereafter begin) unless the court gives leave. Any seizure of the company's assets after commencement of liquidation is void: ss 130 and 128.

(e)   The employees of the company are automatically dismissed. The provisional liquidator assumes the powers of management previously held by the directors.

(f)   Any floating charge crystallises.

(g)   The assets of the company may remain the company's legal property but under the liquidator's control – unless the court vests the assets in the liquidator.

(h)   The business of the company may continue but it is the liquidator's duty to continue it with a view only to realisation, for instance by sale as a going concern.

Within 21 days of the making of the order for winding up (or of the appointment of a provisional liquidator) a statement of affairs must be delivered to the liquidator verified by one or more directors and by the secretary. The statement shows the assets and liabilities of the company and includes a list of creditors with particulars of any security which creditors may hold and how long it has been held: s 131.

Meetings of contributories and creditors

The Official Receiver has twelve weeks to decide whether or not to convene separate meetings of creditors and contributories (members of the company). The purpose of these meetings would be to provide the creditors and contributories with the opportunity to appoint their own nominee as permanent liquidator to replace the Official Receiver, and a liquidation committee as their representative to work with the liquidator. (In cases of conflict, the creditors' nominee takes precedence over the members' nominee.) If the Official Receiver believes there is little interest and that the creditors will be unlikely to appoint a liquidator he can dispense with a meeting, informing the court, the creditors and the contributories of the decision. He must then call a meeting if at least 25% in value of the creditors require him to do so: s 136.

If the creditors do hold a meeting and appoint their own nominee he automatically becomes liquidator subject to a right of objection to the court: s 139. Any person appointed to act as liquidator must be a qualified insolvency practitioner.

At any time after a winding up order is made, the Official Receiver may ask the Secretary of State to appoint a liquidator. Similarly, he may request an appointment if the creditors and members fail to appoint a liquidator: s 137.

1.5 Completion of compulsory liquidation

When the liquidator completes his task he reports to BIS, which examines his accounts. He may apply to the court for an order for dissolution of the company. The order is sent to the registrar who gives notice of it in the London Gazette and dissolves the company: s 205.

Activity 2   **(10 minutes)**

Following an order for compulsory liquidation of a company with debts of £120,000, meetings of the creditors and contributories are held. The creditors nominate P as liquidator, whereas the contributories nominate S. P claims that he can realise the company's assets within a month for £100,000, whereas S claims that she can run the business and sell it as a going concern for £140,000 within six months. If nobody reconsiders his or her position, who will be appointed liquidator? Why is this?

---

2 VOLUNTARY LIQUIDATION

There are two types of voluntary liquidation: a members' voluntary liquidation (where the company is solvent) and a creditors' voluntary liquidation (where the company is insolvent and the members resolve to liquidate in consultation with creditors).

2.1 Members' voluntary liquidation

Rarely, a company's articles provide for liquidation on a specified event by ordinary resolution. More normally, a company may, by special resolution resolve to wind up for any reason.

The winding up commences on the passing of the resolution. A liquidator is usually appointed by the same resolution (or a second resolution passed at the same time).

Declaration of solvency

A voluntary winding up is a members' voluntary winding up only if the directors make and deliver to the registrar a declaration of solvency: s 89. This is a statutory declaration that the directors have made full enquiry into the affairs of the company and are of the opinion that it will be able to pay its debts, together with interest (at the rate applicable under s 189(4)) on those debts, in full, within a specified period not exceeding twelve months. It is a **criminal offence** punishable by fine or imprisonment for a director to make a declaration of solvency without having reasonable grounds for it. The declaration must:

- be made by all the directors or, if there are more than two, by a majority of them.

- include a statement of the company's assets and liabilities as at the latest practicable date before the declaration is made.

The declaration must be:

- made not more than five weeks before the resolution to wind up is passed, and

- delivered to the Registrar within fifteen days after the meeting (s 89).

The company may appoint a liquidator by passing an ordinary resolution to that effect. If the liquidator later concludes that the company will be unable to pay its debts, he must call a meeting of creditors and lay before them a statement of assets and liabilities (s 95).

The liquidator calls special and annual general meetings of contributories to whom he reports. Within three months after each anniversary of the commencement of the winding up the liquidator must call a meeting and lay before it an account of his transactions during the year: s 93. When the liquidation is complete the liquidator calls a meeting to lay before it his final accounts: s 94.

After holding the final meeting the liquidator sends a copy of his accounts to the registrar who dissolves the company three months later by removing its name from the register: s 201.

In a members' voluntary winding up the creditors play no part, since the assumption is that their debts will be paid in full. However, a members' voluntary liquidation may become a creditors' voluntary liquidation where the liquidation process is not progressing to the satisfaction of the company's creditors.

2.2 Creditors' voluntary liquidation

If no declaration of solvency is made and delivered to the Registrar the liquidation proceeds as a creditors' voluntary liquidation even if in the end the company pays its debts in full: s 96. Despite its name, this type of liquidation is *not* initiated by the creditors.

To commence a creditors' voluntary liquidation the directors convene a general meeting of members to pass a resolution. They must also convene a meeting of creditors (s 98), giving at least seven days' notice of this meeting. The notice must be advertised in the *Gazette* and two local newspapers. The notice must either:

(a) Give the name and address of a qualified insolvency practitioner to whom the creditors can apply before the meeting for information about the company, or

(b) State a place in the locality of the company's principal place of business where, on the two business days before the meeting, a list of creditors can be inspected.

The meeting of members is held first and its business is to resolve to wind-up, to appoint a liquidator.

The creditors' meeting should preferably be convened on the same day at a later time than the members' meeting, or on the next day, but in any event within 14 days of it. One of the directors presides at the creditors' meeting and lays before it a full statement of the company's affairs and a list of creditors with the amounts owing to them. The meeting may (if the creditors so wish) nominate a liquidator and a liquidation committee. If the creditors nominate a different person to be liquidator, their choice prevails over the nomination by the members.

It may be the case that the members' nominee takes office as liquidator pending the creditors' meeting. During this period the powers of the members' nominee as liquidator are restricted to

- taking control of the company's property

- disposing of perishable or other goods which might diminish in value if not disposed of immediately, and

- doing all other things necessary for the protection of the company's assets.

This prevents an obliging liquidator selling assets to a new company formed by the members of the insolvent company, in order to defeat the claims of the creditors at minimum cost and enable the same people to continue in business until the next insolvency supervenes. Such a transaction is referred to as 'centrebinding' following *Re Centrebind Ltd 1966*.

Re Centrebind Ltd 1966

The facts: The directors convened a general meeting, without making a statutory declaration of solvency, but failed to call a creditors' meeting for the same or the next day, for which they were liable to pay a small fine. The liquidator chosen by the members had disposed of the assets before the creditors could appoint a liquidator. The creditors' liquidator challenged the sale of the assets (at a low price) as invalid.

Decision: The first liquidator had been in office when he made the sale and so it was a valid exercise of the normal power of sale.

As a result of the restrictions introduced to prevent centrebinding, the members' liquidator is now required to apply to the court for leave if he wishes to perform any other act.

2.3 The effect of voluntary winding-up

> **Activity 3** **(10 minutes)**
>
> Why do the creditors of a company ordinarily have no role in a members' voluntary liquidation?

Unlike a compulsory winding-up, there is no automatic stay of legal proceedings against the company and the employees are not automatically dismissed.

FOR DISCUSSION

What is the point of requiring that all documents state that a company is in liquidation, given that the members and creditors are likely to be aware of that fact?

3 THE ROLE OF THE LIQUIDATOR

Once a liquidator is appointed, whether in a voluntary or a compulsory winding-up, his role is to:

- Settle the list of contributories (ie members who have a liability to contribute in the event of a winding-up)

- Collect and realise the company's assets

- Discharge the company's debts

- Redistribute any surplus to the contributories according to the entitlement rights attached to their shares.

On his appointment, the powers of the directors cease save to the extent that they are permitted to continue by the liquidator or (in a voluntary winding-up) by the company or creditors as appropriate.

Once the liquidation is complete, the liquidator must act as follows:

- In a **voluntary winding-up**, he must prepare an account showing how the winding-up has been dealt with and lay it before a meeting of the members and/or creditors. Within the following week he should then file details with the Registrar who will enter the details on the company's file and the company will be deemed to be dissolved three months thereafter.

- In a **compulsory winding-up** the liquidator must go back to the court which then makes an order dissolving the company. He then files the order and the Registrar records on the company file that the company is dissolved as from the date of the order.

A **liquidation committee** of between three and five creditors may be appointed by all the creditors to assist the liquidator. Voting by the creditors on the selection of committee members is by simple majority, based on the value of each attending creditor's debt. Once on the committee, however, each member has one vote (irrespective of the size of debt) and the committee acts according to single majority decisions. Liquidation committees act to inform the liquidator of creditors' views and assist by providing information from their knowledge of the company. Members of liquidation committees should act in the most appropriate way to further creditors' interests but should not profit from the membership (for example by using information gained through membership to bid for assets of the company).

Where a liquidation committee is formed, it is responsible for determining the liquidator's remuneration. It may also demand verbal or written reports from the liquidator as to the conduct and progress of the liquidation and is required to sanction the liquidator's actions in some cases.

4 AVOIDANCE OF CHARGES

In certain cases, charges or transactions entered into or debts incurred by the company may be invalidated, as follows:

Transaction	Explanation
Charges	Charges not registered within 21 days are void against the liquidator and creditors (and the chargee becomes an unsecured creditor)
Transactions at an undervalue	A transaction 'at an undervalue' is a gift or a transaction in the two years prior to liquidation (or administration), by which the company gives consideration of greater value than it receives, for instance a sale at less than full market price (s 238), unless the company enters into it • In good faith • For the purpose of carrying on its business • Believing on reasonable grounds that it will benefit the company
Preferences	A company 'gives preference' to a creditor or guarantor of its debts if it does anything • By which his position will be benefited if the company goes into insolvent liquidation • And with the intention of producing that result • Six months before the commencement of liquidation with a person unconnected with the company or two years in the case of a connected person ('connected' generally means a director, shadow director or associate) (s 239)
Floating charge	A floating charge created within twelve months prior to winding-up (or two years if given to a connected person) may be void or voidable

If at the time of the undervalue or preference the company was unable to pay its debts, or became so by reason of the transaction (save in the case of a preference with a connected person), and the company later goes into liquidation or administration, the liquidator or the administrator can apply to the court for an order to restore the position to what it would have been if no such transaction had taken place, for example by ordering the return of property or discharging any security.

You will recall that if the liquidator can show that the directors are guilty of wrongful or fraudulent trading the court may order that they be personally liable for some or all of the company's debts (ss 213, 214 IA).

Activity 4 **(20 minutes)**

Trading Ltd has recently begun a process of liquidation (in February 2010) following resolutions by the members and creditors to wind-up the company. Archibold and Duke, the two directors, have been researching insolvency on the internet and it has led them to be concerned over a number of transactions entered into by Trading Ltd over the past few years. They advise you that Trading Ltd has actually been unable to pay its debts since April 2006.

They ask for your advice as to whether the following transactions might be avoided by the liquidator.

A   A floating charge in favour of Adam plc for £100,000 created in March 2008   ☐ Yes   ☐ No

B   A sale of ten cars in March 2008 for £80,000. Archibold and Duke knew that they were probably worth over £90,000 but they honestly believed that the sale would be in the best interest of keeping the company afloat   ☐ Yes   ☐ No

C   A purchase in August 2009 of some car spares for £10,000 which Archibold made as a bit of a favour for the vendor. He suspected that they were only worth £7,500   ☐ Yes   ☐ No

D   A loan that Duke made to the company a few years previously was paid off in June 2009   ☐ Yes   ☐ No

---

5   APPLICATION OF ASSETS IN A WINDING-UP

A liquidator in a compulsory winding-up **must,** and in a voluntary winding-up is **likely to,** adhere to the following prescribed order for distributing the company's assets:

	Priority	Explanation
1	Costs	Including the costs of getting in the assets, liquidator's remuneration and all costs incidental to the liquidation procedure
2	Preferential debts	• Employees' wages (for a prescribed period and subject to a prescribed maximum) • Accrued holiday pay • Contributions to an occupational pension fund These rank equally

	Priority	Explanation
3	Floating charges	Subject to ring-fencing
4	Unsecured ordinary creditors	A certain percentage of assets is 'ring-fenced' for unsecured creditors where there is a minimum fund for distribution of £10,000, namely 50% of the first £10,000 of floating charge realisations and 20% of the floating charge realisations thereafter (subject to a prescribed maximum)
5	Deferred debts	For example dividends declared but not paid and interest accrued on debts since liquidation
6	Members	Any surplus (meaning that the company is in fact solvent) is distributed to members according to their rights under the articles or the terms of issue of their shares.

Note that secured creditors with fixed charges (and indeed floating charges) may appoint a receiver to sell the charged asset, passing any surplus to the liquidator. In the event of a shortfall they must prove for the balance as unsecured creditors. However, a floating chargeholder who faces a shortfall on his secured debt (which is therefore treated as unsecured) cannot share in the ring-fenced part available to unsecured creditors.

Activity 5 **(10 minutes)**

Buffers Ltd has an issued share capital of 5,000 × £1 shares and is in compulsory liquidation. The liquidator has a fund of £8,500 available for distribution and needs to distribute the fund to settle the following claims so far as possible:

- The directors declared a dividend of 10p, six months ago but it has not been paid.

- The liquidation costs, including remuneration, amount to £2,500

- Moneylender plc had a floating charge over the company's stock in trade which has now crystallised and the value is £4,000

- The company's employees have been paid, with the exception of some accrued holiday pay worth £1,200

- Mr Staples, the local stationery supplier is an unsecured creditor and is owed £830.

It is clear that there will not be a surplus for distribution to the members.

A   Which debt will be discharged first?
B   Will Mr Staples receive all of the money owed to him?
C   Will the members receive the dividend?
D   Do the ring-fenced provisions apply?

Following dissolution of a company (by whatever means) its property vests in the Crown as *bona vacantia* (s 1012 Companies Act '06), which means that there is no known person entitled to it. However the Crown has the power to disclaim it, in which case any interested person may apply to the court to have the property vested in them on such terms as the court sees fit.

6 ADMINISTRATION AND RECEIVERSHIP

You should be aware that a company in financial difficulties does not necessarily end up in liquidation. In many cases ways may be found to keep the business going. A company may enter into a 'company voluntary arrangement' or an administrator or receiver may be appointed.

6.1 Administration

Administration is relevant when a company is in financial difficulties but not necessarily insolvent or close to being insolvent. An administrator may be appointed by the court or out of court (in certain circumstances) and will be placed in control of the company, generally taking on the powers previously enjoyed by the directors. The company's creditors are given the opportunity to accept or reject the administrator's proposals for carrying out the administration. The primary aim of administration is to rescue the company as a going concern, failing which the secondary aim is to achieve a better result for the company's creditors than would be the case with a winding up. During an administration, a moratorium arises which means that no legal proceedings can be taken against the company without the consent of the administrator or the court.

6.2 Receivership

Rather confusingly, the term 'receiver' may denote two types of office, one of which was virtually abolished by changes made to the Insolvency Act 1986 by the Enterprise Act 2002, whilst the other remains.

An 'administrative receiver' is appointed by a floating chargeholder and is essentially a manager with control over the whole, or substantial part, of the company's property and extensive powers over its business. However, with some exceptions, administrative receivers can no longer be appointed by holders of floating charges created on or after 15 September 2003 which means that administration and company voluntary arrangements are much more likely to be adopted in the case of company insolvency, as an alternative to liquidation.

The term 'receiver' may also indicate a 'non-administrative receiver' or 'LPA receiver' (so-called because such receivers were traditionally appointed under the Law of Property Act 1925). A receiver may be appointed by the holder of a fixed charge over land in the event of the borrower's default. His role is to collect rent and/or sell the property. The appointment of a receiver may provide a relatively quick and inexpensive remedy for a lender and may be attractive where a straightforward exercise of his power of sale is not appropriate. Although the appointment of a receiver is often followed by liquidation, it is quite possible for the company to remain solvent and to continue in business once the receiver has performed his duties and vacated office.

7 STRIKING OFF

A company may be struck off the register, either by its own application or by the Registrar.

7.1 Defunct companies

The Registrar may strike companies off the Register if he reasonably believes they are not operating (s 1000 Companies Act 2006).

He writes a letter to the company enquiring whether it is still trading. If no reply is received within a month, a registered letter is sent within fourteen days warning them of the situation.

If no answer is received or if the answer confirms that the company is not trading, the Registrar may

- publish a notice in the *Gazette*, and
- send a notice to the company in the post

that the company will be struck off in three months. Unless cause is shown why the company should not be struck off, after three months it may be struck off the register and dissolved.

Any liabilities of directors, officers or members may still be enforced as if the company had not been dissolved.

7.2 Companies being wound up

Similarly, in the case of a company being wound up, if the Registrar believes, that no liquidator is acting or that a company's affairs have been wound up and a liquidator has failed to file the necessary returns for six consecutive months, the Registrar may give notice that the company shall be struck off and dissolved (s 100 CA 2006).

7.3 Non-trading private companies

The directors or a majority of directors of a non-trading private company may apply to have it struck off (s 1003 CA 2006). Certain restrictions apply, for example the company must not have traded for the three prior months and must not be in an arrangement with its creditors or be in receivership or liquidation.

Chapter roundup

- When a company is dissolved, it is removed from the register and ceases to exist. This can happen in several ways, but the most common way is liquidation. In a liquidation, a company's assets are disposed of, its debts are paid so far as possible and any surplus is paid to the members.

- A compulsory liquidation may be petitioned for on any of several grounds, but the most common ground is that the company is unable to pay its debts. A provisional liquidator (usually the Official Receiver) is appointed on the presentation of a petition and, if the court is satisfied, an order for winding up is granted. A statement of affairs is prepared and meetings of contributories and creditors may be held in order to appoint a replacement liquidator. The liquidator reports to BIS on the completion of his work.

- If a company is solvent, it may go into members' voluntary liquidation. The liquidator holds meetings of contributories and prepares final accounts once he has finished his work.

- A creditors' voluntary liquidation is also instigated by the members, but a meeting of the creditors must also be held. The creditors may nominate a liquidator and their choice prevails over the members' choice.

- A liquidation committee may be appointed to work with the liquidator.

Quick quiz

1   Give three grounds on which an order may be made by the court for compulsory liquidation of a company.

2   What grounds may be asserted in a creditor's petition to establish that the company is unable to pay its debts?

3   Give two examples of circumstances which can provide 'just and equitable' grounds for compulsory winding-up.

4   What meetings are called by the Official Receiver?

5   What type of resolution is passed to put a company into voluntary liquidation?

6   How many creditors may be appointed to a liquidation committee?

7   Can the directors of a company which is in the process of being wound up apply to the Registrar to have the company struck off the register in order to speed up the process?

Answers to quick quiz

1   Special resolution
    Unable to pay debts
    Just and equitable to wind-up

2   Written demand for payment of at least £750 remains unpaid for 21 days.

    Judgment obtained but not capable of being enforced

    Proof that company unable to pay its debts (by commercial insolvency or balance sheet test

3   Main purpose of company can no longer be fulfilled

    Illegal or fraudulent purpose

    Deadlock in management

    No confidence by shareholders

4   Meetings of members and creditors to appoint a liquidator.

5   Usually a special resolution.

6   3, 4 or 5.

7   No.

Answers to activities

1   The company was not necessarily unable to pay its debts but was deliberately disputing the amount due.

2   P: the creditors' choice prevails.

3   It is expected that all creditors will be paid in full, so there Is no need for them to interfere.

4   A   No   Floating charges created within the previous 12 months can be avoided

    B   No   It is a transaction at an undervalue within the past two years but it will not be avoided where the company entered into it in good faith for the purposes of carrying on the business and believing it to be in the company's best interests

    C   Yes   This is a transaction at an undervalue within the previous two years

    D   Yes   This is a preference given to a connected person and within the two years prior to liquidation

5   A   The costs of the liquidation, including the liquidator's remuneration

    B   He will receive £800 of the £830 owed, after payment of the costs, holiday pay (being a preferential debt) and floating charge.

    C   No. This is a deferred debt which ranks after unsecured creditors and the fund is insufficient to pay the debt.

    D   No, as the fund available for distribution is below £10,000.

Part C

Consumer Law

Chapter 7 :
CONSUMERS AND
BUSINESS ORGANISATIONS

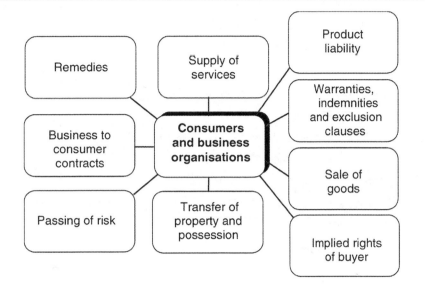

Introduction

A sale of goods is the most common type of commercial transaction. The law relating to sale of goods developed alongside ordinary contract law and was first codified in 1893. Subsequently the law on sale of goods has been consolidated into the Sale of Goods Act 1979, as amended.

A sale of goods may be viewed as a specialised form of contract. There are specific rules governing for example the transfer of property in a contract for the sale of goods, as well as delivery of the goods and remedies available in a case of breach of contract.

You will also meet the Supply of Goods and Services Act 1982, which largely extends the terms of the Sale of Goods Act 1979 to contracts where a service is being purchased. Examples include a contract for the repair of shoes or a contract to purchase the services of a plumber.

Attempts to exclude or restrict liability may be declared void under the Unfair Contract Terms Act 1977 or Unfair Terms in Consumer Contracts Regulations 1999. Unfair commercial practice in the selling of goods are covered by the Consumer Protection from Unfair Trading Regulations 2008. These are both described in this chapter.

Finally in this chapter we introduce the law relating to product liability.

Statutory references in this chapter are to the Sale of Goods Act 1979 unless otherwise noted.

NOTES

Your objectives

In this chapter you will learn about the following.

(a) What constitutes a sale of goods

(b) What terms are implied by the Sale of Goods Act 1979 (as amended)

(c) The significance of the seller's title and the consequences of defective title

(d) What is meant by the description of goods, and the implied conditions in a sale by sample

(e) What is meant by satisfactory quality and by fitness for purpose

(f) When property and risk pass to the buyer

(g) The rules on delivery

(h) The limits on the buyer's right to reject the goods

(i) What remedies the parties may have against each other

(j) The effect of the Supply of Goods and Services Act 1982

(k) The effect of warranties, indemnities and exclusion clauses

(l) Rules that apply only in business to consumer contracts

(m) Rules governing unfair commercial practices

(n) Product liability and the remedies of the consumer against a producer of defective goods

1 SALE OF GOODS

1.1 Definition

> A **contract for the sale of goods** is 'a contract by which the seller transfers, or agrees to transfer, the property in goods to a buyer for a money consideration, called the price' s 2 (1).

Sale includes both an immediate sale, such as purchase of goods in a shop, and an agreement by which the seller is to transfer ownership (in this context called 'property') in goods to the buyer at a future date.

1.2 Goods

There are various 'types of goods' which are set out below. These distinctions are important as title ('property') in some goods cannot be transferred until the goods are identified.

(a) **Existing goods** are those which exist and are owned by the seller at the time when the contract is made. **Future goods** are those which do not exist or which the seller does not yet own when he contracts to sell them. The main point of this distinction is that **property** (the ownership of the goods) **cannot usually pass from seller to buyer unless, or until, the goods exist as specific or ascertained goods.**

(b) **Specific goods** are those which are identified as the goods to be sold at the time when the contract is made, such as 'my Ford Focus, registration no WX 59 BPP'. Goods which are not specific are **unascertained** and become **ascertained** goods when they are subsequently identified as the goods to be sold under the contract.

Goods which have perished

In a contract for sale of specific goods there are rules laid down regarding the contract's status if the goods are perishable.

(a)   If, unknown to the seller, the goods have perished at the time when the contract is made, the contract is void: s 6.

(b)   If the goods perish after the contract is made, without fault of either party and before the risk (that is, the responsibility for loss or damage) passes to the buyer, the contract is avoided: s 7.

'Perished' may mean destroyed completely, or also deteriorated to a point so as to lose their commercial identity.

1.3   Price

The definition states that there should be 'a money consideration, called the price'. This means that an exchange (barter) for other goods does not give rise to a sale of goods. The implication of that is that the parties in such a contract would not be subject to the Sale of Goods Act. However, provided some money changes hands, as with a trade-in arrangement for a car, there is a contract for the sale of goods even though goods are also given.

The price 'may be fixed by the contract, left to be fixed in a manner agreed by the contract, or may be determined by the course of dealing between the parties': s 8(1).

Where the price is not determined in such a manner, 'the buyer must pay a reasonable price': s 8(2). The measure of what is reasonable depends on the circumstances of each case.

Unless the contract's terms imply a different intention, the time of payment is not treated as being of the essence of a contract for sale. (this means that any delay in payment does not automatically entitle the payee to treat the contract as discharged).

In the case of a contract for the supply of goods or services (subject to limited exceptions) which is made between two parties in the course of business, the Late Payment of Commercial Debts (Interest) Act 1998 (LPCDA) provides that the seller may charge interest on sums that become overdue at a rate that is prescribed by statute (currently 8% above base). The parties can, however, oust the provisions of the Act as long as the contract contains an alternative provision that constitutes a substantial contractual remedy for late payment.

2   IMPLIED RIGHTS OF BUYER

The Sale of Goods Act 1979 implies a number of terms into contracts for the sale of goods. In some cases, it states whether these terms are conditions or warranties.

If you want to refresh your memory on conditions and warranties, refer to the relevant chapter of the course book for Business Law.

2.1   Title (s 12)

It is an implied **condition** that the seller has, or will have at the time when property (that is, ownership) in the goods is to be transferred, a right to sell the goods: s 12(1). This is probably one of the single most important sections of the Sale of Goods Act.

In the ordinary way the seller satisfies this condition if he has title to the goods at the moment when property is to pass to the buyer. (In this statutory code 'title' and 'property' are both used in different contexts to mean the same thing, ownership.) But the condition is broken if the seller, although he owns the goods, can be stopped by a third party from selling them: the right to transfer ownership is essential.

> *Rowland v Divall 1923*
>
> *The facts:* D bought a car from a third party and then sold it on to R a dealer. It subsequently transpired that the car had been stolen from its original owner, before it was sold to D. The car was then returned to its original owner, and R sued D for the recovery of the price he had paid to the latter.
>
> *Decision:* D had been in breach of what is now s12 Sale of Goods Act 1979, as he did not have title to the car at the time he sold it to R. D had to repay the entire price, with no deduction for the period of use.

Implied warranty of quiet possession

The seller also gives implied **warranties** that the buyer shall have quiet possession of the goods and that the goods are free of any encumbrance or challenge by a third party (unless disclosed to the buyer when the contract is made): s 12(2).

> *Microbeads A. C. v Vinhurst Road Markings 1975*
>
> *The facts:* A road marking machine was sold by the defendant to the claimant. Unbeknown to either of them, a third party was at that point applying for a patent on the machine. This meant that use of the machine by the purchaser was an infringement of that patent, and the owner of the patent was able to demand royalties from the purchaser.
>
> *Decision:* This constituted a breach by the seller of the implied warranty of quiet possession in S12, and the purchaser was able to claim damages.

> *Rubicon Computer Systems v United Paints Ltd 2000*
>
> *The facts:* A computer system was supplied by Rubicon and a dispute arose because Rubicon, who continued to have access to the system after the installation had taken place, had wrongfully attached a time lock to it which, when it was activated, denied United Paints access to it.
>
> *Decision:* Rubicon were in breach of s 12(2) by preventing United Paints from having quiet possession.

Exclusion of s 12

Although the seller cannot contract out of these terms by stipulating that they shall not apply, he can achieve a rather similar result by undertaking to transfer only such title as he (or some third party from whom he acquired the goods) may have (or have had). This stipulation puts the buyer on notice that the seller is uncertain of title. Furthermore, the seller must disclose to the buyer any charges or encumbrances of which the seller knows. But if the buyer is prepared to buy the goods on that basis he gets what he bargained for, and there is no breach of contract if the seller's title is imperfect.

Activity 1   (10 minutes)

A and B are in dispute over which of them owns some corn which is in A's possession. A sells the corn to C (who is unaware of the dispute) for £1,000. The dispute is then resolved in favour of B, who obtains possession of the corn from C. By that time its value has fallen to £800. Advise C as to his legal position.

2.2 Description (s 13)

In a contract for sale of goods by description, a **condition** is implied that the goods will correspond to the description (s 13(1)). There are a number of issues that need to be resolved should there be a dispute about goods sold by description.

Does the description amount to a contractual term?

The leading case on this is as follows.

> *Ashington Piggeries v Christopher Hill Ltd 1972*
> *The facts:* The defendant (D) supplied the claimant (P) with a herring meal on the basis that it was suitable for feeding to P's minks. The herring meal turned out to be contaminated with another substance that made it unsuitable for the minks. P argued that this constituted a breach of s 13.
>
> *Decision:* No breach of s 13 had occurred as the feed had been correctly described as herring meal. P's remedy rested with the implied term as to quality under s 14, which we shall see shortly. As to whether the description amounted to a contractual term, the judge was of the view that the only descriptive words which were caught by s 13 were those that identified the subject matter of the contract. He further said that parties could use a description that was as broad or narrow as they chose but ultimately the key was whether the buyer could fairly and reasonably refuse to buy the goods on the ground that their failure to comply with what was said about them made them goods of a different kind from those he intended to buy.

The buyer must therefore place some reliance on the description offered if it is to be raised to the status of a contract term. If the buyer did not place such reliance then the description will be treated as incidental to the main body of the contract.

What is meant by a 'sale by description'?

The buyer must have agreed to buy what has been described to him and his reliance upon the description must have been significant in his decision, even where he had inspected the goods.

> *Beale v Taylor 1967*
> *The facts:* The defendant advertised a Triumph as a 'Herald convertible, white, 1961'. The claimant came to inspect the car and subsequently bought it. After buying the car he found that only the back half corresponded with the description. It had been welded to a front half which was part of an earlier Herald 948 model. The defendant relied on the buyer's inspection and argued that it was not a sale by description.
>
> *Decision:* The advertisement described the car as a 1961 Herald, and this formed part of the contract description. It was a sale by description in spite of the buyer's pre-contract inspection.

By way of contrast, another well-known case demonstrates that where examination has taken place it will be more difficult to prove that there has been a sale by description.

> *Harlington & Leinster Ltd v Christopher Hull Fine Art 1991*
> *The facts:* The buyer, an art dealer, wished to purchase a painting by a given artist. Subsequently the painting turned out to be a worthless forgery and the buyer alleged breach of s 13 by the gallery which sold him the painting.
>
> *Decision:* The buyer had in fact relied upon his own judgment rather than on the description of the painting by the seller and therefore the buyer was unsuccessful.

Sale by sample

Where the sale is by sample as well as by description, the bulk must correspond to the sample and the description.

Compliance with the description must be complete and exact.

> *Arcos v E and A Ronaasen and Son 1933*
> *The facts:* The contract was for half-inch wooden staves. Some of the staves delivered by the seller were thicker than the measurements described.
>
> *Decision:* The buyer was entitled to reject the consignment.

'Description' is widely interpreted to include ingredients, age, date of shipment, packing, quantity, and so on.

> *Re Moore & Co and Landauer & Co 1921*
> *The facts:* The buyers agreed to buy 3,000 tins of Australian canned fruit packed in cases of 30 tins. The correct total quantity was delivered, but it was found that half the goods were packed in cases of 24 tins.
>
> *Decision:* Although there was no difference in value there had been a breach of s 13 and the buyers were entitled to reject.

In this case it did not matter that there was no effect on the value of the goods.

If the seller uses a false description he may also commit an offence punishable under the Consumer Protection from Unfair Trading Regulations 2005 (which are described at 8.4 below).

2.3 Sample (s 15)

In a sale by sample there are implied **conditions** that:

(a)   The bulk corresponds in quality with the sample

(b)   The goods are free of any defect rendering them unsatisfactory which would not be apparent on a reasonable examination of the sample.

> **Activity 2**   **(10 minutes)**
>
> There is a contract for the sale of '200 cases of 1958 Bordeaux wine'. If the seller were to supply wine made in 1959, is it likely that he could force the buyer to proceed with the purchase? Give reasons for your answer.

2.4 Quality (s 14 (2))

There is an implied **condition** that where goods are sold **in the course of a business,** goods supplied under a contract are of **satisfactory quality**. The seller must be carrying on a business or profession and make the sale in connection with that activity. Goods sold privately by a seller who is not selling in the course of a business therefore fall outside the scope of this section. It does not apply, for example, to goods bought at jumble sales or car boot sales.

The condition applies to all 'goods supplied under the contract': not only to the goods themselves, therefore, but also to the packaging in which they are sold and also to any instructions provided for the use of the goods.

The condition that the goods supplied under the contract are of satisfactory quality is excluded if the buyer's attention is drawn to defects before the contract is made or the buyer examines the goods before the contract is made, and that examination ought to reveal the defects. Similarly, on a sale by sample, if the defect would have been apparent on a reasonable examination of the sample, there is no breach of condition.

The buyer does not have to show that he relied upon the seller's skill or judgment in any way to gain a remedy under s 14(2), but where the goods supplied are to the buyer's specification and this specification makes them inherently unsatisfactory then the buyer will find it difficult to argue a breach of s 14(2).

Satisfactory quality

Satisfactory quality is met if the goods 'meet the standard that a reasonable person would regard as satisfactory, taking account of any description of the goods, the price (if relevant) and all other relevant circumstances'. When the buyer is a consumer, the latter include any public statement made by the seller in respect of the goods' specific characteristics.

The Act (s 14(2B)) identifies factors which may in appropriate cases be aspects of the quality of goods.

(a) **Fitness for ALL the purposes for which goods of the kind in question are commonly supplied.** If the goods are fit for one purpose, but not others, that is not acceptable.

(b) **Appearance and finish.** Until recently, goods with superficial damage but which operated properly could be of satisfactory quality. This aspect is likely to affect such matters as sales of new motor cars, an area in which there was much dissatisfaction with the old law.

(c) **Freedom from minor defects.** A series of minor defects could, under existing case law, render goods of unsatisfactory quality. Under statute, the goods must be free of minor defects.

(d) **Safety.** This is a new aspect, as there is no clear case law on this.

(e) **Durability.** Goods will have to remain of satisfactory quality for a period which could be expected by a reasonable person.

Fitness for purpose (s 14(3))

Again, this condition applies only to goods sold 'in the course of business'.

Where the buyer expressly or by implication makes known to the seller any particular purpose for which the goods are bought, it is an implied condition that the goods supplied under the contract are reasonably fit for that purpose (whether or not that is the common purpose of such goods), unless the circumstances show that the buyer does not rely, or that it is unreasonable for him to rely, on the skill or judgement of the seller.

Jewson v Boyhan 2003
The facts: The seller provided electrical heating equipment to the buyer and the buyer alleged breach of s 14(2) and s 14(3) because the equipment reduced the energy efficiency ratings of the flat conversions where it was installed.

Decision: The heating equipment did work and therefore there was no breach of s 14(2), and the buyer did not rely on the seller in respect of the energy efficiency issue and therefore there was no breach of s 14(3).

MacGill v Talbot 2002
The facts: In this consumer case, C was a classic car collector and he advised D, a commercial dealer, that he was intending to buy a Rolls Royce in order to restore it. D provided a car and estimated that it would cost £23,500 to restore it. In fact it cost more than £85,000 to restore and C claimed the difference.

Decision: C had made known a particular purpose in the light of previous dealings between the parties.

A buyer may specify the '**particular purpose**' quite broadly without listing all possible uses within that particular purpose. Thus where a substance is commonly used as fertiliser or as animal feedstuff it is sufficient to specify the latter without naming each kind of animal to which it might be fed.

Ashington Piggeries v Christopher Hill 1972
The facts: B gave S a recipe for mink food and requested that S should mix the food in accordance with the recipe and supply it to B. S told B that they had never supplied mink food before although they were manufacturers of animal foodstuffs. One of the ingredients was herring meal which had been stored in a chemical which created a poisonous substance damaging to all animals but particularly damaging to mink. As a result many of the mink died.

Decision: Since the poison affected all animals the food was unfit for its disclosed purpose since B relied on S's skill and judgement to the extent that S was an animal food manufacturer and should not have supplied a generally harmful food. If the poison had only affected mink, then B's skill and judgement demonstrated by its supply of a recipe would have made it unreasonable to rely on S's skill or judgement.

If the goods have only **one obvious purpose,** the buyer by implication makes known his purpose merely by asking for the goods.

Priest v Last 1903
The facts: A customer at a chemist's shop asked for a hot water bottle and was told, in answer to a question, that it would withstand hot water but should not be filled with boiling water. It burst after only five days in use.

Decision: If there is only one purpose, that particular purpose is disclosed by buying the goods. Because it was not an effective hot water bottle, there was a breach of s 14(3). (This was followed by *Frost v Aylesbury Dairy Co 1905:* in the purchase of milk supplied to a domestic address the buyer discloses his purpose, which is human consumption.)

There are two further variations on the interpretation of 'particular purpose'. Where goods are required for a particular purpose which is **not obvious** to the seller or where they are required for a particular purpose known to the seller but there is **some peculiarity** about that purpose, the buyer must make clear to the seller the particular purpose or the peculiarity involved.

Manchester Liners v Rea 1922
The facts: The defendant supplied coal for a particular ship. The coal was unsuitable for that ship but would have been suitable for other ships.

Decision: Coal merchants knew well enough that ships differed in their types and requirements. If a merchant undertook to supply coal for a particular ship, he must supply coal suitable for that ship.

Griffiths v Peter Conway Ltd 1939
The facts: The claimant contracted dermatitis from a Harris Tweed coat purchased from the defendants. She had an unusually sensitive skin and the coat would not have harmed a normal person.

Decision: The claimant's sensitive skin rendered the required use so special that she had not made known the particular purpose for which the coat was to be used.

Activity 4   **(10 minutes)**

R buys a filing cabinet from S, who runs an office furniture shop. R tells S that he will use the cabinet to store land certificates issued by the Land Registry, and asks S whether the cabinet is of the right size for such certificates. S replies that he does not know how large land certificates are, but R goes ahead and buys the cabinet. If the cabinet proved to be too small, why could R not claim that S had breached the condition of reasonable fitness?

---

3 TRANSFER OF PROPERTY AND POSSESSION

Remember that in this context 'property' is ownership.

There are a number of statutory rules about when ownership of the goods actually passes to the buyer.

3.1 Unascertained goods

No property can pass in goods which are unascertained and not yet identified as the goods to be sold under the contract: s 16.

3.2 Specified goods/ascertained goods

The property in specific or ascertained goods is transferred to the buyer at the time when the parties **intend** it to be transferred. Their intention may be deduced from the terms of the contract, the conduct of the parties and the circumstances of the case: s 17.

Unless a different intention appears (and the parties can agree upon whatever terms they like) the rules of s 18 are applied **to ascertain what their intention is** on the passing of property to the buyer.

Many contracts for the supply of goods contain a clause stating that title to the goods remains with the seller until the contract price is paid. Such 'retention of title' or 'Romalpa' clauses are a common example of the s 17 rule that title to specific goods passes when the parties so intend.

3.3 Rules on ascertaining intention

Section 18 of the Sale of Goods Act lists a number of precise rules on the passing of property.

(a) *Rule 1* – If the contract is unconditional and the goods are specific or identified, property passes when the contract is made. It is immaterial that the seller has not yet delivered the goods or that the buyer has not yet paid the price. However, the seller may, and often does, stipulate that property shall not pass until the price is paid (a retention of title clause).

If the seller insists on retaining the goods or documents relating to them (such as the registration book of a car which has been sold) until the price is paid then it will readily be inferred that he intended (and the buyer agreed) that property would not pass on making the contract, but only on payment of the price.

(b) *Rule 2* – If, under a contract for sale of specific goods, the seller is bound to do something to put the goods into a deliverable state, property does not pass until the seller has done what is required of him and the buyer has notice of this.

Underwood v Burgh Castle Brick and Cement Syndicate 1922
The facts: The claimants entered into a contract for the sale of a condensing engine to be loaded onto a railway wagon. At the time of making the contract the engine, which weighed over 30 tons, was embedded in cement foundations at a factory. It was expected that it would take the sellers about two weeks to dismantle it. In loading it into the railway wagon the sellers broke part of the machine. The buyers refused to accept it.

Decision: Property had not passed when the contract was made, because the engine was not in such a condition that the defendants had to take delivery of it. At the time of the damage the engine was still in the sellers' ownership and so at their risk. The buyers were entitled to reject it in its damaged state and to refuse to pay the price.

(c) *Rule 3* – Where there is a contract for the sale of specific goods in a deliverable state but the seller is bound to weigh, measure or test them to fix the price, property passes when he has done so and the buyer has notice of this. The rule does not apply when it is the buyer who must take this action.

(d) *Rule 4* – When goods are delivered to the buyer on approval, that is on sale or return terms, the property passes to the buyer when:

(i)   He signifies to the seller that he approves, or indicates approval by dealing with them or

(ii)   He retains the goods beyond the time fixed for their return without giving notice of rejection or, if no time has been fixed, if he retains them beyond a reasonable time.

(e)   *Rule 5* – When there is a contract for the sale of unascertained or future goods by description, and goods of that description and in a deliverable state are unconditionally appropriated to the contract by the seller with the assent of the buyer, or by the buyer with the assent of the seller, the property then passes to the buyer.

Such assent may be express or implied and given before or after the appropriation is made. For example, if the buyer orders goods to be supplied from the seller's stock he gives implied assent to the seller to make an appropriation from his stock.

To bring rule 5 into operation, something more definite is required than merely selecting or setting aside goods for delivery to the buyer. The act must be irrevocable, for example where the seller sets aside goods and also informs the buyer that they are ready for collection.

Delivery of goods to the buyer, or to a carrier for transmission to the buyer, without reserving to the seller a right of disposal, is an unconditional appropriation which brings rule 5 into operation. However, delivery to a carrier does not pass the property if identical goods destined to be sent to different buyers are mixed and need to be counted or sorted by the carrier.

Healey v Howlett & Sons 1917
The facts: The defendant ordered twenty boxes of mackerel from the claimant. 190 boxes were despatched, instructions being given to railway officials to set aside twenty for the defendant and the rest for two other buyers. The train was delayed before this was done and by the time the officials were ready to set them aside the fish had deteriorated badly.

Decision: Neither property nor risk had passed before the boxes were set aside.

Rule 5 only applies to appropriation of goods in a deliverable state.

Philip Head & Sons v Showfronts 1970
The facts: The parties entered into a contract for supply and laying of carpet at the buyer's premises. A roll of carpet was delivered but it was stolen before it could be laid.

Decision: The carpet was deliverable to the buyer when laid and not before. It was the seller's property when stolen. The risk of loss remained with him.

Activity 5   **(10 minutes)**

On Monday, a contract is made for the sale of goods which are unascertained at that time. On Tuesday, the seller takes goods from stock and decides that these are the goods to be supplied to the buyer. However, the goods must first be packed. This is done on Wednesday and the buyer is notified on Thursday that this has been done and that the goods are ready for collection. Identify the day on which property in the goods passes to the buyer.

NOTES

Sale of Goods (Amendment) Act 1995

The Sale of Goods (Amendment) Act 1995 deals with the passing of ownership in goods which are unascertained in the sense that they have not been set aside for the buyer but are nevertheless to come from an ascertained source – 'I will buy twenty boxes of goods out of the stock of 60 boxes being transported to Doncaster by train.'

If there is no appropriation of a particular twenty boxes to the buyer, the ownership remains with the seller and if the seller goes insolvent, the goods are available for sale by the relevant insolvency practitioner. This is particularly unfortunate where the buyer has made a whole or partial pre-payment. The goods do not belong to him and he cannot recover the pre-payment but only some form of dividend in the insolvency which may be worthless.

This is a problem which those engaged in commerce have long recognised as an injustice. The Sale of Goods (Amendment) Act 1995 effects a change in the above situation where the buyer has made a whole or partial part payment. In such a case, he becomes a co-owner with others having a claim on the entire bulk. The bulk does not then pass into the control of an insolvency practitioner on the seller's insolvency. The right of the buyer to claim damages for injury to the goods is also enhanced by this provision.

3.4 Title

The general rule is that only the owner, or an agent acting with his authority, can transfer the title in goods to a buyer. This is expressed in the Latin maxim *nemo dat quod non habet*: no one can give what he does not have. To the general rule there are a number of exceptions to protect an honest buyer against loss.

(a) **Agency (s 21).** If an ordinary agent (that is, someone acting on behalf of someone else) sells goods without actual or apparent authority, there is usually no transfer of title to the buyer. But a mercantile agent, that is an agent whose business is selling goods for others, may have possession of goods (or documents of title to them) with the owner's consent. He can then sell them, in the ordinary course of his business, to a buyer who buys in good faith and without notice that the agent had no authority to sell (or was exceeding his authority). The buyer acquires title to the goods: s 21.

(b) **Estoppel.** If, by his conduct, the true owner leads the buyer to believe that the person who makes the sale owns the goods, the true owner is prevented (estopped) from denying the seller's authority to sell. Merely to put goods in the possession of another is not to represent that he is the owner.

(c) **Sale under voidable title (s 23).** A person may acquire goods under a contract which is voidable, say for misrepresentation. He then has title to the goods until the contract is avoided. If, before the sale to him is avoided, he re-sells to a person who buys in good faith and without notice of his defective title, that buyer obtains a good title to the goods. Normally the first contract of sale is not avoided until the person entitled to avoid it communicates his decision to the other party but if that party has disappeared other evidence of intention to avoid the first sale, such as reporting the matter to the police, will suffice.

(d) **Re-sale by seller in possession (s 24).** If a seller, or a mercantile agent acting for him, continues in possession of the goods (or documents of title to them) after a sale, and he makes a delivery of them to a person who receives them in good faith and without notice of the previous sale, the transaction takes effect as if the seller were authorised for that purpose.

Suppose that A sells specific goods to B and B, to whom the ownership of the goods passes, immediately leaves them in A's possession until B can collect them. A by mistake then re-sells the goods and delivers them to C, who is unaware of the previous sale to B. C gets good title to the goods; B's only remedy is to sue A. But if A does not actually deliver the goods to C, B has the better right.

(e) **Re-sale by a buyer in possession (s 25).** The seller may permit the buyer to take possession of the goods before ownership has passed to the buyer, as when the seller makes delivery but retains title until the price is paid. If the buyer then makes a re-sale or other disposition in the normal course of business as mercantile agent, with actual delivery or transfer of the goods (or documents of title), to a person who takes them in good faith and without notice of the original seller's rights, title passes to that person as if the buyer had acted as a mercantile agent. This applies even if the buyer has a voidable title which is actually avoided (say by notifying police of the buyer's lack of title).

Newtons of Wembley v Williams 1965
The facts: X purchased a car and paid the price by cheque. The seller stipulated that title to the car should not pass until the cheque was cleared, but allowed X to take possession of the car. The cheque was dishonoured and the sellers informed the police and thereby avoided the sale to X in the only way available to them. But X sold the car for cash in an established secondhand car market to Y who took delivery forthwith.

Decision: Y acquired good title since X was a buyer in possession with the seller's consent and the re-sale in the market was a disposition in the ordinary course of business of a mercantile agent. The loss must fall on the original seller if he could not recover from X.

To be a buyer in possession, the person must have obtained possession of the goods or documents of title to goods with the seller's consent. It is immaterial that the seller withdraws consent after the buyer has obtained possession, and that the latter obtains possession after contracting to sell to the innocent purchaser. He is a buyer in possession provided he obtains possession before delivering possession to the innocent purchaser.

However, s 25 does not allow good title to be given to an innocent purchaser from a buyer in possession if the latter had obtained possession from a 'seller' not entitled to sell, that is, a thief.

(f) **The sale of a motor vehicle acquired under hire purchase.** By the Hire Purchase Act 1964 a private (but not a trade) purchaser of a motor vehicle sold by a hirer under a hire purchase agreement or a buyer under a conditional sale agreement obtains good title (even though the seller had none) if the purchaser takes the vehicle in good faith and without notice that it was only let on hire purchase. The innocent buyer's purchase may be an ordinary sale or a hire purchase or conditional sale agreement. If there are intermediaries who are not private purchasers, the protection is available only to the first private purchaser. For example, A, who has a car under a hire purchase agreement, purports to sell it to B, a car dealer, who sells it to C, a private purchaser. B does not obtain title but C does. This is so even if B is a car dealer buying a vehicle for private, not business, purposes.

> **Activity 6** (10 minutes)
>
> R buys a car and pays with a fraudulent cheque. The seller is unable to communicate with him, but informs the police and the AA of the fraud. R resells the car to J. Does J get good title to the car?

(g) **Special powers of sale.** The court may order goods to be sold. Various persons, such as pawnbrokers, unpaid sellers, hotel keepers and bailees (such as dry cleaners) in possession of abandoned goods for which charges are owing, have specific powers of sale.

4 PASSING OF RISK

In the previous section, we looked at the rules applying to when ownership of goods passes under a contract for the sale of goods. Here we will consider the issue of when 'risk', or 'responsibility' for the goods passes to the buyer. This may be an important issue, for example, in terms of insuring the goods, and the timing of risk passing is not **necessarily** the same as when property in them passes.

4.1 General rule

Unless otherwise agreed, the goods remain at the seller's risk until the property in them is transferred to the buyer but when the property in them is transferred to the buyer the goods are at the buyer's risk whether delivery has been made or not: s 20(1).

The general rule is therefore that property and risk pass at the same time. However, sometimes risk passes to the other party at a different time.

Where delivery has been delayed through the fault of either buyer or seller the goods are at the risk for the part at fault as regards any loss which might not have occurred but for such fault: s 20(2).

There are a number of rules relating to delivery and non-acceptance of goods, which we shall look at now.

4.2 Delivery

Unless otherwise agreed, it is the duty of the seller to deliver the goods, and for the buyer to accept and pay for them (s 27). Unless the parties agree otherwise, delivery and payment are concurrent conditions, ie each party must be ready and willing to deliver or pay (as appropriate) in exchange for the other party's performance (s 28). The parties may agree on whatever delivery arrangements may suit them. But unless otherwise agreed the following rules apply.

(a) **Method.** Delivery is the voluntary transfer of possession from one person to another (s 61). It may be by physical transfer of possession, or of the means of control (such as the key of a warehouse) or by arranging that a third party who has the goods acknowledges ('attorns') to the buyer that he holds them on his behalf, or by delivery of a document of title to the goods.

(b) **Place.** Delivery is to be made at the seller's place of business (s 29(2)) or, if he has none, at his residence, unless the goods are specific and, to the knowledge of both parties when the contract is made, the goods are at some other place. Delivery is, in those circumstances, to be at that other place.

(c) **Time**. If no time is agreed, delivery is to be made within a reasonable time (s 29(3)) and at a reasonable hour: s 29(4).

(d) **Expense**. The seller bears the expense of putting the goods into a deliverable state (for example by packing or bagging them): s 29(5).

Delivery by instalment

Unless otherwise agreed the buyer is *not* obliged to accept delivery by instalments: s 31(1). He may reject a delivery of part only of the goods.

If the contract does provide for delivery by instalments with separate payment for each instalment, the contract is severable or divisible. If one or more instalments under a severable contract are defective, this may amount to repudiation of the entire contract or it may merely give a right to claim compensation for the defective deliveries only. It depends on the ratio of defective to sound deliveries and the likelihood or otherwise that future instalments will also be defective.

Wrong delivery

If the seller delivers the wrong quantity the buyer may reject the whole quantity or any surplus, but if he accepts what is delivered he must pay at the contract rate for the quantity accepted. However, a buyer who does not deal as a consumer may not reject goods where the shortfall or excess (as the case may be) is so slight that it would be unreasonable for him to do so.

Where the contract requires that the goods be moved in the course of delivery:

(a) Delivery to a carrier for transmission to the buyer is deemed to be delivery to the buyer unless the contrary intention appears, as when the seller consigns the goods to himself or his agent at their destination: s 32

(b) The seller must make a reasonable arrangement with the carrier and (if the goods are sent by sea) give the buyer notice in time to permit the buyer to arrange insurance: s 32

(c) The buyer must bear the risk of any deterioration necessarily incidental to the course of transit: s 33

4.3 Acceptance of goods

Acceptance of goods or part of them, deprives the buyer of his right to treat the contract as discharged by breach of condition (for example, as to the quality of the goods) on the part of the seller in relation to those goods. But he may claim damages.

However, if a breach of condition on the seller's part entitles the buyer to reject goods but the buyer accepts goods unaffected by the breach, he is not thereby excluded from rejecting the rest of the goods: s 35 A.

Time of acceptance

The seller is obliged to comply with a request from the buyer to have a reasonable opportunity of examining the goods for the purpose of ascertaining whether they are in conformity with the contract or to compare the bulk with the sample: s 34. The buyer is deemed to have accepted the goods in the following circumstances (s 35, as amended by Sale and Supply of Goods Act 1994):

(a) When he intimates to the seller that he has accepted them, provided that he has had a reasonable opportunity of ascertaining whether they are in conformity with the contract

(b)   When the goods have been delivered to the buyer and he does any act in relation to them which is inconsistent with the ownership of the seller, for example, using or reselling them

(c)   When after the lapse of a reasonable time he retains the goods without intimating to the seller that he has rejected them. In determining whether a reasonable time has elapsed, one factor is whether the buyer has been afforded a reasonable opportunity of examination, for example by use. For example, if A buys a car which is not of satisfactory quality but continues to drive it for 5,000 miles, he would probably at that point be unable to rescind the contract.

When goods are delivered to the buyer and he has not previously examined them then he is not deemed to have accepted them until he has had a reasonable opportunity to examine them for the purposes of ascertaining whether they are in conformity with the contract and, where there is a sale by sample, comparing the bulk with the sample.

Where the seller has breached a condition the buyer may treat the contract as repudiated and hence reject the goods. The buyer does not have to return the goods to the seller – he merely has to inform the seller of his rejection: s 36.

The buyer loses his right to reject goods if:

(a)   He waives the breached condition

(b)   He elects to treat the breach of condition as a breach of warranty

(c)   He has accepted the goods or

(d)   He is unable to return the goods because, for example, he has sold them on to a buyer who keeps them.

Activity 7   (10 minutes)

Peter sells a car bearing the distinctive registration number DAWN 10 to Dawn Smith, who tells her friend Dawn Jones that she has just bought this car. The car is still with Peter when Dawn Jones calls on him, and attempts to buy the same car. Peter confuses the two Dawns, accepts Dawn Jones's cash and allows her to take the car away. When Dawn Smith claims the car from her, Dawn Jones relies on Section 24 of the Sale of Goods Act 1979 to retain the car.

Consider whether the car belongs to Dawn Jones or Dawn Smith.

Activity 8   (10 minutes)

The parties to a contract for the sale of non-perishable goods agree that the goods shall be delivered to the buyer's premises 'during normal business hours'. The seller then states that the only time of day that the goods can be delivered is 10 pm and that the goods must be accepted or rejected immediately on delivery. At that time a caretaker will be present to receive the goods, but he is not competent to inspect them. In what ways has the seller failed to meet his legal obligations?

5 REMEDIES

As with any other contract, one for sale of goods may be breached. Aside from the usual common law remedies (damages, action for the price, and so on) the parties have rights peculiar to this type of contract. They are categorised as:

- The seller's remedies against the goods
- The seller's remedies against the buyer
- The buyer's remedies against the seller

The remedies which are against goods are described as ' real remedies' (*action in rem*); all others are called ' personal remedies' (*action in personam*).

5.1 Real remedies: seller

Ownership of goods often passes to the buyer before they are delivered to the buyer in exchange for the price. If the buyer then defaults, for example by failing to pay the price when due, the seller is given rights against the goods in his possession or under his control although those goods are now owned by the buyer. It is usually more satisfactory to him to retain the goods than merely to sue a buyer, who may well be insolvent, for breach of contract.

These rights are given only to an 'unpaid seller' (s 38). He is unpaid if either:

- The whole of the price has not been paid or tendered to him or
- He has received a bill of exchange and the bill has been dishonoured.

An unpaid seller of goods which are now the property of the buyer has the following statutory rights in respect of the goods (s 39):

- A lien on the goods so long as they are in his possession
- A right of stoppage in transit if the buyer is insolvent and the goods are in the hands of a carrier
- A right of resale in certain circumstances

Lien

Definition

> **Lien**: the seller's right to retain the goods in his possession until the price is paid or tendered (s 41).

The unpaid seller's right of lien applies:

- Where the goods are sold without any stipulation as to credit
- Where they have been sold on credit terms but the credit period has expired or
- Where the buyer becomes insolvent

Even if part of the goods have been delivered to the buyer, the unpaid seller has a lien on the rest unless part delivery indicates his agreement to give up his lien altogether: s 42.

The unpaid seller loses his lien when he delivers the goods to a carrier or warehouseman for transmission to the buyer (unless the seller reserves a right of disposal), or when the buyer or his agent lawfully obtains possession of the goods, or when the seller waives his lien: s 43.

Lien merely gives a right to retain possession until the price is paid. It does not rescind the contract, deprive the buyer of his ownership nor entitle the seller to re-sell the goods.

Stoppage in transit

The right of stoppage in transit (s 44–45) exists when the buyer becomes insolvent. He is insolvent if he has ceased to pay his debts in the ordinary course of business or cannot pay his debts as they fall due: it is not necessary to wait until he becomes bankrupt.

While goods are in transit, neither seller nor buyer has possession of the goods since they are in the possession of a carrier. The unpaid seller may stop the goods in transit by issuing an order to the carrier. The goods cease to be in transit and the seller's right of stoppage ends:

(a) On delivery to the buyer or his agent (whether at the appointed destination or before)

(b) If the carrier acknowledges to the buyer or his agent that the goods (arrived at their original destination) are now held on behalf of the buyer. It is immaterial that the buyer may have indicated to the carrier that the goods are to be taken on to a further destination or

(c) If the carrier wrongfully refuses to make delivery to the buyer or his agent.

But if the buyer refuses to accept the goods which remain in the possession of the carrier, they are still in transit

Right of resale

As between the unpaid seller and the buyer of the goods, the seller has a right of resale:

- If the goods are of a perishable nature
- If the seller gives notice to the buyer of his intention to re-sell and the buyer fails within a reasonable time to pay or tender the price or
- If the seller reserves a right of resale under the contract

If the seller does not, by resale, recover the full amount of his loss he may sue the buyer for damages for breach of contract: s 48. On a sale in these circumstances the second buyer gets good title to the goods.

Retention of title clauses

Many commercial contracts now contain a retention of title clause, often known as a Romalpa clause after the case discussed below. Under such a clause, possession may pass to the buyer but ownership does not pass until the price is paid.

Aluminium Industrie Vaassen BV v Romalpa Ltd 1976
The facts: Romalpa purchased aluminium foil on terms that the stock of foil (and any proceeds of sale) should be the property of the Dutch supplier until the company had paid to the supplier all that it owed. Romalpa got into financial difficulties and a receiver was appointed. The receiver found that the company still held aluminium foil and proceeds of selling other stocks of foil, and had not paid its debt to the supplier. The receiver applied to the court to determine whether or not the foil and the cash were assets of the company under his control as receiver.

Decision: The conditions of sale were valid. The relevant assets, although in the possession of the company, did not belong to it. The receiver could not deal with these assets since his authority under the floating charge was restricted to assets of the company.

The extent to which a Romalpa clause protects an unpaid seller depends to a great extent on the wording of the actual clause. A retention of title clause may be effective even though goods are resold or incorporated into the buyer's products so as to lose their identity if it expressly states that they can be used in these ways before title has passed: *Clough Mill Ltd v Martin 1985.*

Unless the clause expressly retains title even after resale or incorporation, the supplier is not entitled to a proportionate part of the sale proceeds of the manufactured product: *Borden (UK) Ltd v Scottish Timber Products Ltd 1979.* Where there is no express provision, resale or incorporation is conversion of the supplier's property but a third party will still get good title.

If the buyer resells the goods when there is an express provision allowing resale before title passes, the proceeds of sale are held by the buyer as trustee for the supplier.

A reservation of title clause can cover, besides the price of the goods specifically subject of the particular contract of sale, other debts due to the seller under unrelated contracts.

> *Armour and Carron Co Ltd v Thyssen Edelstahlwerke AG 1990*
> *The facts:* The defendants transferred possession in steel strip to a buyer under a contract of sale. The buyer agreed that it would not acquire the property (ownership) until all amounts due to the defendant had been paid. The claimants were appointed receivers of the assets of the buyer; the steel strip had not been paid for. The buyer argued that the clause was an attempt to create a security over moveable property and that it was therefore void.
>
> *Decision:* It was not possible to create a security over goods which you did not own. Under Sale of Goods Act s 19(1) 'where there is a contract for the sale of specific goods ... the seller may ... reserve the right to disposal of the goods until certain conditions are fulfilled'. The defendant had reserved this right until fulfilment of the condition that all the buyer's debts had been paid, including those due under other contracts. They therefore remained owners of the steel strip.

FOR DISCUSSION

Who should insure goods sold under a contract containing a Romalpa clause?

5.2 Personal remedies: seller

The seller has two possible remedies against the buyer personally.

   (a)   He may bring an **action for the price** if:

       (i)   The ownership of the goods has passed to the buyer and he wrongfully neglects or refuses to pay the price according to the terms of the contract or

       (ii)   The price is payable on a certain day (regardless of delivery) and the buyer wrongfully neglects or refuses to pay it.

   (b)   The seller may sue for **damages** for non-acceptance if the buyer wrongfully refuses or neglects to accept and pay for the goods. In this case the claim may include any expense incurred by the seller (for example in storing the goods) caused by the buyer's failure to take delivery after being requested to do so.

The basis for damages is the 'available market' for the goods in question: s 50. If there is one the measure of the damages is ascertained by the difference between the contract price and the market or current price at the time when the goods ought to have been accepted or (if no time was fixed for acceptance) at the time of the refusal to accept. It is also likely that a buyer would be liable for any direct costs incurred by the seller as a result of the buyer's refusal to accept the goods or pay for them.

Activity 9   **(10 minutes)**

Some nuts and bolts are sold to Z Ltd subject to a retention of title clause, the full text of which is as follows.

'Property in the goods shall not pass to the buyer until the buyer has paid for the goods in full'.

Before paying for the nuts and bolts, Z Ltd incorporates them into electric motors which are sold. If Z Ltd fails to pay for the nuts and bolts, what remedy might the supplier seek?

5.3 Personal remedies: buyer

Breach of condition

If the seller is in **breach of an express or implied condition** of the contract, the buyer may reject the goods unless he has lost his right to do so by accepting the goods. In addition he may claim damages under s 53.

If the buyer has paid the price and the consideration has failed entirely, for example if the seller has no title or delivers goods which the buyer is entitled to reject, the buyer may sue to recover the price: s 54.

Breach of warranty

If there is a **breach of warranty** by the seller, or if the buyer is obliged (or prefers) to deal with a breach of a condition by a claim for damages, the buyer may either reduce the amount paid to the seller by an allowance for the breach or sue for damages. The amount of damages is determined on principles similar to those of the seller's claim against the buyer.

It is open to the buyer to base his claim on any circumstances within the general scope of these rules.

> *Mason v Burningham 1949*
> *The facts:* The claimant had been sold a typewriter which turned out to be stolen property. She had to return it to the owner. In addition to the price paid she claimed damages for breach of implied warranty of quiet enjoyment including her expenditure in having the typewriter overhauled.
>
> *Decision:* Damages should be awarded as claimed.

A buyer may also claim damages for non-delivery, calculated on the same principles as described earlier when a seller claims damages. This claim may be made if the seller either fails to deliver altogether or delivers goods which the buyer is entitled to, and does, reject.

The buyer's claim for damages for loss of profit or liability for damages arising on that contract is not affected by a resale by him, unless it can be shown that the parties to the original sale contemplated that there would be a resale.

Williams v Agius 1914
The facts: There was a contract for the sale of coal at 16s 3d per ton. The buyers resold at 19s 6d per ton. The market price at the date for delivery was 23s 6d. per ton. The sellers failed to deliver. The sellers contended that the buyer's actual loss was the difference between the contract price (16s. 3d) and the resale price (19s. 6d) per ton only.

Decision: The buyers should be awarded damages of 7s 3d per ton, the full difference between the market price and the contract price; the resale contract should be ignored.

In an action for breach of contract to deliver specific or ascertained goods, the court may order **specific performance** or delivery of the goods: s 52. But it will only do so if damages would be an inadequate remedy.

We shall look at improved remedies for buyers in consumer contracts later in this chapter.

6 SUPPLY OF SERVICES

6.1 Supply of Goods and Services Act 1982

The Supply of Goods and Services Act 1982 (SGSA 1982) applies to certain contracts which do not fall within the definition of a sale of goods even though they do involve a transfer of ownership.

Transactions covered

(a) **Contracts of exchange or barter:** these are not contracts of sale of goods because there is no money consideration involved

(b) **Contracts of repair:** although some goods are supplied (for example spare parts) the substance of the contract is the provision of services (see below)

(c) **Contracts of hire:** these are not contracts for the sale of goods because they contain no provision for ownership to pass to the hirer

(d) **Collateral contracts to the sale of goods:** for example, where a person buys a car and receives a free set of seat covers as part of a special deal, the purchase of the car is governed by the Sale of Goods Act 1979 but the seat covers, for which consideration was given by buying the car, are part of a collateral contract governed by the Supply of Goods and Services Act 1982

The Act specifically does not cover contracts of apprenticeship or employment (s 12).

If the main purpose of a contract is, for example, the provision of skilled labour, whilst an ancillary object is the transfer of ownership of goods (such as a spare part for a washing machine), the contract is one governed by the 1982 Act.

6.2 Implied rights

The general effect of the Act is to provide safeguards similar to those provided by the Sale of Goods Act in respect of contracts for sale of goods. Where the supply of goods is a part of the transaction, ss 2–5 of the 1982 Act imply certain terms relating to the goods.

NOTES

The terms implied relate to the goods supplied and are similar to those of the Sale of Goods Act 1979, dealing with strict liability regarding:

- Title, freedom from encumbrances and quiet possession (s 2)
- Description (s 3)
- Satisfactory quality and fitness for purpose (s 4)
- Sample (s 5)

Under the Unfair Contract Terms Act 1977, clauses purporting to exclude or restrict liability under these headings are subject to the same rules as similar exclusion clauses in sale of goods contracts.

Where the contract is wholly or substantially for the provision of services, the 1982 Act implies a number of further terms.

(a) Where the supplier of the service is acting in the course of a business, there are implied terms that he will carry out the service with **reasonable care and skill** (s 13) and **within a reasonable time** (s 14).

(b) Where the consideration is not determined by the contract, there is an implied term that the party contracting with the supplier will pay a **reasonable charge** (s 15).

These terms are implied whether there is a supply of goods or not. But they are not conditions of strict liability, and may be excluded so long as such exclusion complies with the reasonableness requirement of the Unfair Contract Terms Act 1977: s 16 SGSA 1982.

This implied term only applies where the supplier is acting in the course of his business. The level of care and skill will be determined by reference to the test set out in the well-known case of *Bolan v Friern Hospital Management Committee 1957*: the supplier will be expected to exercise the ordinary skill of an ordinary competent man exercising that particular art. If the supplier has any special expertise the level may well be higher, such as when a solicitor drafts a legal document. Nevertheless, it is important to note that a supplier will not typically contract for a given end result, so that a surgeon will not be in breach of this term if his patient dies provided he has used reasonable care and skill when treating him.

Of course the parties will always be free to contract to a higher standard and in such a case they will be held to it.

One of the more difficult issues concerning this implied term is the overlap between it and the implied terms of satisfactory quality and fitness for purpose in agreements for the supply of services which also involve the supply of goods and materials, for example the supply and fitting of a carpet. Arguably the standard of reasonable care and skill in supplying the service is at a lesser standard than the 'satisfactory quality' rule applied to goods, so it is important to determine whether the contract is for the sale of goods or the supply of services. This is done by identifying the component parts of the contract and by treating them separately, so the supply of goods is subject to the tests of satisfactory quality and fitness for purpose, and the supply of services is subject to the standard of reasonable care and skill.

On this basis the following are examples of the supply of goods:

- the supply and fitting of a carpet
- the delivery and erection of an agricultural feeding tank

At the same time the following are examples of the supply of services:

- the fitting of brake pads to a car
- the preparation of a document by a solicitor

Perhaps the most topical example of this is the treatment of software. In *St Albans City & District Council v International Computers Limited 1996* it was held that when software is incorporated onto a disk or CD it constitutes goods, but if what is supplied is solely the program then it will not be goods.

6.3 Remedies for breach of s 13

The implied term of reasonable care and skill is only classified as a term and not as a condition. Therefore, it is what is known as an innominate term and so the remedies available will depend on the significance of the breach. In order to terminate the contract it would be necessary to show that the breach undermined the entire contract. Consequently it is far more likely that action would lie in damages.

Activity 10   **(10 minutes)**

Robinson v Graves 1935 concerned a contract to paint a portrait. *Marcel (Furriers) Ltd v Tapper 1953* concerned a contract for the supply of a mink jacket of a special style made to the customer's requirements. In both cases materials were worked on by skilled persons, but in one case it was held that there was a sale of goods and in the other case it was held that there was a supply of services. In which case do you think it was held that there was a sale of goods?

---

7 WARRANTIES, INDEMNITIES AND EXCLUSION CLAUSES

It is common for contracts for the sale and supply of goods and services, especially those between businesses (business to business contracts), to contain clauses that are intended to adjust the balance of power between the parties and their rights and obligations.

(a) A **warranty** in a sale of goods is usually of the 'extended warranty' kind, that is it warrants that the goods shall be free from specific defects for, say, three years; should defects occur, the seller will be liable to rectify them.

(b) An **indemnity** provides that, should one party incur costs or obligations of a specific kind, the other party will make good or 'indemnify' those costs. An example is where Seller A contracts to Seller B who immediately sells them on to Buyer C. A term in B's contract with A could specify that if C has a particular claim against B regarding these goods, B's costs in respect of it will be indemnified by A.

(c) An **exclusion clause** seeks to exclude liability which arises under the contract whether expressly or via an implied term.

7.1 Warranties

Warranties can be given by either party depending on the nature of the contract. The general position is that the party giving the warranty will want to limit its scope as far as possible, whilst the party relying on the warranty will want to ensure that is has as wide a scope as possible.

NOTES

Definition

> **Warranty**: an agreement with reference to goods which are the subject of a contract of sale, but collateral to the main purpose of such a contract, the breach of which gives rise to a claim for damages but not a right to reject the goods and treat the contract as repudiate: s 61 SGA.

While the Unfair Contract Terms Act affects business to consumer contracts, as we shall see shortly, generally parties to a non-consumer contract are free to agree such warranties as they consider appropriate. Some examples of the kinds of express warranty that may typically be found in a commercial contract are as follows.

(a) **Warranty of authority**: an individual warrants that he has authority to sign the contract on behalf of the party that he represents as an agent. This is normally implied by the mere fact of his signing the document. Such a warranty is often included in contracts with international companies whose status may be governed by a different law. The individual concerned will be personally liable for any breach of either the implied or the express warranty.

(b) **Warranty of compliance with laws**: such a warranty is often imposed to encourage the supplier to act in a lawful manner and to provide the innocent party with a remedy in the case of breach. It also imposes on the supplier the obligation to obtain all necessary consents and permissions required by law. Export licences and regulatory consents would be covered here.

(c) **Warranty relating to the quality of goods**: to provide more certainty to both parties, express warranties relating to equality may be preferable to relying in the implied terms of SGA. Where both parties have agreed to an express remedy, the supplier is likely to incorporate an additional clause specifying that this is the only remedy available and all other remedies, such as the right to compensation, are excluded.

(d) **Warranty relating to intellectual property rights**: supply contracts often include a warranty that the goods supplied do not infringe third party intellectual property rights, and provide for express remedies in such a case, such as the supplier being given an opportunity to alter the goods so that they no longer infringe any intellectual property rights. The warranty sets out the procedure and remedies to be followed in the event of infringement occurring, and normally provides that the supplier will conduct any third party claim at its own expense, reimbursing the buyer for any loss. The buyer is usually prohibited from settling or compromising the claim.

7.2 Indemnities

Indemnities have become increasingly popular in recent years and are now regularly included within commercial contracts.

Definition

> **Indemnity**: an obligation on the part of one party to pay to another such amount as is required to protect that other party from a specified loss.

An indemnity clause may contain some agreed mechanism, formula or amount to calculate the identified loss. There are three main different types of indemnity:

(a) **Unilateral indemnities**: one party asks the other party to assume a described risk and to pay for a specified kind of loss. For example in the sale of a company, indemnity would cover unexpected liabilities to taxation which relates to events or transactions prior to completion.

(b) **Reciprocal indemnities**: both parties promise not to do certain things, and the party who breaks his promise must indemnify the other party.

(c) **Mutual indemnities** ('knock for knock' clauses): effectively these are mutual promises not to sue in respect of specified types of claim.

A claim for a breach of indemnity has a number of advantages when compared to claims for breach of warranty or condition.

(a) A claim can be triggered by events and does not necessarily require either party to be at fault.

(b) The party relying on the indemnity merely needs to demonstrate that there is a claim.

(c) They are easier to enforce than claims for breach of warranty or condition.

(d) Generally there is no duty on the party relying on the indemnity to mitigate their loss.

7.3 Exclusion clauses in business to business contracts

All businesses are exposed to an element of risk in their day-to-day activities and so try and reduce this risk as far as possible. Consequently it is common practice for business to business contracts to contain clauses that seek to limit the effect of breaches of contract by the parties to it.

Definition

> **Exclusion clause**: a term in a contract that seeks to restrict the rights of the parties to the contract.

Exclusion clauses generally fall into one of these categories:

(a) **True exclusion clause**: the clauses recognises a potential breach of the contract, and then excuses liability for the breach. Alternatively, the clause is constructed in such a way that it only requires reasonable care in performing duties of one of the parties.

(b) **Litigation clause**: the clause places a limit on the amount that can be claimed for a breach of contract, regardless of the actual loss. This may be a time limitation clause, stating that an action for a claim must be commenced within a certain period of time or the cause of action becomes extinguished.

Such clauses are fertile grounds for disputes, and the courts are regularly called upon to interpret their meaning; they usually take a narrow approach.

7.4 Unfair Contract Terms Act 1977 (UCTA)

UCTA is the principal statute that deals with issues surrounding exclusion clauses. It deals with both business to business and business to consumer contracts. It is supplemented in regard to business to consumer contracts by the Unfair Terms in Consumer Contracts Regulations 1999 (UTRs), which we shall consider later in this chapter.

UCTA takes the approach of prohibiting some types of clause entirely, and requiring the remainder to be subject to a test of reasonableness.

Prohibited exclusion clauses are:

- any attempt to exclude liability in any transaction for death or personal injury caused by negligence: s 2

- any attempt to exclude a warranty of good title and quiet possession on sale of goods and on the supply of goods under contracts of work and materials: s 6

- in *business to consumer contracts* any attempt to exclude the implied warranties as to satisfactory quality, fitness for purpose, conformance with description or sample, whether for sale of goods, supply of work and materials or hire of goods: s 6

Test of reasonableness

General exclusion clauses, or restricted warranties and indemnities, that attempt to exclude liability in *business to business contracts* for any loss or damage other than death or personal injury caused by negligence are subject to a test of reasonableness: s 2.

Exclusion in *business to business contracts* of the implied warranties as to satisfactory quality, fitness for purpose, conformance with description or sample, whether for sale of goods, supply of work and materials or hire of goods may only be excluded if they satisfy the reasonableness test: s 6.

If a consumer in a *business to consumer contract* deals with a business on that business's written standard terms then a term will be subject to the test of reasonableness where the business seeks thereby to exclude liability in respect of a breach of contract, or claims to render a performance substantially different to what was reasonably expected, or fails to perform his obligations at all: s 6.

The test of reasonableness is that the term should be a fair and reasonable one having regard to the circumstances which were, or ought reasonably to have been, known to or in the contemplation of the parties when the contract was made.

In a sale or supply of goods the issue of reasonableness relies on consider of the following points.

(a) The strength of the bargaining position of the parties, taking into account alternative means by which the buyer's requirements could have been met.

(b) Whether the buyer received an inducement to agree to the term, or in accepting it had the opportunity to enter into a similar contract with other persons, but without having to accept a similar term.

(c) Whether the buyer knew or ought reasonably to have known of the existence and extent of the term.

(d) Where the term excludes or restricts any relevant liability if some condition is not complied with, whether it was reasonable at the time of the contract to expect that compliance with the condition would be practicable.

(e) Whether the goods were manufactured, processed or adapted to the special order of the buyer.

If one party is seeking to limit his liability to a specified sum of money then the test of reasonableness will also consider that party's access to resources to meet the liability should it arise, and the extent to which the liability could be covered by insurance.

The two cases below show that in *business to business contracts* where experienced business people representing substantial companies of equal bargaining power negotiate an agreement, they will be taken to have had regard to the matters known to them. The court will consider them to be the best judges on the question of whether the terms of the agreement are reasonable. The court should not assume that either party is likely to commit their company to an agreement which they think is unfair, or which they think includes unreasonable terms. Unless satisfied that one party has in fact taken advantage of the other party – or that term is so unreasonable that it cannot properly have been understood or considered – the court should not interfere.

St Albans City and District Council v International Computers Ltd 1996
The facts: St Albans entered into a contract with ICL for the provision of a software system to be used in collection of the community charge. The system was faulty and overstated the relevant population in the area, and as a result St Albans set the community charge too low and incurred a loss. St Albans brought an action against ICL for about £1.3m. ICL sought to rely upon an exclusion and limitation of liability clause contained in their standard terms and conditions which limited the amount recoverable to £100,000.

Decision: ICL was liable and could not rely upon the limitation of liability clause. Both the High Court and the Court of Appeal held that this particular term was not reasonable because ICL was a large company with substantial assets and insurance cover of up to £50 million, and was in a better position to bear losses than St Albans, which would have met losses out of an increased community charge. The limitation of £100,000 bore no relation to ICL's insurance cover of £50 million. In addition, ICL was in a stronger bargaining position. Whilst St Albans had objected to the limitation clause during negotiations they were persuaded to accept it when they were told that any amendment would need to be approved and that would lead to a delay. Any delay would have meant St Albans would not have been able to meet the community charge timetable. Finally St Albans had not been offered any inducement, such as a reduction in price, to accept the limitation and it had no opportunity to get the service elsewhere as other supplies were offering similar terms.

Watford Electronics Ltd v Sanderson CFL Ltd 2001
The facts: In 1992 Watford purchased a software system from Sanderson to use in its mail order business. The agreement was contained in three negotiated contracts, all of which incorporated Sanderson's standard terms: an 'entire agreement' clause, a warranty that the equipment/software would meet its specifications, and a limitation of liability clause. This excluded both parties'

liability for indirect or consequential loss, and limited Sanderson's liability to the price paid by Watford for the equipment/software (approximately £104, 596). Sanderson agreed to use its best endeavours to minimise any losses that might arise from the contract. The software system did not perform satisfactorily and Watford issued proceedings claiming misrepresentation, breach of implied warranties, breach of contract and negligence. Watford claimed £5.5 million for loss of profits and increased costs of working.

Decision: The Court of Appeal decided that the limitation of liability clauses were reasonable. In reaching their decision they considered two questions:

(a) Was it fair and reasonable having regard to the circumstances which were, or ought reasonably to have been, in the contemplation of the parties when the contact was made, to include a term which sought to exclude contractual claims for indirect/inconsequential losses?

- The court held the exclusion was reasonable given the facts of this particular case. Determining factors when reaching this decision were as follows.

    - The contracts were agreed by an experienced buyer and an experienced seller, between whom there was no inequality of bargaining power or bargaining skill.

    - Watford knew of the existence and significance of the exclusion clause. In fact Watford's own standard terms of business contained a similar restriction on liability and stated that its prices were determined in accordance with the restriction on liability. This showed Watford was well aware of the commercial considerations which lead a supplier to include a provision restricting liability for indirect or inconsequential loss and, in particular, was well aware that a supplier would be likely to determine the price at which it was prepared to sell its products by reference to its exposure to the risk of unquantifiable claims to indirect or consequential losses which might be suffered by the customer if things went wrong.

    - The buyer had sought substantial amendments to the exclusion clause and had managed to quality it by an addendum to the contract so that it would not exclude indirect or consequential loss resulting from the breach of warranty unless Sanderson used its best endeavours to ensure that the equipment and software complied with the warranty. The court said it would not intervene where the contracting parties have agreed on the allocation of risk and the price agreed reflected that allocation of risk.

    - The market, albeit for an integrated package not readily available elsewhere, was sufficiently a buyer's market for Watford to have been able to talk down the price by a significant amount.

(b) Was it fair and reasonable, having regard to those circumstances, to include a term which sought to restrict loss directly and naturally occurring from a breach of warranty to the price paid for the equipment and software?

- The court felt that the limitation of liability clause was an attempt to peg the value which the goods would have had if the warranty had been fulfilled to the price paid by the buyer.

8 BUSINESS TO CONSUMER CONTRACTS

We have already seen that in respect of *business to consumer contracts* it is not possible to exclude the SGA implied terms or warranties in a contract, and that courts tend to adopt a favourable view when faced with a consumer complaining of an alleged breach of one of these implied terms. We need now to look at some further aspects of the law that relate specifically to business to consumer contracts.

8.1 Remedies for customers

Remedies are available to consumers under the Sale and Supply of Goods to Consumers Regulations 2002 (SSGCR). These regulations came into force in 2003, implementing an EU Directive on the sale of consumer goods. They offer additional remedies in respect of goods which do not confirm with the contract under the consumer protection provisions of SGA and SGSA 1982.

Previously a consumer had three main remedies in respect of faulty goods.

(a) Rejection of goods: consumers could reject faulty goods and require their money back provided that they complained within a reasonable period of time. 'Reasonable' was never defined in the SGA but was generally thought to equate to 'short'. However, the consumer had to be given an opportunity to examine the goods and the courts would decide the reasonableness of this on a case by case basis.

(b) Compensation by way of damages: this remedy was usually available either where rejection was not possible, or as an alternative to rejection. Damages would typically be aimed at recovering all or any of the following if a claim was brought within six years form the date of sale:

- actual losses – typically the cost of repair or replacement (with goods of a similar age)

- losses arising directly from the consumer being supplied with the faulty goods

- cost of default being remedies by a third party

(c) Claim under the manufacturer's warranty/guarantee: assuming that one had been given in the first place and that it had not subsequently expired.

These remedies are still available, but since April 2003 a consumer can, instead of rejecting goods or claiming compensation, ask for one of the following where the goods do not conform to the contract at the time of delivery:

- Repair
- Replacement
- Partial refund
- Full refund

A retailer can decline to offer repair or replacement if he can show that the cost involved would be disproportionate compared to full or partial refund. Whether refund is appropriate will depend on how long the consumer has had the item in question, and what use he has had out of it.

A retailer is under an obligation to provide a remedy within a reasonable period of time and without significant inconvenience to the consumer. A consumer cannot pursue more than one remedy at any one time and also cannot switch from one remedy to another without giving the retailer a reasonable opportunity to provide the first remedy requested. Under the Limitation Act 1980, a case based on breach of contract (as these claims are) should be brought within six years. (That does not mean that all goods must last for six years and, particularly where low cost goods or those with a short projected lifespan are concerned, an action brought in the later stages of this limitation period is likely to be unsuccessful.) In addition, by virtue of the EU directive from which the regulations derive, retailers are obliged to honour the additional four remedies for at least two years.

Before the SSGCR were implemented the burden of proof rested squarely on the consumer to demonstrate that a fault was present at the time of sale. Now when the consumer seeks repair or replacement or, thereafter, a full or partial refund within six months of the time of sale then the onus in on the retailer to prove that the goods were in conformity with the contract at the time of sale.

The remedies do not cover fair wear and tear and the consumer will have to prove non-conformity once the first six months have expired.

8.2 Unfair terms

The Unfair Terms in Consumer Contracts Regulations 1999 (the 'UTRs') came into force in October 1999 and relate only to *business to consumer contracts*. Under the UTRs a consumer is not bound by a standard term in a contract with a seller of goods or supplier of services if the term is unfair. The Office of Fair Trading (OFT) has produced a considerable amount of guidance concerning the UTRs and this can be found on their website at www.oft.gov.uk.

Definitions

Consumer: an individual not acting for the purpose of his or her business or profession.

Standard terms: those devised by a business in advance, not individually negotiated with the consumer. They do not have to be in writing but typically they are found in the 'small print' on the back of order forms and bills and so on. While the UTRs do not apply to any term that can be shown to have been individually negotiated, they do apply to any standard terms in the same contract.

Seller or supplier: any person or organisation acting for the purposes of their business. This includes any trade or profession, and the activities of government and other public bodies.

A standard term is unfair when:

(a) it creates a **significant imbalance in the parties' rights and obligations** under the contract: examples given by the OFT are terms that aim to stop consumers from making certain sorts of legal claim against the business which they could otherwise have made, or that give the business rights against the consumer that it would not otherwise have had, and

(b) a **detriment is thereby caused to the consumer** (the mere fact that there is a significant imbalance is not conclusive in determining that a term is unfair, rather the imbalance must cause or be capable of causing a detriment to consumers), and

(c) **this is contrary to the requirement of good faith**. The good faith requirement is based on the idea that consumers should be dealt with fairly and equitably by businesses in such a way as to protect their legitimate interests. The standard requires more than the avoidance of deceit, rather it places a burden on the business to consider whether the term in question should have properly been included in the contract at all.

The UTRs set out the following examples of terms which will generally be considered as being unfair, all of which have the aim or effect of reducing the consumer's rights under the ordinary rules of contract or the general law:

(a) excluding or limiting the legal liability of a seller or supplier in the event of the death of a consumer or personal injury to the latter resulting from an act or omission of that seller or supplier;

(b) inappropriately excluding or limiting the legal rights of the consumer in the event of total or partial non-performance or inadequate performance by the seller;

(c) making an agreement binding on the consumer whereas providing services by the seller is subject to a condition whose realisation depends on the supplier's own will alone;

(d) permitting the seller to retain sums paid by the consumer where the latter decides not to include or perform the contract, without providing for the consumer to receive compensation of an equivalent amount from the seller where the latter is the party cancelling the contract;

(e) requiring any consumer who fails to fulfil his obligation to pay a disproportionately high sum in compensation;

(f) authorising the seller to dissolve the contract on a discretionary basis where the same facility is not granted to the consumer, or permitting the seller to retain the sums paid for services not yet supplied by him where it is the seller himself who dissolves the contract;

(g) enabling the seller to terminate a contract of indeterminate duration without reasonable notice except where there are serious grounds for doing so;

(h) automatically extending a contract of fixed duration where the consumer does not indicate otherwise, when the deadline fixed for the consumer to express his desire not to extend the contract is unreasonably early;

(i) irrecoverably binding the consumer to terms with which he had no real opportunity of becoming acquainted before the conclusion of the contract;

(j) enabling the seller to alter the terms of the contract unilaterally without a valid reason which is specified in the contract;

(k) enabling the seller to alter unilaterally without a valid reason any characteristics of the product or service to be provided;

(l) providing for the price of goods to be determined at the time of delivery or allowing a seller to increase their price without in both cases giving the consumer the corresponding right to cancel the contract if the price is too high in relation to the price agreed when the contact was concluded;

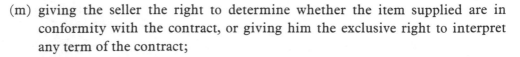
(m) giving the seller the right to determine whether the item supplied are in conformity with the contract, or giving him the exclusive right to interpret any term of the contract;

(n) limiting the seller's obligations to respect commitments undertaken by his agents or making his commitments subject to compliance with a particular formality;

(o) obliging the consumer to fulfil all his obligations where the seller does not perform his;

(p) giving the seller the responsibility of transferring his rights and obligations under the contract, where this may serve to reduce the guarantees for the consumer, without the latter's agreement;

(q) excluding or hindering the consumer's rights to take legal action or exercise any other legal remedy, particularly by requiring the consumer to take disputes exclusively to arbitration not covered by legal provisions, unduly restricting the evidence available to him or imposing on him a burden of proof which, according to the applicable law, should lie with another party to the contract.

If a term is found to be unfair then it is not legally binding on the consumer. This means that if an unfair term requires consumers to do something, they cannot be made to do it; similarly, if an unfair terms seeks to prevent a consumer from doing something, it will not be upheld in court. If an unfair term seeks to exclude or limit liability for unsatisfactory goods or poor workmanship then a consumer can sue for compensation regardless of it.

But just because an unfair term is unenforceable does not mean that the rest of the contract is void, unless it is unworkable without the unfair term.

Under the UTRs, if a business refuses to accept that the term is unfair, then a consumer can seek help from a court. If the court agrees with the consumer, the business will not be allowed to rely on that term against the consumer.

8.3 Unfair Contract Terms Bill

The Law Commission published a report in 2005 on the confused relationship between UCTA and the UTRs and on which it drew the following conclusions:

(a) UCTA is notoriously complicated and difficult to follow

(b) The combination of legislation has led to a widespread confusion amongst consumers and businesses

(c) UCTA is focused narrowly on exclusion clauses but deals with both consumers and businesses, while the UTRs have a wider focus but are limited to consumers only

The Law Commission produced a draft Bill that included its recommendations that:

(a) all areas of protection currently set out in the UTRs should be retained (although the UTRs themselves would be repeated);

(b) the current prohibition in UCTA on terms limiting liability for death or personal injury or excluding the implied terms of Sale of Goods Act against consumers should be retained (although the Act itself would be repeated)

(c) these protections should be extended from standard terms to include negotiated terms as well

(d) new provisions are needed to the effect that where a consumer brings a claim then the burden will be on the business to prove that the term is fair

(e) protection should be extended to small businesses. At present a small business may challenge unfair exclusion clauses but the Law Commission's view is that small businesses are routinely asked to sign up to other unfair terms which currently cannot be challenged. Examples cited are: price variation clauses, indemnity clauses, forfeits of deposits and unequal termination rights. In such cases the small business is either not aware of the significance of the term or does not have the ability to challenge it due to the inequality of bargaining strength between the parties. The recommendation is that small or 'micro' businesses with nine or less employees should be able to challenge any term of any contract that has not been altered through negotiation and that does not relate to price or the main subject matter of the contract. Some contracts would be excluded form this protection, including contracts for financial services, contracts worth over £500,000 and situations where the apparently small business is associated with larger enterprises.

At the time of writing (July 2010) it is still unclear as to when these proposed changes will be enacted.

8.4 Unfair commercial practices

The Consumer Protection from Unfair Trading Regulations 2008 ('CPRs') came into force in May 2008. These regulations implement the Unfair Commercial Practices Directive and part of the Sale of Goods Directive 1999. The CPRs contain a general prohibition on unfair commercial practices, prohibit aggressive or misleading commercial practices and set out an indicative list of 31 banned practices that are always unfair.

The CPRs apply to unfair business-to-consumer commercial practices before, during and after a commercial transaction in relation to a product. They prohibit unfair commercial practices, including practices that contravene the requirements of professional diligence, misleading actions or omissions and aggressive commercial practices. Breach of the prohibition constitutes a criminal offence (with limited exceptions) and there are defences available of due diligence and innocent publication of advertisements.

(You should be aware that there are also regulations which deal with traders who enter into a contract with a consumer at the consumer's home or workplace or on an excursion arranged by the seller away from his business premises (the Cancellation of Contracts made in a Consumers' Home or Place of Work etc Regulations 2008) which came into force in October 2008 (also known as the Doorstep Selling Regulations).)

NOTES

Definitions

Consumer: any individual who in relation to a commercial practice is acting for purposes which are outside his trade, business, craft or profession. (Companies are not treated as consumers).

Trader: any natural or legal person who, in relation to a commercial practice, is acting for purposes relating to his trade, business, craft or profession and anyone acting in the name of or on behalf of a trader. This includes individuals who regularly sell new goods from their homes on the internet using platforms such as e-bay when this is done as a business rather than merely disposing of unwanted goods for a small financial gain.

Product: any good or service, including immoveable property, rights and obligations (including the sale or lease of property).

Business-to-consumer commercial practice: any act, omission, course of conduct or representation, commercial communication including advertising and marketing, by a trader, directly connected with the promotion, sale or supply of a product to or from consumers whether occurring before, during or after a commercial transaction (if any) in relation to a product.

Material distortion: using a commercial practice to appreciably impair the consumer's ability to make an informed decision, thereby causing the consumer to take a transactional decision (broadly, a purchase) that he would not have taken otherwise.

Professional diligence: the standard of special skill and care which a trader may reasonably be expected to exercise towards consumers, commensurate with honest market practice and/or the general principle of good faith in the trader's field of activity. This is an objective standard to be judged against the expectations of the reasonable man in line with honest market practice or good faith. It does not have to be shown that the trader knew he was involved in an unfair commercial practice. ('Honest market practice' and 'good faith' are not specifically defined).

There are two main elements to a **commercial practice**:

- something is done or not done by a trader before, during or after the transaction, and

- the act or omission is directly related to the promotion, supply or sale of a product to or from consumers

This definition of a commercial practice can apply to traders further up the supply chain even if they themselves do not deal directly with consumers. For example, if a manufacturer or wholesaler applies labels to goods falsely describing their composition, knowing that those goods could ultimately be sold to consumers, then the acts of the manufacturer and wholesaler would be 'directly connected with the promotion, sale or supply of a product to consumers'.

Unfair commercial practice

Unfair commercial practice are prohibited (reg 3). A commercial practice is unfair if it is contrary to the requirements of *professional diligence*, and it *materially distorts* or is likely to materially distort the economic behaviour with regard to the product of the *average consumer* whom it reaches or to whom it is addressed, or of the average member of the group when a commercial practice is directed to a particular *group of consumers*.

Let us consider each key factor (denoted in italics in the paragraph above) in turn.

- **Professional diligence** is determined by considering the standard of behaviour that a trader would be reasonably expected to show towards consumers. Consequently as long as a trader reaches this standard then the practice in question will not be viewed as unfair.

- **Material distortion**. The main principles to be taken into consideration here when deciding whether there has been material distortion itself are the following:

  - has the practice impaired the consumer's ability to make an informed decision?

  - was the impairment so great as to have changed the average consumer's decision?

- **'Average consumer'** is a consumer who is reasonably well-informed and who is reasonably observant and circumspect.

- **Group of consumers.** The CPRs assess material distortion against the standards of the average consumer. Where the practice is directed to a particular group of consumers. The average consumer is taken to refer to the average member of the group. Where a clearly identifiable group of consumers is particularly vulnerable to the practice or the underlying product because of their mental or physical infirmity, age or credulity in a way which the trader could reasonably be expected to foresee and the practice is likely to materially distort the economic behaviour only of that group, the average consumer is taken to be the average member of that group. This is without prejudice to the common and legitimate advertising practice of making exaggerated statements or statements which are not meant to be taken literally.

Remember that if the trader acts in a professionally diligent manner then his practice is not unfair, irrespective as to the impact it has on the vulnerable.

There are two tests of reasonableness attached to the vulnerable consumer:

(a) what impact is reasonably foreseeable?
(b) what action is required of a professionally diligent trader?

A trader should only be expected to do what is reasonable, both in considering whether the practice would have an unfair impact on any clearly identifiable group of vulnerable consumers, and in taking steps to mitigate any such impact.

What 'reasonable precautions' are appropriate will depend on the circumstances of the case. However, they should not represent a substantial change in trader behaviour, an example of this being that a trader would be unlikely to be required to alter a marketing campaign to meet the needs of a small number of extremely gullible consumers.

In addition, a commercial practice is unfair if it is either:

- a misleading action
- a misleading omission
- aggressive or
- listed in Schedule 1

Misleading actions

Regulation 5 of the CPRs set out the circumstances in which a practice is considered to be unfair because it misleads through the information it contains. If either of the following two conditions is satisfied, the commercial practice will constitute a misleading action, or if it deceives or is likely to deceive the average consumer (even if the information is factually correct) as to any of the matters listed below.

(1)
- it contains false information or
- if it (or its overall presentation) deceives or is likely to deceive the average consumer, even if the information is factually correct.
- and (in either case) it causes or is likely to cause the average consumer to take a transactional decision he would not have taken otherwise, or

(2) if it concerns any marketing of a product, including comparative advertising, which creates confusion with any products, trade marks, trade names or other distinguishing marks of a competitor or

- any non-compliance with a commitment in a code of conduct with which the trader has undertaken to be bound, where the commitment is not aspirational but is firm and capable of being verified and the trader indicates in a commercial practice that he is bound by the code.
- and, in either case it causes or is likely to cause the average consumer to take a transactional decision he would not have taken otherwise.

The matters referred to in (1) above concerning misleading or deceiving information are as follows:

(a) Existence or nature of the product

(b) Main characters of the product such as:

- Availability
- Benefits and risks
- Execution
- Composition
- Accessories
- After-sale customer assistance and complaint handling
- Method and date of manufacture or provision
- Delivery
- Fitness for purpose
- Usage

- Quantity

- Specification

- Geographical or commercial origins

- Results to be expected from its use

- Results and material features of tests or checks carried out on the product

(c) Extent of the trader's commitments, the motives for the commercial practices and the nature of the sales process, any statement or symbol in relation to direct or indirect sponsorship or approval of the trader or the product

(d) Price or the manner in which the price is calculated, or the existence of a specific price advantage

(e) Need for service, part, replacement or repair

(f) Nature, attributes and rights of the trader or his agent, such as his identity and assets, his qualifications, status, approval, affiliation or connection and ownership of industrial, commercial or intellectual property rights or his awards and distinctions

(g) Consumer's rights or the risks he may face

Misleading omissions

Failure to provide consumers with the information they need so as to make an informed choice may also be misleading. Regulation 6 of the CPRs provides that a commercial practice is misleading if it omits material information that the average consumer needs, according to the context, to take an informed transactional decision and thereby causes or is likely to cause the average consumer to take a transactional decision he would not have taken otherwise.

Any practice which hides material information or provides it in an unclear unintelligible, ambiguous or untimely manner or which fails to identify its commercial intent (unless that is apparent from the context) is also treated as a misleading omission.

The CPRs recognise that certain media (eg television and radio) have time constraints in terms of how much information they can reasonably provide. In such cases any decision about whether material information has been omitted will be considered in the light of any other steps taken by the trader to bring the information to the consumer's attention.

Omissions where there is an invitation to purchase

Where there is an invitation to the consumer actually to purchase goods or services, a number of core information items are always regarded as material and must be provided if they could impact on the transactional decision of the average consumer, except where these are already apparent from the context.

These core information items are as follows:

(a) the main characteristics of the product (to an extent appropriate to the medium and the product);

(b) the geographical address and the identity of the trader, such as his trading name and, where applicable, the geographical address and the identity of the trader on whose behalf he is acting;

(c) the price, inclusive of taxes, or where the nature of the product means that the price cannot reasonably be calculated in advance, the manner in which the price is calculated, as well as, where appropriate, all additional freight, delivery or postal charges or, where these charges cannot be reasonably calculated in advance, the fact that such additional charges may be payable;

(d) the arrangements for payment, delivery, performance and complaint handling policy, if they depart from the requirements of professional diligence;

(e) for products and transactions involving a right of withdrawal or cancellation, the existence of such a right.

Aggressive commercial practices

Regulation 7 of the CPRs provide that a commercial practice shall be regarded as aggressive if, in its factual context, taking account of all the features and circumstances, by harassment, coercion (including the use of physical force), or undue influence, it significantly impairs or is likely to significantly impair the average consumer's freedom of choice or conduct with regard to the product and thereby causes him or is likely to cause him to take a transactional decision that he would not have taken otherwise.

Undue influence in this context means exploiting a position of power in relation to the consumer so as to apply pressure, even without using or threatening to use physical force, in a way which significantly limits the consumer's ability to make an informed decision. An example of undue influence arises where a consumer is in debt to a trader and behind with payments. A trader would be using undue influence (by exploiting a position of power) if he said that he would reschedule the debt if the consumer bought another product from him.

The following factors will be taken into account in determining whether a commercial practice uses harassment, coercion or undue influence:

(a) its timing, location, nature or persistence;

(b) the use of threatening or abusive language or behaviour;

(c) exploitation by the trader of any specific misfortune or circumstance of such gravity as to impair the consumer's judgement, of which the trader is aware, to influence the consumer's decision with regard to the product;

(d) any onerous or disproportionate non-contractual barriers imposed by the trader where a consumer wishes to exercise rights under the contract, including rights to terminate a contract or switch to another product or trader;

(e) any threat to take any action that cannot legally be taken.

Prohibited commercial practices: Schedule 1

Schedule 1 sets out a list of 31 practices that are always unfair. Examples of these practices include:

- falsely claiming that a trader (including his commercial practices) or the products he is selling have been approved by a recognised body

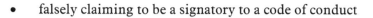
- falsely claiming to be a signatory to a code of conduct

- holding bogus closing down sales

- creating the impression that the consumer cannot leave the premises until a contract is formed

- creating a false impression that the consumer has won a prize

- falsely stating that a product will only be available for a limited time

Some of these prohibitions already exist in English law while others will provide new protections or clarify existing ones.

With very limited exceptions, carrying on a commercial practice in contravention of the CPRs is a criminal offence, punishable by fine and/or up to two years' imprisonment.

It is a defence to show that the offence was committed due to a mistake or accident or another person or a cause beyond the defendant's control provided that the perpetrator of the offence can also show that he took all reasonable precautions and exercised all due diligence to avoid the commission of the offence. It is also an offence, where an offence is committed by the publication of an advertisement, to show that the advertisement was received and published in the ordinary course of business and that the defendant neither knew nor suspected that publication would constitute an offence.

9 PRODUCT LIABILITY

A person who suffers injury or loss in connection with defective or dangerous goods may have remedies as follows.

(a) Remedies in contract
(b) Remedies in tort
(c) Remedies under Part I of the Consumer Protection Act 1987

9.1 Contract

If he is the purchaser he can probably recover damages from the vendor for breach of the statutory implied conditions of quality imposed by the Sale of Goods Act 1979. If he deals as consumer he cannot be deprived of these safeguards; in any other case an attempt to exclude or restrict them is void unless it satisfies a test of reasonableness: Unfair Contract Terms Act 1977.

9.2 Tort

If he suffers personal injury or damage to property which is caused by a defective product he may be able to recover damages for *negligence* from the manufacturer under the law of tort. Any attempt to exclude liability for personal injury or death due to negligence is void and exemption from other liability is usually subject to a test of reasonableness: Unfair Contract Terms Act 1977.

In either case the supplier or manufacturer may dispute the liability. Except for cases covered by SSGCR (see 8.1 above), the claimant must prove breach of contract or negligence as the case may be.

Negligence is covered in the Business Law Course Book.

9.3 Consumer Protection Act 1987 (CPA 1987)

Part I of the Consumer Protection Act 1987 deals with liability for defective products. It covers strict liability for death, personal injury and damage to consumer property. For the consumer, the Act has the advantage that he does not have to prove negligence, nor that there was any privity of contract between him and the person he is suing. In other words the Act imposes strict civil liability, and this liability cannot be excluded by any disclaimer.

Strict product liability

Claims for losses caused by defects in a product may be brought against any of the following.

(a) The manufacturer of the end-product

(b) The manufacturer of a defective component (although he has a defence if he can show that he followed the instructions or specifications of the manufacturer of the end-product)

(c) An importer into the EC (the principle behind this is that anybody responsible who is outside the EC may be much more difficult to find)

(d) An 'own-brander'

(e) A supplier, who is usually a retailer

Because of the potential liability of the parties above, it is usual for a supplier only to be liable if he will not disclose the identity of the importer or manufacturer.

The burden of proof is on the consumer to prove that:

(a) the product contained a defect
(b) he suffered damage
(c) the damage resulted from the defect *and*
(d) the defendant was either the producer or some other person listed above

Proving causation on the balance of probabilities, remoteness of damage and reasonable foresight have the same difficulties as under the law of tort.

Product

The products covered by CPA 1987 include all products including component parts and raw materials. Product is defined as 'any goods or electricity', goods including substances (natural or artificial in solid, liquid or gaseous form), growing crops, things comprised in land by virtue of being attached to it, ships, aircraft and vehicles. It does not include primary (non-processed) agricultural products but includes both raw and cooked food.

'Defective' product

A product will be found to be unsafe where it is not as safe as it is reasonable to expect. This standard of relative safety requires a court to take into account all circumstances surrounding the product – the way it is advertised, the time at which it was supplied, its anticipated normal use, the provision of instructions for use, even its likely misuse – in establishing the standard required. Also the benefit to society and the cost of making the product safer can be considered.

Scope of the Act

Consumers and other users (such as the donee of an electric iron received as a gift), but not business users, can claim compensation for death, personal injury or damage to other property (not to the product itself nor for economic loss, ie caused by the product not working). There is unlimited liability but the following limitations apply in respect of bringing an action.

(a) A claim must be brought within three years of (broadly speaking) the fault becoming apparent

(b) No claim may be brought more than ten years after the original supply

(c) Where the claim is for damage to property, it must not be business property which is damaged and the amount of the damage must be more than £275

Defences

The defendant in a case under the CPA 1987 has six possible defences:

(a) The product complied with mandatory statutory or EC standards (see Piper v JRI (Manufacturing) Ltd 2006, Control of Appeal where the defence was successfully pleaded.

(b) The product was not at any time supplied to another.

(c) The supply was otherwise than in the course of a business.

(d) The defect did not exist in the product when originally supplied.

(e) 'Development risk' – the state of knowledge at the time of manufacture and supply was such that no manufacturer could have been expected to detect the fault. The inclusion of this defence in the Act means that many victims of drugs which had damaging side-effects may be left without a remedy. The defence was kept so as not to discourage medical research.

(f) The defect was wholly attributable to the design of a subsequent product into which the product in question was incorporated.

The fifth of these defences is known as the 'state of the art' defence. This challenges directly the concept of strict liability for defective products and its inclusion has been controversial. In fact the provision affording this defence was challenged before the European Court of Justice (ECJ) in 1997 by the European Commission as being inconsistent with the directive and proposed regime of strict liability. The ECJ ruled in favour of the UK on the grounds that the wording itself did not exclude the courts from interpreting it in a manner consistent with the directive (no cases had come before the courts at that time). The Court did, however, make it clear that the test was to be an objective one, ie that a producer would have to show that the objective state of technical and scientific knowledge at an advanced level, at the time the product was made available, was not sufficient to have enabled the defect to be discovered.

Although liability under the CPA 1987 to a person who has suffered damage cannot be excluded or limited by any contract term or by a notice, parties other than the person damaged who are in the chain of distribution are free to adjust the liabilities between themselves, subject to any common law or statutory controls, such as the Unfair Contract Terms 1977.

The CPA 1987 was a significant step towards protection against unsafe goods. Producers and other distributors have to ensure that they are protected by insurance in their business contracts; careful record-keeping is also required so that the other people in the distribution chain are adequately identified.

BPP
LEARNING MEDIA

9.4   Consumer safety

The general safety requirement, originally imposed under Part II CPA 1987 was replaced by the General Product Safety Regulations 2005 (see below). Section II CPA 1987, however, empowers the Secretary of State to make regulations designed to ensure the safety of goods (with some exceptions such as growing crops, food and controlled drugs). Generally speaking, contravention of such regulations is a criminal offence and enforcement authorities may issue suspension and prohibition notices against persons alleged to be breach.

Regulations made under the provision generally concern very specific products. Examples include the following:

(a)   Cooking Utensils (Safety) Regulations 1972. These govern the proportion of lead permitted in kitchen utensils used for cooking food.

(b)   Electrical Equipment (Safety) Regulations 1994. These requires that various items of electrical equipment shall comply with appropriate British Standards.

(c)   Pencils and Graphic Instruments (Safety) Regulations 1998. These control the maximum amounts of arsenic, cadmium, chromium, mercury, antimony, lead and barium permitted in pencils, pens, brushes, crayons and chalk.

The General Product Safety Regulations 2005

These regulations came into effect in October 2005 and apply to all products which are intended for consumers or likey to be used by consumers and which are supplied in the cause of a commercial activity, save to the extent that the safety of such products is covered by other specific provisions. The regulations do not apply to second-hand products which are supplied as products to be repaired or reconditioned before use, provided that the supplier clearly informs the customer of this.

The regulations impose a general safety requirement that no producer shall supply or place on the market (or offer or agree to do so) any product unless it is a safe product. The term 'producer' includes manufacturers of goods in the EU, anyone who presents themselves as the manufacturer by putting a name or trade mark on the product, importers into the EU (where the manufacturer is outside the EU and has no representative in the EU) and certain others in the supply chain.

A 'safe product' is a product which, under normal or reasonably foreseeable conditions of use, presents no, or minimal, risk. This must be consistent with a high degree of protection for persons' health and safety. Four factors are taken into account in particular:

(a)   The characteristics of the product, eg packaging and instructions for assembly

(b)   The effect of the product on other products (where it is reasonably foreseeable that it will be used with other products)

(c)   The presentation of the product, eg labelling, warnings and instructions for use

(d)   The categories of consumer (eg children) at risk.

A product may be deemed to be safe if it complies with specific UK laws concerning the product. In other cases, the conformity of a product to the general safety requirement may be assessed having regard to various factors, including relevant safety codes of good practice, the state of the art and technology and reasonable consumer expectations concerning safety.

Producers are required to provide relevant information to enable consumers to assess the risks inherent in a product throughout its normal or reasonably foreseeable useful life and to take precautions against those risks. They must also take measures (eg use of batch numbers) to assess the risks a product presents and enable withdrawal from sale.

Distributors are required to act with due care in order to help ensure compliance with producers' obligations. A distributor is any professional in the supply chain whose activity does not affect the safety properties of a product.

Producers and distributors must fully inform the enforcement authority in the event of a suspected breach of the general safety requirement.

The regulations permit a defence of due diligence where a producer has taken all reasonable steps and exercised all due diligence to avoid committing an offence.

District and county councils are given powers of enforcement and they may issue appropriate notices by way of enforcement, including suspension, withdrawal and recall notices. Powers to make test purchases and powers of entry and search are also included. Enforcement officers may also apply to court for an order for the forfeiture of a product which they consider to be a dangerous product.

Breach of the general safety requirement is a criminal offence, punishable by a fine up to £20,000 and/or up to 12 months' imprisonment. The regulations do not confer any right of action in civil proceedings.

Chapter roundup

- Contracts for the sale of goods are subject to the Sale of Goods Act 1979 as amended by the Sale and Supply of Goods Act 1994. In considering such contracts, we must distinguish between existing and future goods, and between specific and unascertained goods.

- If the price for goods is not determined by the contract then a reasonable price must be paid.

- The Sale of Goods Act 1979 implies several terms into contracts for the sale of goods, and the Unfair Contract Terms Act 1977 limits the extent to which these implied terms may be restricted or excluded.

- There is an implied condition that the seller of goods has a right to sell, but the seller may put the buyer on notice that his title may be defective.

- In a sale by description, the goods must match the description given. In a sale by sample, the bulk must correspond to the sample.

- Goods are of satisfactory quality if they meet the standard that a reasonable person would regard as satisfactory.

- If the seller of goods knows the purpose for which the goods are being bought, it is normally an implied condition that the goods are reasonably fit for that purpose.

- The property in goods passes when the parties intend that it shall pass. Where such intention is not otherwise made clear, the rules of s 18 Sale of Goods Act 1979 apply to fix the time. Goods are generally at the buyer's risk from the time that property passes.

NOTES

Chapter roundup continued

- A person not owning goods cannot in general transfer title to a buyer. However, there are several exceptions to protect an innocent buyer.

- Goods must be delivered as agreed, but there are rules which apply in the absence of agreement.

- A buyer must be given an opportunity to inspect and if necessary reject goods, but once he has accepted the goods, either explicitly or by conduct, he cannot later reject them.

- An unpaid seller of goods may be able to retrieve the goods even if title has passed to the buyer. He may also attempt to protect his position by retaining title until he has been paid. Failing such remedies, the seller may sue the buyer. If the seller breaches a condition of the contract, the buyer may reject the goods. The buyer may also sue the seller for breach of condition or warranty.

- The Sale of Goods Act 1979 applies only to sales of goods. The Supply of Goods and Services Act 1982 makes similar provisions for contracts outside the scope of the 1979 Act.

- Contracts for the sale and supply of goods and services, especially business to business contracts, often contain warranties, indemnities and exclusion clauses that are intended to adjust the balance of power between the parties and their rights and obligations.

- Some exclusion or limitation clauses are prohibited entirely, whilst others are subject to a test of reasonableness. Consumer contracts are regulated by the Unfair Terms in Consumer Contracts Regulations, which specifies the circumstances when a term in a consumer contract will be deemed unfair, and which gives examples of these.

- An unfair term is not legally binding on the consumer through the rest of the contract may still be valid.

- In business to consumer contracts the consumer may seek the remedies of repair, replacement or full or partial refund from the party which supplied defective goods.

- Unfair commercial practices, including both actions and misleading information as well as aggressive practices, are regulated Protection from Unfair Trading Regulations 2008.

- A person who suffers injury or loss in connection with defective or dangerous goods may have three types of remedy. The purchaser of goods may resort to the terms implied by the Sale of Goods Act 1979. Any party may seek to recover damages for negligence from the manufacturer under the law of tort. A remedy may also be available under Part I of the Consumer Protection Act 1987, which imposes strict liability for death, personal injury and damage to consumer property.

- Under the General Product Safety Regulations 2005, it is an offence punishable under criminal law to supply consumer goods which fail to comply with a general safety requirement.

Quick quiz

1 What terms are covered by statutory conditions implied (as part of the contract) by the Sale of Goods Act 1979?

2 What is the implied condition as to the seller's right to sell the goods?

3 What is a sale of goods by description and what is implied in such a sale?

4 What is satisfactory quality?

5 When are defects of quality not a breach of the condition of satisfactory quality?

6 Give three exceptions to the rule *nemo dat quod non habet.*

7 What is a severable contract?

8 When is a buyer deemed to have accepted goods?

9 What are the seller's remedies if he is not paid?

10 What is a retention of title clause?

11 What are the buyer's remedies for breach of contract?

12 What terms are implied into a contract which is wholly or substantially for the provision of services?

13 Against what parties may a claim be brought for defects in a product under the principles of strict product liability?

14 What are the six defences available to a defendant under Part I CPA 1987?

15 Can a consumer sue a supplier under the Consumer Protection from Unfair Trading Regulations or the General Product Safety Regulations 2005?

16 What is a 'safe product'?

Answers to quick quiz

1 Title
   Description of goods
   Sale by sample
   Quantity of goods
   Fitness for purpose of the goods

2 That the seller has the right to sell the goods, ie he can pass good title.

3 Implied condition that goods will correspond to the description of them, where they are sold by description.

4 Goods 'meet the standard a reasonable person would regard as satisfactory'.

5 When goods are used not for the particular purpose sold, or for an unusual purpose.

NOTES

6 Agency
Estoppel
Sale under/buyer voidable title
Resale by seller/buyer in possession
Sale of motor vehicle acquired under hire purchase
Special powers of sale

7 A contract where delivery is made by instalments.

8 Once he has had a reasonable opportunity of examining them and intimates acceptance by his word, or conduct.

9 Lien
Stoppage in transit
Right of resale
Retention of title

10 A clause stating that possession of goods does not pass to the buyer until he has paid for them.

11 Recovery of the price
Rejection of the goods
Damages for non-delivery
Specific performance

12 Implied term that the provider of the service will carry it out with reasonable care and skill and within a reasonable time.

Implied term that a reasonable charge will be paid

13 The manufacturer of the end product; the manufacturer of a defective part; an importer into the EC; an own-brander or a supplier (usually a retailer).

14 See the list in paragraph 9.3.

15 No. Both sets of regulations provide for criminal offence which are enforced by the relevant enforcement authorities, not the consumer.

16 Consumer goods which comply with the general safety requirement imposed provided by the General Product Safety Regulations 2005

Answers to activities

1 C may recover the entire price (£1,000) from the seller, A, because C did not receive ownership of the corn and the depreciation in value is irrelevant.

2 No: although 1959 is very close to 1958, the exact year is crucial for wine.

3 P's argument would fail because, although the pen can be made to write with difficulty, this is not the standard of quality expected from an expensive pen.

4 S made it clear that he did not have the skill or judgement on which R sought to rely.

5 Property passes on Thursday under Rule 2 of s 18 Sale of Goods Act 1979.

6 No: This is a case of sale under voidable title and the seller has rescinded the contract by taking all reasonable steps.

7   The car belongs to Dawn Smith because Dawn Jones has attempted to purchase the car while having notice of the previous sale and acting in bad faith. Section 24 does not apply.

8   10 pm is not during normal business hours and the seller has not given the buyer a reasonable opportunity to inspect the goods.

9   The seller may bring an action for the price. The retention of title clause does not mention incorporation into Z Ltd's products, so it cannot be relied upon in this case.

10   *Marcel (Furriers) Ltd v Tapper 1953.*

Part C: Consumer Law

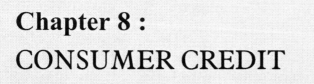

Chapter 8 :
CONSUMER CREDIT

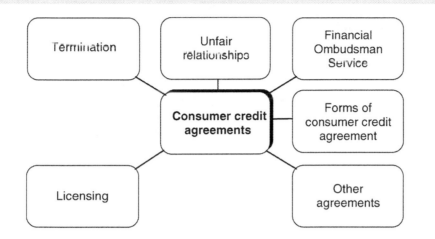

Introduction

The Consumer Credit Act 1974 as amended by the Consumer Credit Act 2006 protects consumers by supporting the concept of 'truth in lending'. The Act applies to any defined lending transactions to individuals, not to companies, and its main provisions govern all consumer credit and consumer hire agreements unless exempted. As an example of its scope, all lending institutions regulated by the Act must inform borrowers of all charges connected with regulated lending, and the rate of interest must be calculated and quoted in a similar way. These are the twin phenomena of the Total Charge for Credit and the Annual Percentage Rate.

Typical problems encountered before the Act were inaccurate advertising, canvassing and the charging of exorbitant rates of interest by lenders. The Act is a complex piece of legislation and seeks to regulate transactions (those which are not exempt, such as mortgages of land) including hire purchase agreements, conditional sale transactions, credit sales and personal loans.

The Consumer Credit Act 2006 reforms the 1974 Act, in particular by enabling debtors to challenge unfair relationships with creditors, and providing for an Ombudsman scheme to hear complaints about licensed businesses.

Statutory references in this section are to the Consumer Credit Act 1974 unless otherwise noted.

Your objectives

In this chapter you will learn about the following.

- (a) Forms of consumer credit agreement
- (b) Other specific agreements involving credit
- (c) The system of consumer credit licensing

(d)   How a consumer credit agreement may be terminated

(e)   Enforcement of consumer credit agreements and the rights of the creditor in the event of default

(f)   Regulation of unfair relationships

(g)   The role of the Financial Ombudsman service

1   CONSUMER CREDIT AGREEMENTS

Consumer credit takes a variety of forms. The simplest form is a loan to a customer which he may use to purchase whatever goods or services he requires. But the creditor often prefers to supply goods himself to the consumer on hire purchase terms so that the goods remain the creditor's property until the consumer has paid the price including credit charges, and can be recovered if the debtor defaults. It is a common business practice for a trader to sell his goods to a finance company so that the latter, in providing credit to a customer of the trader, can do so under a hire purchase or related transaction. There are also other special forms of credit transaction such as those involving bank credit cards, shop budget accounts, loans by pawnbrokers on the security of chattels deposited with them, and so on.

The Consumer Credit Act 1974 (CCA) as amended regulates the provision of credit. 'Credit' includes a cash loan and any other form of financial benefit including hire purchase, conditional sale and credit sale agreements.

A consumer credit agreement is a regulated agreement within the meaning of the Act if it is not an exempt agreement: s 8(3). A consumer hire agreement is a regulated agreement if it is not an exempt agreement: s 15(2).

Definition

A **consumer credit agreement** is an agreement between an individual ('the debtor') and any other person ('the creditor') by which the creditor provides the debtor with credit of any amount: s 8(1). Note that 'individual' includes sole traders and partnerships of tow or three partners.

A **consumer credit agreement** is a personal credit agreement by which the creditor provides the debtor with credit.

1.1   Restricted use of credit

A distinction is made in s 11 between an agreement whereby the creditor exercises some control over the use of his finance and one where he has no power of restriction.

A **restricted-use credit agreement** is a regulated consumer credit agreement to finance:

(a)   A transaction between the debtor and the creditor (whether forming part of that agreement or not), or

(b)   A transaction between the debtor and a person (the 'supplier') other than the creditor, or

(c)   (To refinance) any existing indebtedness of the debtor's, whether to the creditor or another person

1.2 Unrestricted use of credit

The residual category is unrestricted use credit. The debtor can use the funds as he sees fit. An **unrestricted-use credit agreement** is a regulated consumer credit agreement which is not a restricted-use credit agreement.

In addition to its classification as restricted or unrestricted use, a credit agreement can be described as running account or fixed sum.

Running-account credit is a facility under a personal credit agreement whereby the debtor is enabled to receive from time to time from the creditor or a third party cash, goods and services to an amount of value such that, taking into account payments made by or to the credit of the debtor, the credit limit (if any) is not at any time exceeded, for example, a personal account with a mail-order company or a credit card. At least every twelve months the creditor must send the debtor statements about their account, which must include specified information about the consequences of failing to make repayments, or of only making the minimum repayment.

Fixed-sum credit is any other facility under a personal credit agreement whereby the debtor is enabled to receive credit, for example, a cash loan. Creditors must provide such debtors with an annual statement of their indebtedness.

1.3 Debtor-creditor-supplier agreements

A **debtor-creditor supplier agreement** is a regulated consumer credit agreement being a restricted-use credit agreement under (a) and (b) (under pre-existing arrangements, or in contemplation of future arrangements, made between creditor and supplier) above, or an unrestricted-use credit agreement (made under pre-existing arrangements between creditor and supplier in the knowledge that the credit is to be used to finance a transaction between the debtor and the supplier). In other words, there are arrangements so that the creditor and supplier of goods are linked, through a linked finance house.

1.4 A debtor-creditor agreement

A **debtor-creditor agreement** is a regulated consumer credit agreement being a restricted-use credit agreement under (b) (not made by the creditor under pre-existing arrangements with the supplier) and (c) above, or an unrestricted-use credit agreements (similarly not made under pre-existing arrangements with the supplier). In other words, there is no connection between the finance and the supplier, such as, taking out a bank loan to buy a car.

1.5 Protection of the debtor

Before the agreement is signed

It often happens that a 'negotiator' is involved in the 'antecedent negotiations' of a consumer credit agreement. This can happen in two ways.

  (a)   A person buying, say, a motor car and wishing to finance it by a hire purchase agreement will obtain the car from a dealer. The dealer will arrange the finance on behalf of the purchaser through a credit institution. In effect, the car dealer, acting as negotiator, is a credit broker.

  (b)   A person buys goods from a shop and pays by credit card.

In these cases s 56 provides of the Act that the 'negotiator' (the car dealer or the shop) is the agent of the creditor. This has two effects. The creditor is liable for any misrepresentations made by the negotiator as though he had made them himself, and any money paid by the debtor to the negotiator will be regarded as having been received by the creditor.

Two further rules protect the debtor who has not yet entered into a binding regulated agreement.

(a) A debtor is not bound by any prior agreement to enter into a regulated agreement, such as an option (s 59). Without this protection, the detailed rules covering regulated agreements could be circumvented by a prior promise to enter into obligations.

(b) The debtor may withdraw from the agreement at any time before all the formalities are completed by giving notice to the creditor, the negotiator or the creditor's agent (s 57). Thus he may withdraw up to the time when the agreement is fully executed.

At the time the agreement is made

To protect the debtor at the time the agreement is being made the Act lays down detailed requirements as to the formalities of execution and the provision of copies.

Formalities of execution

The agreement must be in writing and its form (printed) and content are prescribed by regulations to ensure that the debtor is made aware of his rights and obligations, particularly his rights of cancellation and termination. The terms of the agreement must be complete and legible and all necessary insertion of particulars in blank spaces must be made before the debtor signs the agreement. Signature must be made in the 'signature box'.

The debtor must be supplied with all 'relevant information' relating to the agreement, including the cash price, the deposit paid, the timing and number of instalments, the total charge for credit (TCC) and the annual percentage rate (APR).

Failure to comply with the required formalities in making a consumer credit agreement makes it an improperly executed agreement. It can still be enforced by the debtor but the creditor may find it difficult to enforce. The court has a discretion to refuse enforcement having regard to the prejudice caused by the contravention in question and the degree of culpability for it. It may also allow enforcement but reduce the debtor's liability as a result of the contravention.

The provision of copies

When the agreement is sent or presented to the debtor for his signature, he must be provided with a copy (which he may keep) of the agreement and of any document (such as conditions of sale of goods) referred to in the agreement. If, unusually, the creditor signs at the same time, this will be the only copy the debtor receives. If, as is common practice, the agreement has to be signed by the creditor or some other person, such as a guarantor, after the debtor has signed, the debtor is entitled within seven days of the agreement becoming completely executed (being signed by all parties) to receive a **second copy** of the executed agreement and all documents referred to in it.

> **Activity 1** **(10 minutes)**
>
> What types of insertions in blank spaces might an unscrupulous creditor try to make after a debtor has signed an agreement, were it not for the law against doing so?

Provision of information after the agreement is made

The 2006 Act concentrates on the creditor providing information to the debtor after the agreement has been made. Where the credit agreement is a fixed sum one, creditors must provide debtors with annual statements while there are still amounts to be paid, starting no later than one year after the agreement is made. If the creditor fails to do so then the agreement is unenforceable by him until he complies, and the debtor need not pay any interest during this period. There is a similar requirement to set out the consequences of failing to make repayments, or of only making minimum repayments.

Creditors and owners of hired items must give debtors/hirers notice of any sums that are in arrears in respect of fixed sum, running credit or hire agreements not less than 14 days after the debtor/hirer has fallen into arrears. They must also give notice of any default sums, which are sums payable by the debtor/hirer in connection with his breach of a regulated agreement, such as a late payment penalty on a credit card. Along with this notice the debtor/hirer is also entitled to receive information sheets prepared by the OFT about arrears and default under a consumer credit agreement. Again, if the creditor fails to provide this information then the agreement is unenforceable by him until he complies, and the debtor need not pay any interest during this period.

Interest may only be charged on any default sum after 28 days from the time that notice was given of it.

2 OTHER AGREEMENTS

In section 1 we looked at the main classifications that are used to describe consumer credit agreements. In this section we introduce a number of additional types of agreement.

2.1 Exempt agreements

Typically, an **exempt agreement** is a consumer credit agreement made with an individual by a local authority or either a specified body (for example, a building society), in relation to land or dwellings on land and mortgages.

Other types of agreement may be exempted by order of the Secretary of State. For example, under an order that came into force in April 2008, an agreement may be exempt if it contains a qualifying statement as to the debtor's high net worth.

In addition, an agreement is exempt where the debtor or hirer enters into the agreement for business purposes and the credit provided or payment to be made exceeds £25,000 (s 16B).

2.2 Small agreements

A **small agreement** is a regulated consumer credit agreement for credit not exceeding £50 and is exempt from some, but not all, of the CCA 1974. The rules on formation of credit agreements do not apply, for example.

2.3 Multiple agreements

The Consumer Credit Act includes provisions which prevent lenders exploiting a loophole to bundle together different loan agreements in order to exceed the financial limit for loans to be covered by the Act. These are referred to as multiple agreements.

Legitimate multiple agreements can be found in credit card agreements. Credit card companies may, for example, quote different APRs for purchases, balance transfers and cash advances, but these remain part of a single agreement.

2.4 Linked transactions

A 'linked transaction' is one which is subsidiary to but in some way connected with the main credit transaction: s 19. It is thus automatically terminated if the main transaction is cancelled etc. The following are examples of linked transactions.

(a) An agreement to sell an item which is financed by a (main) D-C-S credit agreement.

(b) An agreement entered into in order to comply with a term in the main credit agreement (such as the term often seen in hire-purchase of a car that the purchaser will insure it for the creditor's benefit).

(c) A preliminary agreement entered into by the debtor so that the creditor will then enter into the main agreement.

2.5 Cancellable agreements

Even after the agreement has been made and the provisions as to formalities and copies have been met the debtor is protected to a limited extent by virtue of the fact that certain agreements are cancellable.

A cancellable agreement is one (other than most agreements for loans made in land transactions to which alternative safeguards apply) made in the following circumstances.

(a) There have been **oral representations**, for example statements concerning the terms of the loan or the quality of the goods, made in the presence of the debtor by or on behalf of the person with whom the debtor negotiates before the agreement is made.

(b) The agreement is signed by the debtor **elsewhere than at the place of business** of the creditor, supplier of the goods or other negotiator: s 67.

This rather involved definition is designed to protect the debtor who may have been persuaded to enter into the agreement by a sales representative or other agent, usually in the course of a visit to the debtor's house. In such cases the debtor has a limited opportunity to cancel the agreement even after he has signed it. But if the debtor goes to the creditor's office to sign the agreement that is treated as a deliberate act, no longer influenced by salesmanship, and the debtor has no right of cancellation.

Notice and cooling off

The debtor must be given written notice of his right to cancel a cancellable agreement. If he is entitled, as he usually is, to receive a second copy of the agreement when executed, it suffices to send him by post that copy which must include a statement of his rights. If, however, he is not entitled to a second copy of the agreement (because debtor and creditor sign together), he must be sent by post a separate notice of his right of cancellation within the same period of seven days after the agreement is made.

On receiving notice of his right of cancellation the debtor has a five-day 'cooling off' period in which he may exercise it. If he decides to cancel he must give notice in writing to the appropriate person (designated in the notice of his cancellation rights). It takes effect as soon as it is posted.

If the procedures for notification of rights of cancellation are not observed, the creditor may not enforce the agreement against the debtor without obtaining the leave of the court.

The effect of cancellation

The effect of cancelling an agreement depends in part on the particular circumstances. In a debtor-creditor-supplier agreement for restricted use credit (such as a hire purchase agreement):

(a)   The debtor is no longer bound to make payments under the agreement and may recover any payments made (or goods which he has supplied in part exchange: in some circumstances he may have their value instead)

(b)   Any goods supplied to the debtor may be collected from him at his address by the creditor; while waiting for recovery the debtor must for 21 days take reasonable care of the goods and he has a lien on them for any money or goods (see (a) above) to be returned to him.

Where there is simply a debtor-creditor agreement for unrestricted use credit (such as a cash loan), cancellation means that the debtor must repay that amount of the loan already received with interest. The agreement continues in force in relation to repayment of the debt and interest (including terms relating to timing and method), although if he repays the loan either within one month of cancellation or before the date of the first instalment due the debtor will not have to repay interest.

Activity 2   **(10 minutes)**

S signs a credit agreement on 4 May. The notice of her right of cancellation is posted to her on 7 May and she receives it on 9 May. She posts a notice of cancellation on 13 May and it is received on 16 May. Is her notice of cancellation effective?

---

3   CONSUMER CREDIT LICENSING

3.1   Licensing consumer credit

Part III of the CCA relates to persons conducting a business dealing with regulated agreements. The aim of these provisions is to establish a system of licensing for:

(a)   consumer credit businesses and consumer hire businesses; and
(b)   ancillary businesses.

The first category above includes not only finance companies, but also any retailer who sells his goods on credit sale, conditional sale or hire purchase. The second category includes such businesses as credit-brokerage, debt-collecting, debt administration, credit information services and operating a credit reference agency. It follows that the retailer who arranges finance for his customer through a finance house is included, because he is in effect acting as a credit broker. All these businesses are required to be licensed under a system operated by the Office of Fair Trading (OFT). Anyone carrying on such a business without a licence commits an offence.

When applying to the OFT for a standard licence the applicant must specify what businesses they want the licence to cover, and must satisfy the OFT that they are 'fit' to do everything they have applied for. In determining whether or not they are fit, the OFT has regard to the skills, knowledge and experience of the applicant and of anyone who will work with them under the licence, and the practices and procedures they will follow. The OFT will also consider whether the applicant or an associate:

- has committed an offence involving fraud, other dishonesty or violence

- has previously contravened the 1974 Act, the Financial Services and Markets Act 2000 or any other laws relating to consumer credit

- has practised discrimination

- has engaged in deceitful, oppressive, unfair or improper business practices, including irresponsible lending

The OFT has powers to vary, suspend, renew and withdraw licences, and to require access to premises so as to observe the licensee's conduct of business. A regulated agreement made by an unlicensed business or through the agency of an unlicensed credit broker will generally be unenforceable against the customer. Similarly, any agreement for the services of an unlicensed ancillary business will be unenforceable against the client.

Standard licences are generally issued for indefinite periods that do not exceed five years.

3.2 Advertising consumer credit

The Consumer Credit (Advertisements) Regulations 2004 control advertisements aimed at providing credit to non-business customers. The objective of these regulations is to ensure that consumers have a fair impression of the product offered and a means of comparison between different products. He or she must therefore have adequate and sufficient information.

The advertisement must be phrased so as to fall into one of the following three categories – simple, intermediate or full.

(a) A *simple* advertisement neither specifies a price nor contains an indication that credit or hire products are available.

(b) An *intermediate* advertisement must, at the very least, contain an indication as to where full written credit details can be obtained.

(c) A *full* advertisement must contain a great deal of information, the most important of which is the APR.

Warnings as to the consequences of giving security for regulated agreements are also required. For example, it is compulsory when advertising home mortgages to include the warning 'Your home may be at risk if you do not keep up repayments on a mortgage or other loan secured on it.' Although such warnings are aimed at unscrupulous lenders, the government is keen to be seen to encourage careful borrowing.

Regard should also be had to the Consumer Protection from Unfair Trading Regulations 2008 (described in the previous chapter) which also apply to credit advertisements.

3.3   Canvassing consumer credit

'Canvassing' can be defined as 'orally soliciting an individual to enter into a credit agreement'. This is permitted if it occurs on the trade premises of either the debtor or the creditor (s 48) but it is greatly restricted '*off trade premises*'.

Canvassing off trade premises by making representations to induce a customer to make a regulated agreement involves:

(a)   making oral representations during a visit by the canvasser for that purpose; *and*

(b)   making that visit to somewhere other than the business premises of the canvasser, creditor, supplier or consumer; *and*

(c)   *not* making that visit in response to a request made on a previous occasion.

The fact that the visit was made *for the purposes* of canvassing exempts a casual conversation at, say, a squash game which leads to a loan being recommended.

The controls on canvassing off trade premises, as defined above, are as follows:

(a)   canvassing D-C agreements off trade premises – such as cash loans – is a criminal offence: s 49. It will still be an offence even if made in response to a request unless that request is in writing and signed;

(b)   canvassing other regulated agreements off trade premises can only be done under a licence expressly authorising such activity: s 23.

One important exception relates to overdrafts on current accounts where the canvasser is the creditor or an employee of the creditor (eg of a bank). Such an activity is not banned nor does it require a special licence.

4   TERMINATION

Once it has come into operation, a consumer credit agreement may be terminated before it is fully performed because:

(a)   the debtor elects to pay off the credit early;

(b)   the debtor elects to terminate it; or

(c)   the creditor terminates it for breach of its terms and/or default by the debtor.

4.1   Debtor's election to pay off credit

No provision in a consumer credit agreement may prevent the debtor from paying off the entire amount of credit early. He will obtain a rebate of the interest which he is required to pay under the agreement but which is not yet due. He may either give notice of his intention to repay or merely pay the balance less the rebate. In the latter case the notice immediately takes effect (although some future date may be specified on which it is to take effect).

4.2   Debtor's election to terminate

The debtor has a statutory right (which cannot be excluded by the agreement) to terminate a hire purchase or conditional sale agreement at any time, if he pays an amount which raises his aggregate payments to one half of the total price plus the whole of any installation charge: s 100.

Suppose, for example, that the total price is £100 and the installation charge £10. The debtor has paid instalments of £30 in all, plus the installation charge and owes an instalment of £10. The debtor may terminate the agreement and must raise the aggregate of his payment to £60 (half £100 plus £10). As he has paid £40 already his liability on giving notice of termination is to pay a further £20. If he had paid instalments of £50 in aggregate plus the installation charge and owed £10 as an overdue instalment he would be liable to pay that £10 since (although he has already paid half the total price) it is a payment due at the time of termination.

If the debtor considers that the above formula produces an excessive amount, he may apply to the court to order a reduction.

The debtor must of course permit the creditor to retake possession of the goods. If the debtor has not taken reasonable care of the goods while in his possession, the creditor is entitled (in addition to the sums payable as described above) to recover compensation for the damage to his goods caused by the debtor's failure to take care of them.

Note that following the 2006 Act the OFT may exempt certain agreement from this provision if it appears to be in the hirer's interests to do so.

A debtor or hirer may apply to a court for a time order by which the court may reschedule any payments due under a regulated agreement: s 129. He may do this after having received notice of sums in arrears (see above) or after having received a default notice (see below). A debtor who has received a notice of sums in arrears may only apply to the court for a time order fourteen days after he has responded to the notice by providing certain required information to the creditor/owner, setting out a proposal for how he will make payments under the agreement and specifying that he will apply for a time order.

4.3 Creditor's right to terminate

By s 98 the creditor is allowed to terminate the agreement if the debtor is in breach of one of the contract's terms other than that relating to repayment. For example, he may terminate where the debtor made misrepresentations, where the debtor has become insolvent or where the goods are destroyed. The creditor usually then has the right to repossess the goods and the debtor must pay up to one-half of the price. Seven days notice must be given.

Default notices

If the creditor is entitled to terminate the agreement by reason of the debtor's failure to maintain the agreed payments, the creditor must first serve on the debtor a 'default notice' which:

(a) specifies the default alleged;

(b) requires it to be remedied if remediable or demands compensation (if any is required) if irremediable; and

(c) specifies a period of not less than fourteen days in which action is to be taken as required under (b). This gives the debtor time to apply to the court if he decides to do so: s 87.

Repossession of goods

If the debtor is in breach of a hire purchase or conditional sale agreement and he has paid at least one third of the total price for the goods (plus the whole of any installation charges) the goods are then *'protected goods'* which the creditor may only re-possess from the debtor after obtaining an order of the court: s 90.

If the creditor recovers possession of protected goods without a court order, the regulated agreement is terminated and *the debtor is released from all liability under the agreement - he may even recover all sums he has paid under it: s 91.*

Whether or not the goods are protected the creditor may not enter premises to take possession of them except under an order of the court: s 92.

5 UNFAIR RELATIONSHIPS

The 1974 Act allowed the court to reopen what it called 'extortionate credit bargains', which were agreements that required the debtor to make payments that were grossly exorbitant or that otherwise grossly contravened ordinarily principles of fair dealing. When looking at these agreements, typically between 'loan sharks' and people who were least able to pay the charges, the court considered prevailing interest rates, the debtor's age, experience and degree of financial pressure, and the creditor's risk and reward under the agreement.

The 2006 Act repeals the sections of the 1974 Act on extortionate credit bargains, and talks instead about 'unfair relationships' between debtors and creditors. Except in relation to agreements secured on land, the court can consider whether the relationship between the parties arising out a specific agreement is unfair to the debtor because of the agreement's terms, or the way in which it is operated in every respect by the creditor. If the court finds the relationship to be unfair it can make a wide range of orders, including the creditor repaying the debtor some of what has been paid over, and the debtor being discharged form any further duty to make payments.

A creditor who has fallen foul of the provisions relating to unfair relationships may also have proceedings brought against it by the OFT under competition law, which we will see in Chapter 9 of this course book.

The protection to consumers afforded by these unfair relationship provisions is supplemented by the Consumer Protection from Unfair Trading Regulations 2008 which were described in the previous chapter. These regulations apply to the provision of consumer credit services as they do to the supply of goods and other services. A breach of these regulations may create an unfair relationship which entitles the consumer to bring a court action. The breach may also be actionable under Part 8 of the Enterprise Act 2002 if the business practice can be said to harm the collective interests of consumers. (Note, however, that the Doorstep Selling Regulations, also mentioned in the previous chapter, do not apply to cancellable agreements under CCA 1974 nor to solicited contracts for regulated consumer credit agreements under that Act).

6 FINANCIAL OMBUDSMAN SERVICE

The Financial Ombudsman Service (FOS) is an independent organisation set up in 2001 following the Financial Services and Markets Act 2000 to resolve disputes between consumers and businesses providing financial services. It tries to operate using less formal procedures such as mediation and conciliation, although in complex cases it may produce a formal report. The Consumer Credit Act 2006 extends FOS's jurisdiction to consumer credit licensees. From April 2007 licensed consumer credit businesses must comply with complaints handling requirements in the *Handbook* published by the

NOTES

Financial Services Authority (FSA). They set out the procedures and requirements that businesses must follow when handling complaints from customers, including requirements on:

- acknowledging and responding to complaints
- the time limits for dealing with complaints
- record-keeping and reporting; and
- the right of customers to refer unresolved disputes to the FOS.

Chapter roundup

- The Consumer Credit Act 1974 regulates the provision of credit. Credit includes a cash loan and any other form of financial benefit including hire purchase, conditional sale and credit sale agreements.

- There are two types of credit. Running account credit is also referred to as revolving credit. Fixed-sum credit is a once-only credit such as a single loan. The nature of credit may be restricted use or unrestricted use. Agreements may be debtor-creditor or debtor-creditor-supplier.

- Part III of the Act relates to persons conducting a business dealing with regulated agreements. The aim of these provisions is to establish a system of licensing for consumer credit businesses and consumer hire businesses and ancillary businesses.

- The main object of the Act is the protection of individual debtors. This can be analysed into protection before the agreement is made, at the time the agreement is made and after the agreement has been made.

- Most consumer credit agreements are terminated by performance. They may also be terminated early, in specific circumstances, by debtor or creditor.

- The court has wide powers to intervene in relationships between debtors and creditors that are unfair on debtors.

- Since April 2007 consumer credit licensees have been included in the Financial Ombudsman Scheme.

Quick quiz

1 What are the features of restricted use credit?

2 What is a debtor-credit-supplier agreement?

3 What are the formalities of execution of a consumer credit agreement?

4 What is a cancellable agreement?

5 What is canvassing?

Answers to quick quiz

1   Restricted use credit is used to finance a transaction between a debtor and creditor, or between a debtor and supplier or to enable a debtor to refinance existing indebtedness.

2   A debtor-creditor-supplier agreement is one in which there are three parties and where there is an agreement between the creditor and the supplier of goods or services.

3   The agreement must be in writing and in a prescribed form. Terms must be complete and legible. Signatures must be made in a 'signature box'. The debtor must be supplied with all 'relevant information'.

4   One in which there have been oral representations and in which the agreement is signed elsewhere than at the creditor's place of business.

5   Canvassing is orally soliciting an individual to enter into a credit agreement.

Answers to activities

1   The rate of interest and the levels of penalties for defaults are two obvious examples.

2   Yes: 13 May is within five days of 9 May.

Chapter 9:
MONOPOLIES, MERGERS AND COMPETITION

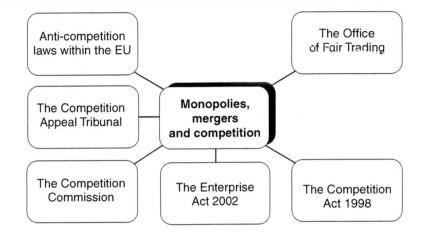

Introduction

In this chapter we examine various aspects of consumer protection law related to ensuring fair competition. The Competition Act 1998 and the Enterprise Act 2002 brought significant changes to this area of the law. There are two broad themes, firstly the control of deceptive or unfair practices, thereby giving the consumer a genuine power of choice, and secondly the promotion of open and fair competition.

Your objectives

In this chapter you will learn about the following.

(a) The role and powers of the Office of Fair Trading

(b) The key provisions of the Competition Act 1998 and Enterprise Act 2002

(c) The law on mergers and market investigations in the UK and the role of the Competition Commission

(d) The impact of EU competition law

1 THE OFFICE OF FAIR TRADING

The Office of Fair Trading (OFT) plays an important role in helping consumers understand their rights and protecting consumer interests in the UK. It also seeks to ensure that business practices are fair and competitive. The powers of the OFT are set out in legislation, principally relating to competition and consumer protection. Its main functions are as follows:

(a) In conjunction with local trading standards offices, identifying and taken action in relation to specific consumer markets for

- Goods, including essential, recreational, industrial and pharmaceutical goods

- Infrastructure and the knowledge economy, including transport, utilities, energy, construction and the creative industries

- Services, including financial, medical and professional services, and estate agencies

(b) Enforcing and supporting regulations, including those on:

- Cartels and the abuse of market power
- Mergers
- credit licensing (see Chapter 8)

(c) Developing consumer skills and raising awareness on issues such as:

- Effective Codes of Practice
- Local authority assured trader schemes
- Con artists and scammers

1.1 Competition enforcement

The OFT plays an important role in enforcing competition law, principally the Competition Act 1998, the EC Treaty (Articles 81 and 82) and the Enterprise Act 2002.

Definition

> A **cartel** is a group of firms or businesses that agree among themselves to 'rig' a market by setting prices at a particular level.

The OFT's role includes the following:

(a) Stopping and deterring cartels and other damaging anti-competitive agreements

(b) Stopping and deterring abuse of dominant market positions

(c) Promoting a strong competitive culture across the economy

(d) Informing business, through a widespread education programme, about new legislation and how to comply with it

The Competition Act 1998 provides for any business involved in a cartel to be fined up to 10% of its UK turnover. Under OFT guidance, the turnover is usually taken to be a company's UK group turnover for each year of the infringement up to a maximum of three years. The Enterprise Act 2002 also provides for criminal prosecution of individuals who dishonestly engage in cartel agreements.

The OFT operates a leniency programme which enables an organisation involved in such agreements to come forward and corporate with the OFT, in return for immunity from, or a reduction in, any financial penalty.

1.2 Consumer protection

In terms of consumer protection, the OFT has a wide jurisdiction. Its role includes the following:

(a) Taking action against rogue traders who trade unfairly

(b) Approving and promoting codes of practice

(c) Warning about and banning estate agents

(d) Applying for enforcement orders against persons who breach consumer protection legislation

Activity 1 **(5 minutes)**

The Enterprise Act 2002 introduces a criminal offence for individuals who dishonestly engage in cartel agreements. In the event of a prosecution, where would a case be heard?

2 THE COMPETITION ACT 1998

The Competition Act 1998 incorporates provisions similar to Articles 81 (on anti-competitive agreements) and 82 (abuse of dominant position) of the Treaty of Amsterdam (covered later in this chapter) and replaced most of existing UK competition law such as the Restrictive Trade Practices Acts 1976 and 1977, the Resale Prices Act 1976 and sections 2 – 10 of the Competition Act 1980. EC and UK competition law are now based upon the same model.

The Act contains two principal provisions:

(a) The *Chapter I prohibition* prohibits anti-competitive agreements which distort competition. Such practices include price restrictions, market sharing agreements, restrictions on customers, information exchange agreements and cartels.

(b) The *Chapter II prohibition* prohibits abuses of market power by dominant companies. A dominant company normally means one having at least 40% of the market by value or volume. It ensures that all customers are treated fairly and, for example, that they are not forced to buy products they did not want in exchange for supplies of the product they need.

2.1 Anti-competitive agreements

The Chapter I prohibition (s 2) prohibits agreements between undertakings, decisions by associations of undertakings or concerted practices which may affect trade within the UK and have as their object or effect the prevention, restriction or distortion of competition within the UK. It applies to agreements, decisions or practices which:

(a) directly or indirectly fix purchase or selling prices or any other trading conditions

(b) limit or control production, markets, technical development or investment

(c) share market or sources of supply

(d) apply dissimilar conditions to equivalent transactions with other trading parties, thereby placing them at a competitive disadvantage

(e) make the conclusion of contracts subject to acceptance of supplementary obligations which have no connection with the main contract.

Scope

Agreements are only caught by the Act if they have an **appreciable effect** on competition. An agreement is unlikely to be considered as having an appreciable effect where the aggregate market share of the parties involved does not exceed 25%. However, agreements to fix prices, impose minimum resale prices or share markets are generally seen as capable of having an appreciable effect even where the parties' combined market share falls below 25%.

Exemptions

Some sectors (such as financial services, public policy, coal and steel) have their own competition regulation and are therefore excluded. Other agreements may be exempted under block exemption provisions or applications for individual exemption.

Breach of the rules renders agreements void. Third parties such as customers or competitors are able to sue for damages, and the competition authorities are able to levy stringent fines of up to 10% of the UK turnover of the business involved. This is the most powerful incentive for compliance under the Act. Smaller businesses, with a combined turnover of up to £20 million, may be relieved from fines under the legislation provided the 'small agreement' is not a price-fixing agreement.

The OFT is the main enforcement body though similar powers are exercisable by regulators in the telecommunications, utilities, rail and air traffic industries. Appeals are held before the Competition Appeals Tribunal.

The OFT and the sector regulators have the following powers:

(a) To enter premises to inspect and copy documents
(b) To use force to enter premises if necessary with a magistrate's warrant

2.2 Abuse of a dominant position

The Chapter II prohibition covers the **abuse of a dominant position** in a market. It stipulates that any conduct which amounts to the abuse of a dominant position in a market is prohibited if it may affect trade within the UK.

A **dominant position** essentially means that the business is able to behave independently of competitive pressures, such as other competitors, in that market. A large market share is the primary indicator of a dominant position but other relevant factors include the economic weakness of competitors, the control of technology and resources and the absence of latent competition.

Note that it is the **abuse** of the dominant position that constitutes an offence, not the **holding** of that position.

The Act gives examples of specific types of conduct that may constitute abuse of a dominant position:

(a)   To impose unfair purchase or selling prices

(b)   To limit production, markets or technical development to the prejudice of consumers

(c)   To apply different trading conditions to equivalent transactions, thereby placing certain parties at a competitive advantage

(d)   To attach unrelated supplementary conditions to contracts

In determining whether or not an undertaking is in a dominant position, the OFT and sector regulators looks first at its market share. Generally, an undertaking is unlikely to be considered dominant if it has a market share of less than 40%. But this does not exclude the possibility that an undertaking with a lower market share may be considered dominant. In assessing this, the OFT considers the number and size of existing competitors as well as the potential for new competitors to enter the market.

An organisation that abuses a dominant position may be relieved from fines under the legislation (providing there is no price fixing) if its turnover in the applicable market is less than £50 million. Other action may still be taken, however, and other businesses might still be able to claim compensation for any loss suffered as a result of an abuse of a dominant market position.

3   THE ENTERPRISE ACT 2002

The Enterprise Act 2002 covers the position where two or more businesses merge and that merger has the effect of reducing competition, usually because the merger results in a significant market share. The Act also empowers the OFT (and others) to refer markets to the Competition Commission where it considers that competition is being restricted or distorted (under provisions which replace the Fair Trading Act 1973).

3.1   Mergers

Mergers are considered by the competition authorities under the Enterprise Act 2002. They are investigated by the OFT provided certain criteria are satisfied, namely:

- two or more business enterprises cease to be distinct

- the merger is either proposed or took place not more than four months ago (although this four month limit may be extended in certain cases) and

- *either* the business being taken over has a turnover in the UK of £70 million or more, *or* the merged businesses together supply or acquire at least 25% of a particular product or service in the UK (or in a substantial part of the UK) and the merger results in the share of supply or consumption being increased.

The OFT must consider whether there is a significant prospect that the merger may be expected to result in a **substantial lessening of the competition**. If the OFT believes that this test is or may be met, then it must (as a general rule) either refer the merger to the Competition Commission or, if appropriate, seek undertakings from the merging parties to remedy the expected adverse effects of the merger. (Undertakings are given voluntarily but, once accepted by the relevant authority, become legally binding and enforceable in the courts). The OFT is not required to refer a merger if it considers either that the market involved is not of sufficient importance to warrant an investigation (for example, where the costs involved would be disproportionally high) or that any lessening of competition would be outweighed by benefits to consumers.

If the merger is referred to the Competition Commission, it will conduct a full investigation to determine whether the merger has caused, or may be expected to cause, a substantial lessening of competition. If so, the Competition Commission will either prohibit the merger or impose remedies, in the form of undertakings from the parties or orders. The Commission should publish a report within 24 weeks from the date of reference, setting out its conclusions on whether a substantial lessening of competition is to be expected and also the remedies which if concludes must be put into effect.

The 2002 Act also provides for mergers to be investigated on grounds of public interest, such as national security, in cases where the Secretary of State serves an intervention notice (provided a reference decision has not already been taken by the OFT). Special public interest cases of merger may be referred even though neither the normal turnover test nor the share of supply test is satisfied.

The OFT will also have a role in monitoring whether parties comply with undertakings and orders following a merger. It will be responsible for maintaining a public register of all undertakings given and orders made.

Certain instances of merger are subject to special rules on the grounds of public interest, for example mergers between newspapers (although the government is under increasing pressure to relax those rules in order to safeguard local media businesses against falling advertising revenues).

3.2 Market investigation references

The prohibition of abuse of a dominant market position in the Competition Act 1998 is the principal weapon against anti-competitive behaviour by monopolies. However, even where there has been no obvious breach of the prohibitions contained in the Competition Act 1998, the OFT (or certain sectoral regulators or, in limited cases, the Secretary of State) may refer to the Competition Commission any circumstances where competition appears to have been prevented, reduced or distorted by either the structure of a particular market or the conduct of any of the persons operating within that market.

Except where the Secretary of State issues a public interest intervention notice, the Competition Commission then has a duty to take such steps as it considers reasonable and practicable to remedy the competition problems that has identified in its investigation, including any detrimental effect on customers. (There are special provisions which apply in certain regulated sectors, such as water, gas and electricity.)

The OFT has issued guidance which explains that it will not make a reference where it considers that other action (for example under the Competition Act 1998) would be more appropriate or that a reference would be inappropriate in view of the potential adverse effects of the perceived problem or the remedies available. A reference may be made, therefore, were there appears to be no actual breach of the 1998 Act (for example, in cases of uncoordinated parallel conduct by several firms) or where taking action under the Act may be inadequate to deal with the adverse effect of the competition identified.

Generally speaking, conduct of a single firm is unlikely to be the subject of a market investigation reference, whether it is dominant or not, unless there are other features of the relevant market that adversely affect competition.

The Competition Commission should carry out its market investigation and publish a report within not more than two years after the reference is made.

4 THE COMPETITION COMMISSION

The Competition Commission is an independent public body established by the Competition Act 1998. It replaced the Monopolies and Mergers Commission.

The Commission conducts in-depth inquiries into mergers, markets and regulation of the major regulated industries. Every inquiry is undertaken in response to a reference made to it by another authority: usually by the OFT. The Commission has no power to conduct inquiries on its own initiative.

As described above, the Enterprise Act 2002 introduced a new regime for the investigation of mergers and markets in the UK. The Commission was also given greatly extended powers (including directing companies to take remedial action) by the 2002 Act, in place of the limited advisory role to the government, which it had previously.

Staffing

The Commission is headed by a Chairman, who chairs the Council (the strategic management board). The Council also includes the Deputy Chairmen, the Chief Executive, and two non-executive Commission members.

Members are appointed by the Secretary of State for Business, Innovations and Skills for an eight-year term following an open competition. They are appointed for their individual experience, ability and diversity of background, not as representatives of particular organisations, interests or political parties. There are usually about 50 members.

Specialist panels

There are specialist panels of members for utilities, communications and newspapers. The utilities panel is the specialist panel for water, energy, gas and electricity inquiries. There is also a Remedies Standing Group to oversee implementation of any remedial action required.

Investigations

Each inquiry is heard by at least three members (usually four or five) and is usually led by the Chairman or one of the Deputy Chairmen. Members are assisted by a specialist staff team on each inquiry. Utility, communications and newspaper inquiries must have at least one member from the appropriate specialist panel.

5 THE COMPETITION APPEAL TRIBUNAL

The Competition Appeal Tribunal (CAT) is a specialist judicial body and is independent of the Competition Commission. It was created by the Enterprise Act 2002. The CAT has the function of hearing appeals of certain decisions taken by the Competition Commission or the OFT or sectoral regulators with the power, among other things, to confirm, set aside or vary the decision, or remit the matter to the OFT (or regulator).

Functions of the CAT

The CAT's functions under the Act are as follows:

(a) Hearing claims for damages where an infringement of competition law has been established (under Chapters I or II of CA98 or UK decisions under Articles 81 or 82 of the EC Treaty)

(b)   Hearing appeals on the merits in respect of decisions made under the Competition Act 1998 by the OFT and the sectoral regulators.

(c)   Reviewing decisions made by the Secretary of State, OFT and the Competition Commission in respect of mergers or market investigation references (or potential references).

(d)   Hearing appeals against certain decisions made by OFCOM and/or the Secretary of State under specific legislation.

The CAT has a president (who is appointed by the Lord Chancellor), a panel of chairmen and a panel of ordinary members. The tribunal for each proceeding must consist of a chairman (who may be the president) and two other members.

Activity 2   **(30 minutes)**

The Competition Commission may make enquiries into particular markets where it appears that the structure of the market or the conduct of suppliers or customers is harming competition. The OFT may make market references (suggesting the necessity for an investigation). A number of 'sectoral regulators' may also make references in relation to designated sectors. Find out who these sectoral regulators are.

---

6   ANTI-COMPETITIVE PRACTICES WITHIN THE EU

Anti-competitive practices which affect only the trade within one member state of the EU are subject only to national legislation. However, where such practices may affect trade between member states, the EU rules on competition come into force. These are similar to the prohibitions contained in the Competition Act 1998 (indeed they were the basis for the 1998 provisions) and are found in Article 81 and Article 82 of the EC Treaty. Both articles apply to any body or person engaged in commercial activities.

Under a 'modernisation regulation' which came into effect in May 2004, the competition authorities and courts in the member states are also responsible for the application and enforcement of the Treaty provisions. They are obliged to apply Articles 81 and 82 in cases where they apply national competition law to agreeing or practices, which may affect trade between member states.

Quotas

Member states of the EC are prevented from restricting competition by the fact that any form of quota is strictly controlled. A quota is a restriction which limits the import, export or through-transit of goods.

Specifically included as justifications for quotas are protection of health and life of humans, animals or plants, protection of national treasures and the protection of industrial and commercial property. If the restriction is arbitrary or greater than is necessary the measure cannot be justified.

6.1 Article 81 – restrictive agreements, decisions and concerted practices

This prohibits all *agreements* between businesses, *decisions* of associations of businesses and *concerted practices* which affect trade between members and prevent, restrict or distort competition. *Any such agreement or decision shall be void.* Activities of particular concern include

(a) fixing prices
(b) limiting production
(c) sharing markets
(d) discriminatory conditions of trading.

'*Agreement*' is not limited to legally binding contracts – any arrangement is caught so long as it is between businesses which are *separate economic entities*. Arrangements between a principal and his agent or parent company and subsidiary are outside the Article.

'*Decision*' is not limited to those which are legally binding on the members of the association – any decision, including a decision to recommend a particular practice by its members, is within the article.

'*Concerted practice*' embraces activities involving 'contact' between the parties but the 'contact' may derive from the practice itself, such as where a number of companies in a common trade share price information. Merely adjusting to the practices of competitors will not constitute a concerted practice.

The activities must 'have as their object or effect the prevention, restriction or distortion of competition'. In essence, this requires evidence that the position in a member state, were it not for the agreement, would be one of more open competition. The most obvious example of an agreement in breach of Article 81 is a cartel agreement between competitors. The European Commission has a 'leniency policy' which means that the first company in a cartel to hand over evidence to the Commission will not be required to pay a fine. The Commission also conducts its own investigations into possible cartel arrangements.

Any agreement may, however, be 'justified' and the prohibition declared to be inapplicable if, generally speaking, it contributes to improving production or distribution or promotes technical or economic progress. If it cannot be justified, it is automatically void. The power to make such declarations is vested in the Commission. (The Article does not apply to agricultural transport, coal, steel and nuclear energy and the public sector.)

Individual agreements, which do not pose any serious threat of distorting competition may be exempted on application by the parties to the Commission and national courts may also refer a question of exemption to the Commission. There is block exemption for agreements relating to research and development and motor vehicle distribution for example. Joint activities such as sharing market research reports, sharing financial consultancy and advice, and sharing production facilities and advertising are also not regarded as distorting competition.

Vertical deals (for example between supplier and distributor) involving a supplier's market share of less than 30% market share may be exempted from the restrictive agreement rules, as are horizontal deals (between companies in the same market sector) with less than 5% market share.

6.2 Article 82 – abuse of dominant position

Any abuse by one or more businesses of a dominant position within the common market shall be prohibited so far as it affects trade between member states. The list of particular abuses is similar to that set out in Article 81.

A business will enjoy a *dominant position* where it has power 'which enables it to hinder the maintenance of effective competition by allowing it to behave independently of its competitors and customers'. Whether a dominant position is enjoyed is dependent upon the definition of the market and the business's overall power in respect of that market.

The 'market' is wider than the mere provision of specific goods or services; thus a supplier of bananas may influence the market for fruit, but not enjoy a dominant position in it. If the market is limited to bananas, he may enjoy a dominant position. The market as a territorial entity is not limited to a particular state. The position must, however, be in a *substantial part* of the common market.

If the business enjoys a monopoly or near monopoly it may be presumed to occupy a dominant position. *A dominant position itself is not reprehensible – only an abuse* of it is an infringement.

Chapter roundup

- The Office of Fair Trading plays an important role in helping consumers understand their rights and protecting consumer interests.

- The Competition Act 1998 includes measures to prohibit anti-competitive agreements and abuses of market power.

- The Competition Commission is an independent public body established by the Competition Act 1998. There is also a Competition Appeal Tribunal.

- EU rules on competition include Article 81 on restrictive agreements, decisions and concerted practice and Article 82 on abuse of a dominant position.

Quick quiz

1   What is a cartel?

2   What type of agreements may be caught by the Competition Act's Chapter I prohibition on anti-competitive agreements?

3   What is a dominant position?

4   What is the role of the Competition Commission?

5   When may an EC quota be justified?

Answers to quick quiz

1 A cartel is a group of firms or businesses that agree among themselves to coordinate prices and/or production in order to reduce competition and so increase profits.

2 Agreements which, directly or indirectly, fix prices or trading conditions; control production, markets, technical development or investment; share market or sources of supply; apply dissimilar conditions to equivalent transactions; impose conditional obligations which have no connection with the main contract.

3 A dominant position essentially means that the business is able to behave independently of competitive pressures, such as other competitors, on that market.

4 The Competition Commission conducts in-depth inquiries into mergers, markets and the regulation of the major regulated industries. Every inquiry is undertaken in response to a reference made to it by another authority: usually by the OFT. The Commission has no power to conduct inquiries on its own initiative.

5 Specifically included as justifications for quotas are protection of health and life of humans, animals or plants, protection of national treasures and the protection of industrial and commercial property. If the restriction is arbitrary or greater than is necessary the measure cannot be justified.

Answers to activities

1 The cartel offence is triable either in a magistrates' court (summary trail), or in a crown court before a jury (trial on indictment). A convicted offender on a summary trial may receive up to six months' imprisonment and/or a fine up to the statutory maximum. On conviction on indictment, an offender may receive a maximum of five years' imprisonment and/or an unlimited fine.

2 The following sectoral regulators may make market investigation references:

- OFCOM (communications sector)
- OFGEM (energy markets)
- OFWAT (water industry)
- OFREG (gas and electricity in Northern Ireland)
- ORR (railway services)
- CAA (air traffic services

Intellectual Property Law

Chapter 10 :
INTELLECTUAL PROPERTY: PATENTS AND TRADE MARKS

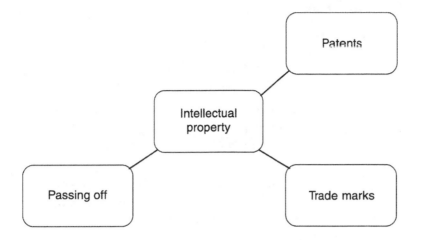

Introduction

Intellectual property is a term covering a number of distinct rights which provide the owner with a form of limited monopoly or degree of exclusivity. Some rights require registration; others are enforceable under common law rules.

In this chapter we examine the law relating to patents and trade marks, and consider actions for passing off.

Your objectives

In this chapter you will learn about the following.

(a)   The protection of inventors by patent legislation

(b)   The rights of patent holders

(c)   The benefits of trade marks and the system of registration

(d)   The rights of trade mark holders

(e)   What is meant by an action in passing off and when it might be resorted to

1 INTELLECTUAL PROPERTY

UK law affords a degree of protection to intellectual property (IP). It is a basic rule of law that *ideas* cannot be protected. It is deemed to be in the public interest that ideas should be allowed to be exploited rather than subjected to monopolistic control.

> *Green v Broadcasting Corporation of New Zealand 1989*
> The claimant had devised a television show and compered it for many years. He wished to prevent the defendants from exploiting his idea without his approval.
>
> *Held:* an idea for the format of a television show could not be the subject of copyright protection.

In spite of this basic position, the law has developed as a combination of statutory principles, common law rules and equitable principles to provide protection to certain specific categories of industrial and intellectual property. Three main categories can be distinguished.

(a) *A patent* is a monopoly right to exploit an invention for a stated period of time. By registering a patent an inventor makes it an offence for other people, without his consent, to cash in on the fruits of his intellectual efforts.

(b) *A trade mark* is a distinctive word, name or other sign which is used to indicate a connection in the course of trade between goods or services and of one undertaking from those of other undertakings. By registering a trade mark, the owner of the mark makes it an offence for other people to use it without consent.

(c) *Copyright* protects authors, artists, composers etc from being deprived of their rewards by unauthorised copying of their works. Unlike patents and trade marks, copyright is not subject to any system of registration: it comes into effect automatically when a work is created.

The official government body responsible for granting IP rights is the UK Intellectual Property Office (known as the Patent Office before April 2007).

2 PATENTS

The law relating to patents is contained in the Patents Act 1977, as amended. The Act sets out a system by which inventors may register their discoveries and in return are granted a period in which they have a monopoly right to exploit them and may prevent all others from making use of them in the country in which the patent is granted. There is of course no obligation on an inventor to register his idea; he may prefer not to publish it and to rely on secrecy as his safeguard against competitors.

There were substantial changes made to the law by the Copyright, Designs and Patents Act 1988 and the Patents Act 2004, but they amended the 1977 Act and did not repeal it. Statutory references in this section, therefore, are to the 1977 Act unless otherwise stated.

2.1 Criteria for patentability

To obtain the grant of a patent, and then to renew it, involves identifying an invention (as below) and then filing an application. Application for registration of a patent is made to the UK Intellectual Property Office in Newport, following the procedure laid down by the Patents Act 1977. The criteria set out in s 1 PA (see below) must be satisfied if the application is to be successful.

There is a fee of £30 for a preliminary examination of the application and there will be a search fee of £100. Searches can take several months and may involve filing foreign applications. A substantive examination (fee £70) will be conducted by the Office after which it will reject or grant the patent. The patent must be renewed annually every five years for the maximum twenty years life of the patent. Failure to renew the patent will mean that the rights of the patent owner lapse.

Section 1 sets out the criteria which an invention must satisfy before the issue of a patent can be considered.

The invention must:

- be functional or technical, relating to how something works, what it does, what it is made of, or how it is made

- be new, and not have been made public in any way, anywhere in the world. Conversations with patent agents, solicitors of UK Intellectual Property Office staff are confidential, so will not make an invention public

- involve an inventive step, and not be obvious to someone with a good knowledge of the subject

- have an industrial use, that is it must be capable of being made or used in an industry, and must work in a way which meets established physical laws

Patents cannot be granted by the UK Intellectual Property Office for:

- a scientific or mathematical discovery, theory or method
- a literary, dramatic, musical or artistic work
- a way of performing a mental act, playing a game or doing business
- the presentation of information, or some computer programs
- an animal or plant variety
- a method of medical treatment, surgery or diagnosis
- anything immoral or contrary to public policy

The criteria above are investigated by the UK Intellectual Property Office when an application is made for registration. It is a complex process to decide whether an invention meets the criteria, and in practice the examination is mainly restricted to prior UK patent specifications. The result of this is that patents may often be granted where the criteria are not satisfied. The validity of such patents may be challenged (see later).

Novelty

'An invention shall be taken to be new if it does not form part of the state of the art' (s 2(1). This means that an invention is not new if, before the date of filing the patent application, any processes, products or information relating to it had been made available to the public. This can lead to problems in fields where many inventors are at work simultaneously. The rule is that if two or more inventors file similar applications, the earlier application is deemed to be included in the state of the art when the later application is being considered.

In some cases, a patent is not invalidated even though information about it had previously been made public. For example, if the prior disclosure was made in breach of confidence it is ignored in assessing the invention's novelty (s 2(4)). But where a clear *anticipation* of the invention has occurred, no patent will be awarded. Guidance on what constitutes anticipation is given in the case of *General Tire and Rubber Co v Firestone Tyre and Rubber Co 1972*: 'a signpost, however clear, upon the road to the patentee's invention will not suffice. The prior inventor must be clearly shown to have planted his flag at the precise destination before the patentee.'

Inventive step

'An invention shall be taken to involve an inventive step if it is not obvious to a person skilled in the art, having regard to any matter which forms part of the state of the art' (s 3). This is an area where there is a great deal of case law. When a patent is challenged many years after it was granted, the state of the art may have made great advances in the meantime. It may appear, looking back, that the new development was obvious enough, and therefore not an inventive step. But the use of hindsight in this way may well be unfair to the patentee and the courts have tried to recognise that what seems a simple step today may not have been so obvious ten years ago.

Merely to combine (collocate) known products or processes in a new way will not normally constitute an inventive step, even though the result may be novel, such as to combine a meat-mincing machine with a pie-filling machine or to produce a pen which is also a torch. But if the collocation produces some real advance or involves the exercise of inventive ingenuity it is patentable. For example, the Black & Decker 'Workmate' was essentially a combination of known devices but it was, patentable.

Industrial applications

An invention shall be taken to be capable of industrial application if it can be made or used in any kind of industry (s 4). For this purpose, agriculture is included as an industry. This provision means that surgical or therapeutic processes and diagnostic methods used in medicine cannot be patented.

2.2 The rights of the patent holder

A patent gives the owner a virtually exclusive monopoly to exploit a product or process for a period of twenty years, provided renewal fees are paid on time. The Act does not, however, specify the rights arising on grant: those can only be derived from considering the infringing activities – anything which is not capable of being infringed is outside the monopoly. If the patent is valid it prevents any other person, even an inventor who independently conceives the same invention, from doing the infringing activities.

After five years the monopoly is enjoyed annually on the payment of renewal fees. Failure to renew the patent results in the lapse of rights. The original patentee or any subsequent owner of a patent may exploit it themselves or, more usually, they will grant licences to others. Others may become interested either through perusal of UK Intellectual Property Office publications or by responding to information about inventions in international journals and on databases or from invention exploitation enterprises.

A patent can be amended after it has been granted and the patentee can sue for pre-amendment infringement.

Infringement

Section 60 Patents Act 1977 states that a patent is infringed if a person, without the consent of the proprietor, takes any of the following actions.

(a)   If the invention is a *product*, he makes, disposes of, offers to dispose of, uses or imports the product or keeps it whether for disposal or otherwise.

(b)   If the invention is a *process*, he uses the process or he offers it for use in the UK when he knows, or it is obvious to a reasonable person in the circumstances, that its use there, without the consent of the proprietor, would be an infringement of the patent.

(c)   If the invention is a *process*, he disposes of, offers to dispose of, uses or imports any product obtained directly by means of that process or keeps any such product whether for disposal or otherwise.

A large number of defences are provided. An act is not an infringement if any of the following can be shown.

(a)   The patentee's rights have become 'exhaustive' under the European Patent Convention – once the patentee has allowed a product onto the market his rights to sue for any subsequent otherwise infringing activity is lost.

(b)   The act is done privately and for non-commercial purposes.

(c)   The act is done for experimental purposes relating to the subject matter of the invention.

(d)   The act consists of the extemporaneous preparation in a pharmacy of a medicine for an individual in accordance with a prescription from a registered medical or dental practitioner or consists of dealing with such a medicine.

(e)   The act is done by a defendant who did the same act before the priority date of the invention or made effective and serious preparation to do such an act.

(f)   It is done with the express or implied consent of the patentee, such as an express licence; an implied licence to repair arises in respect of products distributed with the authority of the patentee and this includes the right to instruct others to make spare parts.

Only a valid patent can be infringed: it is open to a defendant to challenge the validity of a patent. If his defence fails, and an infringement is judged to have taken place, the patentee may apply for an injunction, or for damages, or for surrender of any products infringing the patent, or for all of these. He may also apply for an account of the defendant's profits derived from the infringement and for a declaration that the defendant has been guilty of an infringement.

Damages for infringement

The normal aim of an award of damages is to compensate the claimant for the harm caused him by the legal injury. There are many ways in which particular copyrights and patents may be exploited. A starting point in assessing damages is accordingly to ask whether the claimant and defendant are in actual competition. If they are, the loss to the claimant may also include damages to future prospects, the loss of ancillary supplies and services and possibly even the fact that the defendant is, as a result of the infringement, is able to build up a strong competitive position.

In *Gerber v Lectra 1995*, the defendant who infringed a patent for automatic cutting machines was held liable for the 'associated' damages arising from lost profits on computer-aided design systems sold with the machines, on spare parts for them, servicing contracts and for putting itself in a position, by means of the infringement, to make sales after expiry of the patent.

2.3   Exploitation of patents

The Act encourages exploitation of the patent by 'licences of right' and 'compulsory licences'.

Licences of right

Before the anniversary of the filing date, a patentee may apply to the UK Intellectual Property Office for an entry to be made on the register that licences under patent are to be available as of right; if so endorsed any person will then be entitled to a licence on such terms as are agreed with the patentee or, if there is no agreement on terms imposed, by the Office.

Compulsory licences

After three years from grant any person may apply to the Office for a licence under a patent or the endorsement of a patent with licence of right. There are a number of grounds on which an application may be granted and most require evidence that the invention is not being exploited to a reasonable extent in the light of the demand of the public or industry or commerce. The threat of compulsory licences is an incentive to patentees to exploit inventions themselves and very few compulsory licences are granted.

2.4 Employee inventions

An invention made by an employee is taken to belong to his employer for the purposes of the Patents Act 1977 if:

(a) it was made in the course of the employee's normal duties, or in the course of other duties specifically assigned to him, and the circumstances were such that an invention might reasonably be expected to result; or

(b) it was made in the course of the employee's duties and the employee, because of the nature of his duties and the particular responsibilities arising from them, had a special obligation to further the interests of his employer's undertaking.

All other employee inventions belong to the employee (s 39).

An employee may apply for a ruling that his invention, for which a patent has been granted, is of outstanding benefit to the employer and that it is just that compensation should be paid to him by the employer.

2.5 European Patent Office (EPO)

The European Patent Office is an international authority set up on the basis of the European Patent Convention. Its role is to grant European patents using a unitary and centralised procedure. By filing a single patent application in any of the three official languages – English, French or German – it is possible to obtain patent protection in 27 different European nations.

2.6 World Intellectual Property Organisation (WIPO)

The World Intellectual Property Organisation (WIPO) is an agency of the United Nations dedicated to developing a balanced and accessible international IP system which rewards creativity, stimulates innovation and contributes to economic development while safeguarding the public interest.

WIPO was established in 1967 with a mandate to promote the protection of IP throughout the world through co-operation among states and in collaboration with other international organisations. Its headquarters are in Geneva, Switzerland.

Activity 1   **(5 minutes)**

Consider why the Black and Decker 'workmate' adjustable DIY bench should have been granted a patent.

---

3   TRADE MARKS

UK law attempts to prevent traders from running their business in such a way as to steal a competitor's trade. A business may have spent years building up goodwill with customers and potential customers. It would be unfair if a newly formed business attempted to capitalise on this by making out that its own products or services were those of the established business. Anyone who suffers financial loss as a result of an offence of this kind is entitled to bring a passing off action in the courts claiming compensation for his loss and asking for an injunction against continuance of the deception.

Passing off will be discussed later in this chapter. Such actions suffer from the disadvantage that the related offence is very hard to prove. An injured party is in a stronger position if he can rely on the law relating to trade marks; it may be easier to prove that an infringement of a registered trade mark has taken place. The law relating to trade marks is found in the Trade Marks Act 1994 (TMA) plus regulations.

3.1   Registration

The TMA (s 63) provides for the maintenance (at the UK Intellectual Property Office) of a register of trade marks. Unless a mark is registered, the owner will not be able to institute proceedings for an infringement, though of course he may still have an action for passing off. Trade marks can only be registered in respect of particular goods and/or services or classes of goods and/or services (s 1). Once a trade mark has been registered, its owner is given the exclusive right to use the mark in respect of the goods and/or services concerned (s 9).

Registrable trade marks

A trade mark is a mark used or proposed to be used in relation to goods and/or services so as to indicate a connection in the course of the trade or business between the goods and/or services and the proprietor or licensee of the mark, whether with or without any indication of the identity of that person.

Definition

A **trade mark** is 'any sign capable of being represented graphically which is capable of distinguishing goods or services of one undertaking from those of other undertakings.'

The Act goes on to provide that:

'A trade mark may, in particular, consist of words (including personal names), designs, letters, numerals or the shape of goods or their packaging.'

The following are examples of registrable trade marks.

(a)   **Devices** (for example, the Mercedes three-pointed star).

(b)   **Names** (for example, 'Esso' or 'Gillette').

(c)   **Words** known or invented (for example, 'Crest' or 'Kodak').

(d)   **Letters** (for example, 'BP' and 'EMI').

(e)   **Numerals** (for example, '4711').

(f)   **Colour combinations** have been registered as marks for certain drug capsules: *Smith Kline & French Laboratories Ltd v Sterling-Winthrop Group Ltd 1976*. A trade mark is usually registered for use in all colours, unless the application is limited to certain colours in order to establish distinctiveness (as in the drug capsules case).

(g)   Some **three-dimensional figures** (for example, the Rolls Royce *Spirit of Ecstasy* silver lady).

(h)   **Smells**, provided that they can be depicted graphically (this may sound difficult, but has been in the U.S and in the UK, e.g. the smell of freshly cut grass as applied to tennis balls.).

(i)   **Sounds** such as the 'cavalry charge' jingle which accompanies the Direct Line motor insurance red telephone/computer mouse on wheels as they race across the desk in television commercials.

(j)   **Three-dimensional shapes**, probably the most important change to trade mark law introduced by the 1994 Act.

There are detailed grounds for refusal of registration. These are set out in s 3 of the Act.

(a)   Signs which cannot constitute trade marks, because they do not satisfy the requirements of s 1(1).

(b)   Signs which:

(i)   are devoid of any distinctive character

(ii)   consist exclusively of signs or indications which may serve, in trade, to designate the kind, quality, quantity, intended purpose, value, geographical origin, the time of production of goods or of rendering of services, or other characteristics of goods or services, or

(iii) consist exclusively of signs or indications which have become customary in the current language or in the *bona fide* and established practices of the trade.

(c)   Signs which because:

(i)   they consist exclusively of

(1)   the shape which results from the nature of the goods themselves,

(2)   the shape of goods which is necessary to obtain a technical result, or

(3)   the shape which gives substantial value to the goods;

(ii)   they are contrary to public policy or to accepted principles of morality, or of such a nature as to deceive the public (for instance as to the nature, quality or geographical origin of the goods or service);

(iii) their use is prohibited in the UK by any enactment or rule of law or by any provision of EC law; or

(iv) they are specially protected emblems.

(d) Signs which are applied for in bad faith.

These four groupings constitute the 'absolute' grounds for refusal of registration. There are also 'relative' grounds for refusal of registration, set out in s 5. These provide broadly that a trade mark shall not be registered if it is:

(a) identical with an earlier identical mark in respect of identical goods and/or services, or

(b) identical or similar to an earlier identical or similar trade mark in respect of similar goods and/or services, and there exists a likelihood of confusion on the part of the public, including a likelihood of association or

(c) a identical or similar trade mark in respect of similar and dissimilar goods and/or services and use would take unfair advantage of or be detrimental to the distinctive character of the earlier mark

Collective and certification trade marks

Certification trade marks are granted to owners who do not trade in the goods themselves, but authorise others, in accordance with regulations approved by the Department of Business, Enterprise and Regulatory Reform, to use the mark as a certificate of compliance with certain standards. Examples are the pure wool and wool blend marks of the International Wool Secretariat and the Harris Tweed mark.

Collective marks were introduced by s 49 TMA 1994. A collective mark is 'a mark distinguishing the goods or services of members of the association which is the proprietor of the mark from those of other undertakings.' Unlike certification marks, they can only be used by members of the association which is the proprietor of the mark. A third party who is not a member of the association has no right to use the mark, regardless of the quality or characteristics of the goods or services supplied by that third party.

Owners of very well known invented word marks used to be able to obtain a *defensive registration* of that mark to cover goods in which they did not intend to trade, when use of the mark on those other goods would suggest to the public a trade connection with the trade mark owner. This is no longer possible.

The Community Trade Mark

The Secretary of State has the power to make provisions in connection with the Community Trade Mark Regulation. This Regulation created 'the Community trade mark', which has a unitary effect throughout the EC. Trade mark owners have been able to take advantage of the new system from early 1996, s 16.

The Regulation does not replace the trade mark law of individual member states, but provides an alternative system whereby an applicant can seek Community-wide protection of a mark by means of a single application. The Community trade mark has the same effect in every country in the EC, which means that an application for a Community trade mark must be made, and therefore accepted or rejected, for the whole of the EC.

The result of a successful opposition in a single EC member state means that the Community trade mark will be rejected. Likewise, once registration is obtained, it can be revoked Community-wide if attacked by a single member state. The Office for Harmonisation in the Internal Market (Trademarks and Designs) is located in Alicante in Spain.

Many of the provisions of the Regulation are similar to the provisions of the EC Directive which have been incorporated into the Trade Marks Act itself.

Process of registration

Below is an outline of the steps involved in applying for a registered trade mark under the Trade Marks Act 1994.

(a) **Applicants**

Any person, natural or legal who wishes to use a trade mark for the goods or services specified in the application may apply to the Trade Marks section of the UK Intellectual Property Office to register it. An applicant must affirm on application that they have used or have a bona fide intention of using the Trade Mark for which registration is sought.

(b) **Priority**

It may occasionally happen that two parties quite independently seek to use the same trade mark without either being able to claim priority from prior use. The question of priority is then decided on the basis of which application has the earlier filing date. Under the Paris Convention, an applicant in the UK may claim up to six months priority from an application in another Convention country.

(c) **Classification**

The Trade Marks Register is divided into classes: 34 for goods and 11 for services. The Registrar has the final power to decide which class particular goods or services belong to. Applicants must name all goods and services at the outset for which registration is sought.

(d) **Search and examination**

A search for conflicting trade marks is usually carried out by the applicant. However, the Registrar always conducts a search of previous trade marks and will draw to the Applicant's intention earlier marks where the Register believes there is a conflict. In certain cases, the Registrar may notify the holder/s of an earlier trade mark/s that the Applicant has sought registration of a conflicting Trade Mark.

(e) **Objections**

Oppositions to a proposed registration must be made by third parties within two months of the Trade Mark application being advertised in the Trade Marks Journal. A non-extendible one month extension can be granted to lodge opposition. An opposition must be on either absolute or relative grounds. Absolute grounds relate to distinctiveness and certain public interest objectives. Relative grounds arise because some other trader or proprietor has an earlier conflicting right.

(f) **Appeal**

Appeal against a decision by the Registrar may be made to the High Court or to an 'appointed person', generally a senior barrister. If an appeal is made to the 'appointed person' there is no right of further appeal except in very limited circumstances.

(g) **Term of registration**

Once this procedure is complete, the trade mark is regarded as registered from the date of filing of the application. The right lasts ten years. It is renewable every ten years, provided it not revoked or invalidated, for example on grounds of non-use.

3.2 Rights of trade mark holders

The owner of a registered trade mark has an exclusive right to use of the mark. The right is infringed (s 10) if any other person, without the owner's consent, uses the mark itself or a mark closely resembling it in the course of trade (not in a song, a painting or an instruction manual for instance). The infringement will occur if the offender uses the mark as a trade mark applying to goods or services similar to those for which the trade mark is registered. Infringement may even occur in less blatant circumstances such as in comparative advertising. However, there must be a seriously misleading use of the mark registered.

Barclays Bank v RBS Advanta 1996
Another bank's credit card venture both claimed to have 15 particular advantages and to fare well in a chart of charges which compared eight credit cards by name, including 'Barclaycard'.

Held: a case of material dishonesty had to be made out which went beyond mere 'puffery'.

Against an action by a trade mark owner there are the following defences.

(a) Use of another registered trade mark in relation to goods or services for which that other mark is registered, s 11(1).

(b) *Bona fide* use of one's own name or address, s 11(2).

(c) Use to describe the goods or services, s 11(2). This was found to be a valid defence in *British Sugar plc v James Robertson & Sons 1996*.

(d) Use to indicate the purpose of a product or service, particularly spare parts, s 11(2).

The owner of a registered trademark which has been infringed has the following remedies available to him.

(a) Damages and compensation for the actual damage suffered by the claimant.

(b) An account of profits – a sum representing the profits made by the defendant from his infringing acts (which can be a substantially larger sum than damages).

(c) An injunction (permanent or interlocutory) to prevent the infringement being repeated.

Exhaustion of rights

The Trade Marks Act states that trade marks can be breached by importing goods without the consent of the trade mark owner. Those who own trade marks are therefore in a strong position to prevent imports.

There is a European dimension to this issue, and s 12 TMA sets out the EU principle of *exhaustion of rights* once goods are put on the market in the EU. Under s 12(1): 'A registered trade mark is not infringed by the use of the trade mark in relation to goods which have been [previously] put on the market in the European Economic Area [European Union countries plus Norway, Iceland and Liechtenstein] under that trade mark by the proprietor, or with his consent.' This does not however apply where the owner of the trade mark could legitimately prevent further dealing in the goods, such as where quality has been damaged.

This can also be related to the policy pursued by some companies of *selective distribution*, where they will only sell their goods through high class outlets, in order to keep prices, and company image, high. In the case detailed below, these issues were explored.

> *Silhouette International Schmied GmbH & Co KG v Hartlauer Handelsgesellschaft GmbH 1998*
> In October 1995 the claimant (producer of high price sunglasses) sold 21,000 out-of-fashion frames to a Bulgarian company, on the condition that they were only to be resold in Bulgaria or former USSR countries. Hartlauer (an Austrian seller of cheap sunglasses whom Silhouette had always refused to supply) bought them further down the line of supply, and imported them into Austria in December 1995. Silhouette sued for infringement of trade mark.
>
> *Held:* the court held that Silhouette *could* prevent the resale in the EEA, as the exhaustion of rights principle only applies in relation to goods bought in one EC country (ie not Bulgaria) and resold in another (thus underlining the principle that Europe should be a single market with free circulation of goods, but that that this should not extend to world free trade). The case applied only to *registered trade marks*.

Parallel trading

Some companies have been accused of using the trade mark legislation, in tandem with selective distribution agreements, to stifle competition and boost their prices. *Parallel traders* are challenging this position, and there is some lobbying for a change in the law to protect consumers. EU ministers met recently to discuss a report which found that almost all goods were cheaper in the US than in Europe by some 40 to 50 per cent.

Parallel (or grey) imports are goods obtained through unofficial distribution channels. They should not be confused with *counterfeit goods*, whose import can always be prevented by the TMA and the Trade Descriptions Act 1968.

Parallel traders either take advantage of price differentials in other countries, or decide not to charge such a high margin on the goods. A recent example is provided by the UK supermarkets stocking items such as designer label jeans, perfumes and sportswear at discount prices. The designers have often retaliated with court action. A change in European trade mark law is likely to be slow in coming, but the advent of the Euro may serve to make some price differentials so transparent as to be unsustainable.

Counterfeiting

The Act contains important anti-counterfeiting measures. It is an offence for a person to apply a mark identical to or nearly resembling a registered trade mark to goods, or to material used or intended to be used for labelling, packaging or advertising goods when that person is not entitled to use the mark in question and the goods are not connected in the course of trade with a person so entitled, provided the person acts with a view to benefiting from the counterfeit.

3.3   Exploitation of trade marks

Trade marks have frequently become an indicator of the quality of goods rather than (as originally) an indicator of the origin of the goods. The legislation has influenced this trend, as it allows trading in the mark without the attachment of a relevant part of the business. This means that there does not have to be a single place of origin of the goods: they can be sourced from different locations. This promotes licensing of trade marks.

Licensing

A licence or sub-licence to use a registered trade mark may be granted in respect of some or all of the goods or service for which a trade mark is registered, s 28. Licences may also be granted in relation to use in a particular locality.

All 'registrable transactions', including therefore licences, can be registered: s 25. If the licence is not registered, it will be ineffective 'as against a person acquiring a conflicting interest in or under the registered trade mark in ignorance of it'. If the application to register the licence in not made within six months of the date of the transaction, the licensee will not be awarded any damages for an act of infringement committed between the date of the transaction and the date of registration. It is therefore very important to register the trade mark licence as soon as possible.

Once a licence is registered, any licensee may call on the proprietor of the registered trade mark to commence infringement proceedings and, if the proprietor fails to do so within two months, the licensee may bring the proceedings in his own name, s 30.

An *exclusive licence* is a licence authorising the licensee, to the exclusion of all other persons, including the person granting the licence, to use a registered trade mark in the manner authorised by the licence, s 29. An exclusive licencee has the same rights as if the exclusive licence had been an assignment and hence may bring infringement proceedings in his own name.

Assignment

An assignment must be in writing and signed by the assignor. Like a licence, an assignment must be entered on the Register, otherwise it will be ineffective. An application to record an assignment must also be made within six months of the date of the transaction.

Character merchandising

Character merchandising is a phrase used to describe the position where a trade mark is applied to a wide variety of different goods or services. A trade mark merchandised in this way is often a fictional character, such as Teletubbies. The mark will then appear on a wide range of items such as clothing, stationery and confectionery.

The owners of such marks rarely merchandise the goods themselves, but usually grant licences to others to use the mark in connection with various goods and services. Under the former law, character merchandising licences could not be registered, as the Registrar had to refuse an application for registration of a permitted user if it appeared to him that the grant of registration would tend to facilitate 'trafficking' in a mark.

This position was changed under the 1994 legislation, which recognised character merchandising.

Activity 2   (5 minutes)

Why should a manufacturer of goods, who is the registered owner of a trade mark, wish to license the trade mark?

---

4 PASSING OFF

The courts try to protect traders from unscrupulous competitors who seek to market their own products as being those of a different, and better known, business. Although an action for infringement of a trade mark may be simpler to win, there are cases (when traders have failed to register all their marks or their marks are not registrable) when passing off actions must be resorted to. The unregistered rights which a person may seek to enforce in this way are sometimes referred to as *common law trade marks*.

4.1 The Advocaat case

In *Ervin Warnink BV v J Townend & Sons (Hull) Ltd 1979* (known as the *Advocaat* case), five characteristics were identified as creating a valid cause of action for passing off:

(a) a misrepresentation

(b) made by a trader in the course of a trade

(c) to prospective customers of his or the ultimate consumers of goods and services supplied by him

(d) which it is reasonably foreseeable will injure the goodwill and business of another trader

(e) which causes actual damage to that goodwill or business.

Ervin Warnink BV v J Townend & Sons (Hull) Ltd 1979
The claimants were one of several Dutch manufacturers of the alcoholic drink advocaat. Advocaat could only be sold under that name in the Netherlands if it complied with a certain formula. The defendants sold a drink, which did not comply with the formula, under the name 'Keeling's Old English Advocaat'.

Held: although it was accepted that no purchaser of the defendant's product would believe it to be supplied by the claimants or even to be Dutch, an order was made preventing the use of the name advocaat on any drinks which did not comply with the formula.

The claimant in a passing off action must therefore establish the following.

(a) Because of the reputation attached to his goods or his business, there is a goodwill attached to the marks or names he uses.

(b) The defendant is misrepresenting that the goods he sells are, or are connected with, the goods or business of the claimant.

(c) He has as a result suffered damage to his business or goodwill, or he is likely to suffer damage.

4.2 Reputation

The claimant must first of all establish that he has a reputation or goodwill in the name or mark concerned. This is the principal reason why an action for infringement of trade marks is simpler than an action for passing off: the mere fact of registration disposes of this requirement. In establishing goodwill the trader must show that he has such a distinctive trading style that it should be protected.

Chelsea Man Menswear Ltd v Chelsea Girl Ltd 1987
The claimant operated shops in London and the Midlands selling clothes under the 'Chelsea Man' label. The defendant operated 'Chelsea Girl' stores and wished to open a complementary chain of 'Chelsea Man' stores.

Held: an injunction was granted against the defendant covering the entire UK. The claimant's goodwill extended beyond its area of operation.

Harrods Ltd v Harrodian School 1996
The department store Harrods maintained a sports club since 1929 known as the Harrodian Club for members of their staff. In 1993 the site was purchased and used as a school called 'The Harrodian School'. The claimants claimed that this use of the name constituted passing off, but lost their claim at first instance. The claimants appealed.

Held: the appeal would be dismissed. It was not sufficient to demonstrate some kind of connection between the claimant and the defendant, if that connection would not led the public to suppose that the claimant had made himself responsible for the quality of the defendant's goods or services. A belief that the claimant had sponsored the defendant would not ordinarily give the public that impression.

The goodwill must have continued for some time.

Nationwide Building Society v Nationwide Estate Agents Ltd 1987
The claimant had used the name 'Nationwide' as a building society for some time, and began trading as an estate agency under the 'Nationwide' name in 1987. In 1986 the defendants had set up an estate agents under this name. It was shown that there was clearly confusion in the minds of the public as a result.

Held: the claimant's passing off action failed since neither party had established any substantial goodwill in the estate agency business.

The trader must be careful not to claim too wide a territory for the goodwill, as shown in the *Budweiser* case.

Anheuser-Busch Inc v Budejovicky Budvar NP 1984
The claimants sold 'Budweiser' lager in the United States. The defendants sold 'Budweiser' lager in England. Small numbers of the claimant's cans were exported to England and sold in US military establishments.

Held: although the claimants had achieved some reputation in England, they did not carry on business in England and could not demonstrate any damage to their goodwill. The action failed.

4.3 Misrepresentation

The claimant must show that the trader misrepresented products as being those of another person. This means that:

(a) the impression given must be a false one; and
(b) consumers generally would be confused by the defendant's trading style.

It is not only the source of supply which can constitute misrepresentation; the character and quality of goods can be misrepresented, as can a person's endorsement of a product. Difficulties arise in passing off actions as to whether a misrepresentation has occurred in the following circumstances.

Descriptive names

Businesses often like to use business names which describe what they do, for example 'office cleaning'. It is difficult to protect such names since the courts tend to identify small differences in trading style to distinguish them.

Office Cleaning Services Ltd v Westminster Window and General Cleaners Ltd 1946
The claimants traded as 'Office Cleaning Services' and the defendants as 'Office Cleaning Association'.

Held: the claimants failed. There was a difference between their trading styles. 'Where a trader adopts words in common use, some risk of confusion is inevitable. That risk must be run unless the first user is allowed unfairly to monopolise the words'.

Use of own name

Confusion often arises because many people have the same names and tend to trade under them. Where there is no dishonesty or calculation to cause confusion, the law simply accepts that such confusion is inevitable. 'If a man uses his own name, and uses it honestly and fairly, and is doing nothing more, he cannot be restrained, even if confusion results': *Wright Layman & Umney Ltd v Wright 1949*. Note that the principle applies to individuals who receive names at birth; corporate bodies do not have the same defence of innocently trading under their own names.

Common field of activity

A person who manufactures, say, soap and no other toiletries may decide to institute a passing off action against another trader who causes confusion by using the same name to manufacture and sell, say, shampoo. The difficult point at issue is how far the two parties are in a 'common field of activity'.

Wombles Ltd v Wombles Skips Ltd 1975
The claimants owned the copyright in the *Wombles* stories (the Wombles were a group of furry creatures living on Wimbledon Common and collecting litter). The defendants were using the word in the name of a company connected with refuse containers.

Held: the passing off action failed. There was no common field of activity.

Stringfellow v McCain Foods (GB) Ltd
The claimant owned a restaurant called 'Stringfellows'. The defendants marketed frozen chips under the name 'Stringfellows'.

Held: the claimant was granted a remedy as the court decided that there was some danger of confusion.

United Biscuits (UK) Ltd v Asda Stores Ltd 1997
The defendants sold a chocolate biscuit 'Puffin' with a picture of a puffin. The claimants argued that the name and packaging could cause confusion with the 'Penguin' brand.

Held: Asda was guilty of passing off. The judge ruled that Puffin's packaging could lead to confusion. However, he did not agree that the use of a sea-bird logo with a name similar to 'Penguin' violated the United Biscuits trademark.

However the doctrine of 'common field of activity' may not always be important.

Mirage Studios v Counter-Feat Clothing Co Ltd 1991
The claimants were the owners of copyright in certain drawings of 'Ninja Turtles'. The defendants used the name and other drawings (so no infringement of copyright) on articles of clothing.

Held: restraint of such use was granted, even though there was no common field of activity.

4.4 Damage

Finally, it must be demonstrated that the claimant has actually suffered damage to his business or goodwill, or that he will probably do so. In the latter case, he may seek a *quia timet* injunction.

The scope of passing off

The case below has long been a landmark case in demonstrating the scope of passing off. Before the Trade Marks Act 1994, a container shape could not be registered as a trade mark (see the *Coca-Cola* case above). However a container may be so distinctive that anyone who uses the same shape can be sued for passing off.

> *Reckitt and Colman Products Ltd v Borden Inc 1990*
>
> The claimants had, since 1956, sold lemon juice in yellow plastic containers shaped like lemons under the brand name 'Jif'. In 1985 the defendants introduced products known as Mark I, Mark II and Mark III which were almost identical in shape and colour to the claimant's product. It was shown that, although a shopper could distinguish the two by reading the labels, most would not do so and shoppers would buy the defendant's goods believing them to be 'Jif'.
>
> *Held:* in the House of Lords the three passing off principles were restated as: goodwill or reputation attaching to the goods or services, misrepresentation by the defendant leading to confusion among the public, and damage arising from the misrepresentation. It was found that the claimant had established goodwill and that confusion would arise in the minds of shoppers wishing to buy lemon juice in a lemon-shaped container. The defendant had not taken sufficient steps to eradicate confusion and so an injunction was granted restraining the defendant from using the lemon shape.

If the claimant is successful, his remedies are similar to those relating to an infringement of patent or trade mark.

Significance of passing off

Following the enactment of the Trade Marks Act 1994, actions for passing off became less significant.

(a) Shapes, packaging, sounds, smells and other sensory marks became registrable as trade marks.

(b) The test for registrability as a trade mark was relaxed so that, for example, geographical names and descriptive words may, if distinctive of the proprietor's goods or services, be accepted.

(c) The scope of the infringement action was broadened.

NOTES

Chapter roundup

- A patent is a monopoly right to exploit an invention for a stated period of time. By registering a patent an inventor makes it an offence for other people, without his consent, to benefit from his intellectual efforts.

- The period for which a patent is granted is twenty years. It may during that period be exploited by the granting of licences of right or compulsory licences.

- A trade mark is a distinctive word, name or other mark which is used to indicate a connection in the course of trade between goods or services and their owner. By registering a trade mark, the owner of the mark makes it an offence for other people to use it.

- Trade marks may also be licensed or assigned to other users.

- Where a person seeks to enforce unregistered rights (rights not embodied in a registered trade mark) he may resort to a passing off action. He will have a valid cause of action if he can show that the three conditions laid down in *The Jif Lemon* case are satisfied.

Quick quiz

1   What is the legislation governing patents?

2   What are the three criteria (set out in s 1 of the relevant Act) which an invention must satisfy for a patent to be granted?

3   What rights does a patent give to the owner?

4   List five defences to a claim that a patent has been infringed.

5   Give four examples of registered trade marks.

6   What is a Community Trade Mark?

7   What five characteristics create a valid cause of action for passing off?

8   What were the facts of *Reckitt and Colman Products Ltd v Borden Inc 1990*?

Answers to quick quiz

1 The Patents Act 1977.

2 The invention must be new, involve an inventive step and be capable of industrial application.

3 A patent gives the owner a virtually exclusive monopoly to exploit a product or process for twenty years so long as certain conditions are met.

4 Refer to the list in paragraph 2.2.

5 Any four from devices, names, words, letters, numerals, colour combinations, three-dimensional figures or shapes, smells and sounds.

6 A trade mark which applies throughout the EC.

7 Refer to the list in paragraph 4.1.

8 Refer to the description of the case in paragraph 4.4.

Answers to activities

1 The 'workmate' is one of the best known successfully patented designs of the late twentieth century. Another famous patent in the UK is that granted for the Dyson carpet cleaner. In the US, the original (non-riveted) ringpull used on soft drinks cans was successfully patented.

2 (a) Licensing can help expansion.

(b) Licensing can ensure protection of the goods.

(c) Long-term brand loyalty can be encouraged.

(d) Access to additional manufacturing capacity can be obtained.

(e) Access to new outlets can be obtained without the owner having to manufacture there.

Part D: Intellectual Property Law

Chapter 11 :
INTELLECTUAL PROPERTY: COPYRIGHT LAW

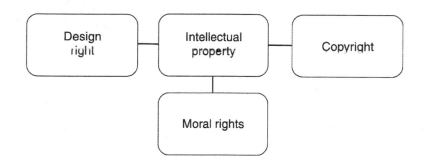

Introduction

In this chapter we continue our review of intellectual property law with a study of the Copyright Designs and Patents Act 1988 (CDPA) as amended where appropriate by the Duration of Copyright and Rights in Performance Regulations 1995 and the Copyright and Related Rights Regulations 2003. We shall also look at the Registered Designs Act 1949, as amended (RDA).

Your objectives

In this chapter you will learn about the following.

    (a)   The scope of copyright legislation

    (b)   The protection afforded by copyright

    (c)   Remedies for infringement of copyright

    (d)   Design rights and moral rights

1 COPYRIGHT

The law of copyright embraces a vast field of human creativity and entrepreneurial activity. The basic notion of copyright is the exclusive right to use one's own work, the corollary of which is the right to stop others from exploiting it. *The basis of protection is to prevent theft of the skill and labour which has gone into the creative production.*

The right has been extended to unauthorised performances of literary and musical works and (because of technological advances) broadcasts and cable transmissions of literary and dramatic works where copying plays no significant part.

An important consequence of the definition is that there must be some form of work or product. An *idea*, which has no tangible product, is not protected from being copied, such as the format for a gameshow (*Green v Broadcasting Corporation of New Zealand 1989*) or a situation comedy.

1.1 Scope of copyright legislation

The Copyright, Designs and Patents Act 1988 repealed all existing copyright legislation. The Act (to which all subsequent references are made) states that copyright is a property right which subsists in the following works.

(a) Original literary, dramatic, musical or artistic works.
(b) Sound recordings, films or broadcasts.
(c) The typographical arrangement of published editions.

Original literary, dramatic, musical and artistic works

Original means that the work emanates from the author and is not copied, although a derivative work, such as a translation, which involves distinct skill and labour, gives rise to a new form of copyright. The term can be taken to mean that skill, judgment and effort should have been taken in producing the work.

A *literary* work is any work, other than one which is dramatic or musical, which is written, spoken or sung. It includes not only novels, poems and plays but also such diverse items as a computer program, a timetable and a database. *Dramatic* works include those which involve dance or mime. But copyright in a literary, dramatic or musical work does not subsist until it is recorded, in writing or otherwise. A *musical* work does not include the words or actions which accompany it. Hence the composer of a West End musical has copyright in the music and the lyricist has copyright in the lyrics.

Artistic work is defined in the Act as being any of the following.

(a) A graphic work, photograph, sculpture or collage, irrespective of artistic quality.

(b) A work of architecture, being a building or a model for a building (the plans are protected as a graphic work).

(c) A work of artistic craftsmanship.

'Work of artistic craftsmanship' appears to mean that there must be some evidence that it is the work of an artist-craftsman, such as a jeweller, but it is possible that it extends to more mundane items too.

Hensher (G) Ltd v Restawhile Upholstery (Lancs) Ltd 1976
The case concerned a prototype consisting of a design for a chair.

Held: although it was not the function of the court to consider artistic merit as such, a work had to have some artistic character over and above being a work of craftsmanship. (The five judges gave different speeches and there was some disagreement over whether a work of artistic craftsmanship could be functional as well as aesthetic.)

Sound recordings, films and broadcasts

Sound recordings include recordings on any medium, such as audio cassettes or CDs. Films include 'still' photographs from films. Broadcasts include any sound or pictures transmitted by means of a broadcast, in other words sent for simultaneous reception by members of the public, or transmitted at a time determined by the person making the transmission for presentation to the public. Save for some exceptions, internet transmissions are not to be treated as broadcasts.

Typographical arrangements of published editions

Often editions of plays, poems or musicals have a distinctive typographical page layout. Copyright can exist in this for a publisher even though the copyright in the work itself has expired.

1.2 Ownership of copyright

The 'author' of a work is the person who creates it. This simple definition is extended as follows.

(a) Sound recordings or films: the person 'by whom the arrangements necessary for the making of the recording or film are undertaken' (not the performers).

(b) A broadcast: the person who makes the broadcast.

(c) A typographical arrangement of a published edition: the publisher.

(d) A literary, dramatic, musical or artistic work which is computer-generated: the author shall be taken to be the person by whom the arrangements necessary for the creation of the work are undertaken.

The author becomes the first owner of any copyright as soon as the work is created and without any formality, subject to certain provisions. In particular, where the work has been made by an employee in the course of his employment, his employer is the first owner: s 11(2).

Joint ownership

There is no provision to vest copyright in the commissioners of works at all, so it remains with the author. Joint ownership is possible, as where a work is co-produced.

Most businesses commission copyright works from time to time, for example using a software company to develop circuitry. Under the 1988 Act, unless the person writing the work is an employee, the rights will not be owned by the person paying for the work.

> *Flyde Microsystems v Key Radio Systems 1998*
> The defendant had asked the plaintiff to develop circuit boards for its mobile radio. The plaintiff did so, spending about twenty man years on the work, and sold £3m worth of the boards to the defendant. The circuit boards contained chips loaded with a certain software written by the plaintiff's employees. The defendant subsequently sold radios to customers which, while not containing the circuit boards, still contained this software. The plaintiff sought an injunction claiming infringement of copyright.

Held: Although it was true that the defendant had spent time, effort and skill in testing the software, this was not enough to make them joint authors. Their skills were more like those of a proof reader. The court granted an injunction restraining the defendant from using the software.

Copyright assignment

It is possible for the normal provisions of 'first ownership' to be set aside by the assignment (transfer of ownership) of copyright in a work *prior* to its creation. It is *always* possible to assign copyright *after* the completion of the work. A valid assignment must be in writing and signed by or on behalf of the copyright owner.

Copyright licensing

No formalities are required for the licensing of a copyright unless it is to be an exclusive licence, in which case the same formalities are required as for an assignment of ownership. A licence, which may be implied, allows the licensee to use the work subject to the owner's copyright. In most cases a person who commissions a work for a particular purpose, such as a graphic illustration for a textbook, has an implied licence to use it.

Duration of copyright

The period of copyright in different works expires as follows.

(a) *Literary, dramatic, musical or artistic works*: at the end of the period of 70 years from the end of the calendar year in which the author dies. If the work is of unknown authorship, it expires at the end of the period of 70 years from the end of the calendar year in which it was first made available to the public. If the work is computer-generated, it expires at the end of a period of 70 years from the end of the calendar year in which it was made. Where a work is one of joint authorship, it expires at the death of the last author to die.

(b) *A sound recording*: at the end of the period of 50 years from the end of the calendar year in which it was made or, if released before the end of that period, 50 years from the end of the calendar year in which it was released. 'Release' means the first public showing, but unauthorised acts are excluded.

(c) A *film:* at the end of the period of 70 years from the end of the calendar year in which the death occurs of the last to die of the following persons, if known:

- the principal director
- the author of the screenplay
- the author of the dialogue, or
- the composer of music specially created for and used in the film

(d) *Broadcasts:* at the end of the period of 50 years from the end of the calendar year in which the broadcast was made. Copyright in a repeat expires at the same time as that of the original broadcast.

(e) *The typographical arrangement of a published edition*: at the end of the period of 25 years from the end of the calendar year in which the edition was first published.

1.3 Rights of the copyright owner

The copyright owner has the exclusive right to do any of the following in the UK: s 16 CDPA 1988.

(a) Copy the work.

(b) Issue copies of the work to the public, or rent or lend the work to the public.

(c) Perform, show or play the work in public.

(d) Communicate the work to the public.

(e) Make an adaptation of the work or do any of the above in relation to an adaptation.

The underlying right is the same in each case. It is a right of the owner to prevent others from reproducing his work. This amounts to an exclusive right to reproduce the work for a fixed period.

Moral rights

The Act provides for certain additional rights, discussed later in this chapter. These apply to certain works only, and can be asserted by the author, director or commissioner of a work, whether or not he is the owner of the copyright.

(a) The right to be identified as the author or director (s 77).
(b) The right to object to derogatory treatment of the work (s 80).
(c) The right to privacy of certain photographs or films (s 85).

1.4 Infringements of copyright

Primary infringements

The copyright is primarily infringed where a person not licensed by the copyright owner does any of the acts restricted by the copyright or authorises another to do them. In order to gain a remedy where there is a primary infringement there is no need to show that the defendant was aware of the infringement.

Copying

Copying may be direct or indirect.

> *British Leyland Motor Corp v Armstrong Patents Co 1986*
> The defendant made copies of the plaintiff's exhaust systems.
>
> *Held:* even though the defendant had never seen the design drawings for these systems, they had infringed the plaintiffs' copyright in the design drawings by making a three-dimensional copy of a three-dimensional model which was itself (legitimately) based on an original drawing.

Copying may relate to the work as a whole or to a substantial part of it, the question of what constitutes a substantial part being a matter of 'quality rather than quantity'. The greater the skill expended in the creation of the work, the less it will be able to be copied, whilst if the work is largely itself a borrowing or commonplace, a large proportion may not be a substantial part.

'Copying' in relation to a literary, dramatic, musical or artistic work means reproducing the work in any material form, including storing it in any medium by electronic means. Some difficulty may arise as to the meaning of 'material form'. A garment knitted according to the pattern of a knitting guide was held not to be an infringement as it was not a reproduction or copy of the guide. The knitted item was an execution of the instructions in the pattern and it stored them only in the sense that by a meticulous counting of the stitches could the contents of the guide be reconstructed.

Public performance

It is a primary infringement to perform a copyright work in public. This is defined very widely to include private performances and the playing of background music in supermarkets, where the performance is done without consent. Provided no charge for admission is made, however, the public showing of a broadcast or cablecast is not an infringement: s 72.

Communication to the public

Communication to the public of the work is a primary infringement of the copyright in a literary, dramatic, musical or artistic work, a sound recording or film, and a broadcast. 'Communication to the public' means communication to the public by electronic transmission, which includes broadcasting the work and making the work available to the public by electronic transmission in such a way that members of the public may access it from a place and at a time individually chosen by them, that is internet transmission.

In addition, a performer's rights are infringed by a person who, without his consent, makes available to the public a recording of the whole or any substantial part of a qualifying performance directly form the live performance, broadcasts live the whole or any substantial part of a qualifying performance, or make a recording of the whole or any substantial party of a qualifying performance directly from a broadcast of the live performance. In each case the performer's rights are infringed when the whole or any substantial part of a qualifying performance is made available by electronic transmission in such as way that members of the public may access the recording from a place and at a time individually chosen by them: s 182.

The right of a performer under this section to authorise or prohibit the making available to the public of a recording is referred to as the 'making available right'.

Adaptation

Infringement by making an *adaptation* includes the following.

(a) A translation of the work.

(b) Converting a dramatic work into a non-dramatic work and vice versa.

(c) Making a version of the story in which the action is conveyed wholly or mainly by pictures.

(d) In relation to a musical work, a transcription or arrangement.

(e) Adaptation in relation to a computer program will include its transfer into a different computer language or code.

(f) Video piracy.

Secondary infringement

A secondary infringement is committed in the following cases.

(a) Where a person imports into the United Kingdom, otherwise than for private or domestic use, an article which he knows or has reason to believe is an infringing copy of the work.

(b) Where a person possesses in the course of a business, sells or lets for hire, or exposes for sale or hire, or in the course of a business exhibits in public, or distributes in the course of a business or otherwise to such an extent as to affect prejudicially the copyright owner, an article which he knows or has reason to believe, is an infringing copy.

(c) Where a person makes, imports into the United Kingdom, possesses in the course of a business or sells or hires an article specifically designed or adapted for making copies of the work, knowing or having reason to believe that it will be used to make infringing copies.

(d) Where a work is infringed at a place of public entertainment, the person who gave permission for that place to be used for the performance is deemed to have infringed the copyright, unless he believed at the time that the performance would not infringe copyright.

(e) Where a person supplies apparatus for making an infringing copy, gives permission for the apparatus to be brought on to his premises, or supplies copies of a sound recording or film for the purposes of infringement, where he knew or had reasonable grounds to know of the infringement, that person is liable for infringement.

The 1988 Act permits the issue by a justice of the peace of a search warrant for the detection of infringing articles. An order can then be made for the delivery up of infringing articles. The copyright owner can, by giving written notice to the Customs, have infringing articles which are being imported seized and forfeited.

Defences to an action for breach of copyright

Sections 29 and 30 contain the three *'fair dealing'* defences.

(a) 'Fair dealing' with a copyright work for the purposes of *research or private study* does not infringe the copyright. The production of multiple copies is thus excluded from the defence. However, the Newspaper Licensing Agency has taken steps to stop multiple copies of newspaper articles being used for internal dissemination or for clients.

(b) A work can be used fairly for the purposes of *criticism or review.*

(c) (Except for photographs) a work can be used for the reporting of *current events.*

Short passages from published literary or dramatic works can be included in a collection intended for use in *educational establishments*. There is no infringement where a copyright work is performed at an educational establishment by a teacher or pupil in the course of the establishment's activities and the audience is composed of teachers or pupils. This does not include the performance of works for an audience of parents. Copies of broadcasts may be made at educational establishments for educational purposes. A limited amount of reprographic copying is allowed in educational establishments, but any licensing arrangements must be adhered to.

There are special provisions for copying to be undertaken by *librarians*. Basically these require that the librarian should be satisfied that the copy is to be used purely for private study or research and that no person should be given more than one copy or more than a reasonable proportion of any particular work. A charge, not less than the cost of the copying and including a contribution to the cost of the general expenses of the library, should be made. Any librarian who does not adhere to the rules is treated as an infringer in the same way as any other.

There is no infringement of copyright where anything is done for the purposes of *judicial or parliamentary proceedings*.

Hiring out copies of sound recordings, films or computer programs is not an infringement if consent has been obtained: s 18(3). Finally *'time-shifting'* – recording a programme to watch at a more convenient time – is no longer an infringement *provided* the copy is erased after 28 days: s 70.

In some cases it may be a defence under s 28A to claim that any copy was temporary, that is transient or incidental. This will be allowed where the copying was an integral and essential part of a technological process, and its sole purpose was either a lawful use of the work which had no independent economic significance, or it was to enable the work to be transmitted in a network between third parties by an intermediary. The 'temporary copy' defence will only apply to:

- a literary work, other than a computer program or a database
- a dramatic, musical or artistic work
- a typographical arrangement of a published edition
- a sound recording or
- a film

Under s 31 copyright in a work is not infringed by its incidental inclusion in an artistic work, sound recording, film or broadcast. However, a musical work, words spoken or sung with music, or so much of a sound recording or broadcast as includes a musical work or such words, is not treated as being incidentally included in another work if it is deliberately included.

In certain circumstances visually impaired people may possess or use a copy of the whole or part of a literary, dramatic, musical or artistic work or a published edition which is not otherwise accessible to them because of the impairment.

Remedies for infringement

Civil remedies for infringement of copyrights are as follows:

Damages

Damages for copyright infringement are assessed on the amount required to compensate the plaintiff for actual harm suffered (such as damage to reputation caused by the poor quality of infringing articles). Damages cannot be awarded against a person who did not know of the copyright's existence.

Account of profits

This may be awarded *instead of* damages, and result in payment of a sum which represents the profits made by the defendant arising from his infringement of copyright; and/or

Injunction

The owner, once he has proved his case, can obtain a permanent injunction restraining the infringement for the duration of the copyright. Because copyright actions often take so long to come to trial, there are also *interlocutory* injunctions available which restrain infringing actions until the case is heard. An injunction may be granted against a service provider (ISP) where that service provider has actual knowledge of another person using their service to infringe copyright.

Anton Piller order

This may be awarded in cases where the plaintiff can make a good prima facie argument that the service of a writ or interlocutory injunction on the defendant will result in the destruction, secretion or removal of evidence vital to the case. The order allows the plaintiff to enter the defendant's premises and seize the relevant material. Surprise is of the essence so usually a petition for an *Anton Piller* order is heard *ex parte* (the defendant is not present);

Delivery up order

A 'delivery up' order requires infringing copies to be delivered up by the defendant, and for instance can allow the plaintiff to seize infringing copies from a street trader. A destruction order allows the infringing articles to be destroyed.

Activity 1   **(5 minutes)**

What is the duration of copyright in the UK?

Criminal offences

The Copyright and Related Rights Regulations 2003 introduced a number of criminal penalties in relation to copyright.

A person who infringes copyright in a work by communicating the work to the public in the course of a business, or if not in the course of a business then to such an extent as to affect prejudicially the owner of the copyright commits an offence if he knows or has reason to believe that, by doing so, he is infringing copyright in that work. This offence can attract a penalty of imprisonment for up to two years or a fine or both.

The same sanction applies to a person who infringes a performer's making available right tin the same circumstances.

2   MORAL RIGHTS

The copyright owner's moral rights of 'paternity' and 'integrity', and rights as to the false attribution of work and the display of photographs, are introduced by the 1988 Act following the United Kingdom's treaty obligations under the Berne Convention.

Any infringement of the author's moral rights is actionable as a breach of statutory duty. In an action for such an infringement the court may grant an injunction prohibiting the doing of any act unless an approved disclaimer is made dissociating the author or director from the treatment of the work.

2.1   Paternity

'Paternity' refers to the right of the author of a copyright literary, dramatic, musical or artistic work and the director of a copyright film to be identified as the author or director of the work whenever the work is published commercially, performed in public, broadcast or communicated to the public, or copies of a film or sound recording are issued to the public. The author may identify himself by means of a pseudonym or initials. The right is not infringed unless the right is asserted and this may be generally or specifically.

There are a number of exceptions to the right. It does not apply to the following.

(a) To a computer program, the design of a typeface or any computer-generated work.

(b) Where anything is done with the authority of the copyright owner where copyright originally vested in the person's employer (where the work was produced in the course of employment).

(c) Where copyright would not be infringed by virtue of various exceptions in the Act (fair dealing, incidental inclusion, in examination questions and parliamentary and judicial proceedings etc).

(d) Where it was included in a periodical or reference work with the author's consent.

2.2 Integrity

'Integrity' is the right to object to derogatory treatment of the work. The author of a copyright literary, dramatic, musical or artistic work, and the director of a copyright film, have the right not to have their work subjected to derogatory treatment. Treatment is defined as 'any addition to, deletion from or alteration to or adaptation of the work' other than a translation of a literary or dramatic work or a transcription of a piece of music. The treatment of a work is derogatory if it amounts to distortion or mutilation of the work or is otherwise prejudicial to the honour or reputation of the author or director.

As with the right to paternity, there are a number of instances where this right, which does not subsist in a computer program or a computer-generated work, is not infringed. It does not apply:

(a) to a work made for the purpose of reporting current events

(b) to publication in a periodical or collective work of reference where the work was made for the purposes of such publication or with the consent of the author for such a purpose

(c) where the treatment is done to avoid the commission of an offence or, especially with regard to BBC broadcasts, of 'avoiding the inclusion in a programme broadcast by them of anything which offends against good taste or decency or which is likely to encourage or incite to crime or to lead to disorder or to be offensive to public feeling' provided that, where the author or director is identified, there is a sufficient disclaimer.

Where a work of architecture in the form of a building is subjected to derogatory treatment the author of such a work has the right to have his name removed from any identification on the building. This right does not, apparently, extend to the physical relocation of his work, or to its destruction. Thus an artist could not invoke this section of the Act to prevent a disgruntled sitter from destroying the canvas for which he has posed and paid.

False attribution of work

Under the 1988 Act a person has the right not to have a literary, dramatic, musical or artistic work attributed to him as an author, or a film attributed to him as a director, if it is not his. This right only extends for twenty years after his death, so it does not extend for the whole of the copyright period in some cases. There may also be an action for passing off here.

Right of privacy in certain photographs and films

Where a person, for private and domestic purposes, commissions the taking of a film or photograph, but does not have copyright in the resulting work, he has the right not to have copies of the work issued to the public, to have the work exhibited or shown publicly, or to have it broadcast. Previously, the commissioner of such a work had the copyright in it and could prevent its dissemination by exercising the copyright owner's rights. The right to privacy now exists in a work commissioned professionally or gratuitously but does not provide any right to inhibit the publication of photographs, say at a wedding, which have been taken with or without permission but not actually commissioned.

Activity 2   **(15 minutes)**

Turn to the introductory pages of a modern novel and find the page containing information about the publisher (the verso page). What copyright information can you see?

---

3 DESIGN RIGHT

There are three separate but overlapping ways in which UK law protects industrial designs, which are defined as designs intended to be used in producing at least 50 items commercially.

Protection	Act	Type of design	Duration
Artistic copyright	CDPA	All designs	Life of creator + 50 years
Design right	CDPA	Functional designs	Up to 15 years
Design registration	RDA	Aesthetic designs	Up to 25 years

The complexity of the law means that a person planning to manufacture to an industrial design must look at the situation in the light of all of the above legislation, while the creator of a design may choose either to protect it actively, by registration, or to rely on the automatic protection of artistic copyright or design right.

The distinction between aesthetic and functional designs has been abolished by the European Parliament and EC Council Directive 98/71/EC on the legal protection of designs.

3.1 Copyright protection

The protection offered by artistic copyright may attach to industrial designs in the following circumstances.

(a) The finished product incorporating the design is itself an artistic work – a building falls into this category, though most industrial designs will not.

(b) The finished product is not an artistic work but has its origins in original design documents – an original drawing, irrespective of artistic merit, attracts artistic copyright. This may be infringed by the following actions.

(i) Making a two dimensional copy of the drawing (eg a photocopy).
(ii) Making a three dimensional model from the design (eg a prototype).
(iii) Making a three dimensional copy of a three dimensional model.

3.2 Design right protection

Design right was a new property right when it was created by CDPA. It arises, like copyright, automatically in a qualifying design: there is no need to register the design. This confers a protection which did not previously exist where no artistic work was created in the course of the design process.

'Design' is defined as meaning the design of any aspect of the shape or configuration (internal or external) of the whole or part of an article: s 211. Design right does not subsist in the following.

(a) A method or principle of construction.

(b) Features of shape or configuration of an article which:

   (i) enable the article to be connected to, or placed in, around or against, another article so that either article may perform its function (this is known as the *must-fit* exception); or

   (ii) are dependent upon the appearance of another article of which the first article is intended by the designer to form an integral part (this is known as the *must-match* exception).

(c) Surface decoration.

The must-fit and must-match exceptions only apply to those features of a design which are necessary to make the article fit or match. While the features which match or fit are not themselves afforded design right protection, the elements which are not so connected are capable of protection.

A design right only subsists in an *original* design and a design is not considered original if it is commonplace in the design field in question at the time of its creation. This test of originality can be more stringent than that imposed in cases of copyright. Design right does not subsist unless and until the design has been recorded in a design document or an article has been made to the design.

Design right subsists for only ten years from the end of the year in which articles made to the design are first put on the market: s 216. There is, however, an overall limit of fifteen years from the end of the year in which the design was first recorded or an article first made. Thus the design should be exploited as soon as possible for the maximum benefit to be obtained from the quite narrow time limits.

Licences to perform all the acts otherwise restricted by design rights are made available to anyone as of right during the final five years of the design period (which is usually ten years). Where, however, there is a reference made under monopoly, merger or competition legislation, the Minister responsible may make an order that licences of right shall be available at any time if it appears to him that the restrictive conditions contained in the licence or the design right holder's refusal to grant a licence on reasonable terms operates against the public interest. Where there is a failure to agree the terms of the licence, these and the royalties payable are determined by the UK Intellectual Property Office.

Ownership of design right

The general rule about the owner of design right is similar to that of copyright: the first owner is the designer who created the design. In the case of computer-generated design it is the person who made the necessary arrangements for the creation of the design to be undertaken.

The rule is subject to more extensive exceptions than is the case in copyright law. A person commissioning a design is the first owner and where a design has been made in the course of employment it generally belongs to the employer: s 214. Where the protection is obtained by first marketing of articles made to that design, the first owner is the person who first markets the articles.

Licences and assignment with regard to design rights are similar to those available for copyright.

The owner of a design right has the exclusive right to reproduce the design for commercial purposes by making articles in accordance with that design or by creating a design document recording that design so that articles may be made from it: s 226.

Infringement of design right

The right is infringed by anyone who reproduces articles exactly or substantially similar to the design without the authority of the holder of the design right. Unauthorised importation, possession for commercial purposes, sale, hire or offer of infringing articles also constitutes an infringement where the defendant knew or had reason to believe that the article was infringing the design holder's rights: s 227. Design right infringement does not give rise to infringement of copyright: the two matters must be considered quite separately.

Remedies for the infringement of design right are analogous to those available for infringement of copyright. Additional damages are available where the circumstances of the infringement are aggravated, eg by flagrancy or a substantial benefit accruing to the infringer.

'Threats' actions

Design right owners must not, like the owners of patent and registered designs, make groundless threats of action for infringement: s 253. The person threatened by an infringement proceeding may bring an action claiming:

(a) a declaration that the threats are unjustifiable;
(b) an injunction against the continuance of the threats; and
(c) damages to recover any losses suffered as a result of the threats.

These forms of relief are available unless the threatener can satisfy the court that the acts with regard to which the proceedings were threatened did actually constitute an infringement. The design right owner can make legitimate threats where the act complained of consists of making or importing an allegedly infringing article. But note that mere notification does not constitute a threat.

3.3 Registered design protection

The main statute is still the Registered Designs Act 1949 (RDA), amended by the 1988 Act and subsequent regulations. Under this, the proprietor of a work who has registered or has permitted the registration of a design embodying the work has monopoly rights in it for a period of up to 25 years.

In order to be registrable, the design must have two facets: novelty and individual character.

Novelty

The design must be new (s 1(2) RDA) which is judged by whether an identical design, or a new design whose features differ in immaterial details, has been made available to the public before the application for registration. Disclosure of the design in confidence will not destroy its novelty and nor will previous use of an artistic work bearing the design in question (in some cases). This means that the owner of an artistic copyright who has already published his work but who later decides to apply it industrially (by applying it to 50 or more articles) in order to register the design can do so.

Individual character

A design has individual character if the overall impression it produces on the informed user differs from the overall impression produced on such a user by any design which has been made available to the public before the relevant date. In determining the extent to which a design has individual character, the degree of freedom of the author in creating the design shall be taken into consideration: s 1B.

A component in a complex product only has individual character if, and to the extent that, it is still visible in the complex product.

A right tin a registered design cannot exist in features of a product's appearance which are only dictated by the product's technical function, or so that it can be mechanically connected to, or placed in, around or against, another product in order that either product may perform its function. In addition, there can be no right tin a registered design for a design which is contrary to public policy or to accepted principles of morality.

A design is registrable only in respect of an article or set of articles to which it is applied – that is, to an item of manufacture and/or to any part of an item of manufacture which is intended to be sold separately, such as spare parts: s 44.

The person entitled to register a design is either the *commissioner* of the design, where it has been done for consideration, or the employer where the design has been created in the course of employment, or the *designer* (proprietor) himself: ss 1 and 2. The right may be assigned.

The term of the registered design lasts for five years from the time when the application is made. The duration may be extended by up to four further periods of five years, provided renewal fees are paid: s 8.

Chapter roundup

- Copyright protects authors from being deprived of their rewards by unauthorised copying of their works. Unlike patents and trade marks, copyright is not subject to any system of registration: it comes into effect automatically when a work is created.

- Copyright is a property which subsists in original literary, dramatic, musical and artistic works, sound recordings, films, broadcasts and the typographical arrangement of published editions. It may also apply to databases, and other information stored on computer.

- The period of copyright varies depending upon the nature of the work; in many cases it is 70 years from the end of the calendar year of the death of the author or from the making of a recording.

- Infringement of a copyright may be primary or secondary. There are three 'fair dealing' defences to an action for breach of copyright.

- The Copyright, Designs and Patents Act 1988 introduced the concept of a copyright owner's moral rights of paternity and integrity. The Act also created a new property right called design right. This is a right distinct from the system of design registration.

Quick quiz

1   What is copyright?

2   What is an artistic work?

3   Give three examples of the author of a work.

4   What rights does the copyright owner have?

5   In what way may a person making an adaptation of a work infringe the copyright in that work?

6   What are the three fair dealing defences?

7   What is paternity?

8   What is 'design' for the purposes of design right?

9   What two facets must a design have to be registrable under RDA 1949?

NOTES

Answers to quick quiz

1   The exclusive right to use one's own work, ie legal protection given to stop others from exploiting it.

2   A graphic work, an architectural work or a work of artistic craftsmanship.

3   Your example could include a publisher, the sound producer on a film or a broadcaster.

4   The copyright owner may copy the work, issue the work to the public, perform, show, broadcast or adapt the work.

5   See the list given in paragraph 1.4.

6   Research or private study; criticism or review; reporting of current events (except photographs).

7   The right of an author to be identified as the author of a work when it is issued to the public.

8   Design is defined as meaning the design of any aspect of the shape or configuration of the whole or part of the article.

9   Novelty and individual character

Answers to activities

1   Copyright in a literary, dramatic, musical or artistic work (including a photograph) lasts until 70 years after the death of the author. The duration of copyright in a film is 70 years after the death of the last to survive of the principal director, the authors of the screenplay and dialogue, and the composer of any music specially created for the film. Sound recordings are generally protected for 50 years from the year of publication. Broadcasts are protected for 50 years and published editions are protected for 25 years.

For copyright works created outside the UK or another country of the European Economic Area, the term of protection may be shorter. There may also be differences for works created before 1 January 1996.

2   There will be a copyright symbol © as on page (ii) of this Course Book. This copyright marking is not essential, but acts as a warning that copyright is valued. There is a presumption in court that it indicates the owner. There may also be a statement to the following effect. 'The right of x to be identified as the author of this work has been asserted by him in accordance with the Copyright, Designs and Patents Act 1988.'

Appendix:
Edexcel Guidelines

This course book, and its companion volume Business Essentials Business Law, between them cover the topics set out in the Edexcel guideline for the HND/HNC Business qualification for:

- Unit 5: Aspects of Contract and Negligence for Business
- Unit 25: English Legal System
- Unit 26: Business Law
- Unit 27: Further Aspects of Contract and Tort
- Unit 28: European Law

The BPP Learning Media Business Essentials course books divide the material between them, one entitled Company and Commercial Law and the other entitled Business Law.

This book covers:

- Unit 25: English Legal System
- Unit 26: Business Law

EDEXCEL GUIDELINES FOR SPECIALIST UNIT 25: ENGLISH LEGAL SYSTEM

Description of the Unit

This unit provides an introduction to the English legal system. It develops learners' knowledge of the court structure, court procedures, funding and legal personnel. Alternative methods of settling disputes are also covered, as are the sources of law, their development and interpretation. It also provides an introduction to the legal formalities required for the formation of the different business entities, their management and dissolution.

Outcomes and assessment criteria

Outcomes	Assessment criteria
	To achieve each outcome a student must demonstrate the ability to:
LO1 Understand the court system and its alternatives	1.1 explain the differences between criminal and civil law
	1.2 analyse the role of individual courts and assess their effectiveness within the court structure
	1.3 evaluate court roles in live cases/case study material and present findings
	1.4 explain the meaning of ADR and analyse its usefulness
LO2 Understand the finance of representation	2.1 explain sources of legal advice
	2.2 assess implications of changes in funding
	2.3 evaluate the role of solicitors, barristers and judges
LO3 Be able to evaluate the different sources of law	3.1 evaluate the current day importance of the sources of law
	3.2 analyse the application of the sources of law in live situations/a case study and present findings
	3.3 assess the effectiveness of the rules of interpretation
LO4 Be able to select an appropriate legal entity	4.1 evaluate the legal principles which influence choice of business entity in a given situation
	4.2 justify your choice of legal entity.

Content	Covered in chapter(s)
1 Understand the court system and its alternatives	
Criminal courts: classification of crimes and methods of trial; magistrates court (jurisdiction, personnel, procedure); Crown court (juries, their role and structure, jurisdiction, procedure); grounds for appeal: Court of Appeal: House of Lords: European Court of Justice	*Covered in Business Essentials Business Law*
Civil courts: small claims court and jurisdiction; county court and High Court (jurisdiction of both, allocation of cases to tracks); grounds for appeal; Court of Appeal; House of Lords; European Court of Justice	
Alternative dispute resolution: meaning; conciliation; mediation; arbitration; advantages and disadvantages; tribunals and enquiries	
2 Understand the finance of representation	
Legal advice and funding: sources of legal advice; duty solicitor scheme; funding; conditional fees	*Covered in Business Essentials Business Law*
Legal personnel: solicitors and barristers; legal executives; paralegals; roles and training; the judiciary	
3 Be able to evaluate the different sources of law	
Sources of law: judicial precedent, statute, delegated legislation (meaning, how they operate, advantages and disadvantages); Rules of Statutory Interpretation; European law (types of law)	*Covered in Business Essentials Business Law*
Differences between common law and equity: role of equity today	
4 Be able to select an appropriate legal entity	
Meaning and examples: sole traders; partnerships; limited liability partnerships; companies	2,
Advantages and disadvantages: of types of legal business entity	3, 5,
Legal requirements: for the formation of sole traders, partnerships, and companies	6
Provisions: relating to the running/management of businesses eg rights/duties of partners, directors and creditors; dissolution of business entities	

Delivery

Each section will require lecturers to provide an introductory factual framework. Learners should then take part in a variety of activities, eg visits, talks, research to access primary sources, case studies, group discussions and moots.

A good starting point for delivery is Outcome 1. Visits to a variety of courts generate discussion and enable learners to visualise the courts, their personnel and the procedures and types of cases dealt with. It may then be preferable to continue with Outcome 3, as some of the cases seen in the courts will generate discussion on the law involved and explanation of Statutes, Judicial Precedent and Delegated Legislation will follow naturally. It is important when looking at the rules of interpretation to use live case examples to explain the different results which can result from the application of different rules. Outcome 2 also follows on from the court visits and looks at where advice can be sought, how it can be funded and what responsibilities the different legal personnel have. Finally, Outcome 4 looks at the formation of businesses and the legal requirements involved. This Outcome is freestanding, but useful in cases where learners are not opting for further law units.

Assessment

The assessment(s) should aim in a structured way to test the different unit outcomes. They will develop and test a variety of skills and encourage use of primary and secondary legal materials. Examples of assessment could include:

- a record of a visit to a court/tribunal with an analysis of the role of that institution

- a case study including a number of incidents which require advice on the particular courts that would deal with the incidents, the availability of advice, funding and personnel

- a case study on a source of law

- a report on proposed or recent legislation

- an oral presentation on some aspect of the legal system

- a case study on a business, including choice of business entity, advantages/disadvantages, management, dissolution.

Links

This unit forms the foundation for all the other specialist law units. It examines the structure of the legal system, the sources of law, funding and personnel. This is an essential introduction to the specialist law units covering contract, tort, European law and business law.

The formation, management and dissolution of business entities is a useful introduction to the company unit.

The sources of law section looks at types of European law and the court structure of the ECJ which is a useful introduction to *Unit 28: European Law*.

Resources

Learners should have access to a learning resource centre with a good range of legal text and case books. These should be supported by journals, statutes and law reports. Good newspapers are also necessary because of the topical nature of law.

Learners will also benefit from visits to courts and parliament. Crown Courts are usually excellent in arranging tours and talks by resident judges. Magistrates, solicitors and barristers are usually willing to talk collectively to groups of learners.

Suggested reading

Textbooks

- Elliot and Quinn. *English Legal System* (Longman, April 2002)

- Slapper and Kelly. *English Legal System* (Cavendish, August 2001)

- Ingman, T. *The English Legal Process* (Blackstone, August 2000)

- Stychin, C. *Legal Method: Text and Materials* (Sweet & Maxwell, April 1999)

- Darbyshire, P. *Nutshells English Legal System* (Sweet & Maxwell, March 2001)

- Smith and Keenan. *Advanced Business Law* (Prentice Hall, January 2000)

- Martin, J. *English Legal System* (Hodder & Stoughton Educational, June 2002)

Websites

World wide websites can be useful in providing information and case studies, for example:

• www.bized.co.uk	Provides case studies appropriate for educational purposes
• www.cps.gov.uk	The Crown Prosecution Service
• www.legalservices.gov.uk	Legal Services Commission
• www.dca.gov.uk	Department for Constitutional Affairs
• www.lawcom.gov.uk	The Law Commission
• www.criminal-justice-system.gov.uk	Criminal Justice System
• www.eurunion.org	European Union in the US
• www.courtservice.gov.uk	The Court Service
• www.bbc.co.uk/law	BBC
• www.cjsonline.org	Criminal Justice System

EDEXCEL GUIDELINES FOR SPECIALIST UNIT 26: BUSINESS LAW

Description of the unit

The aim of this unit is to provide knowledge and application of the law relating to sale of goods, consumer credit, monopolies and intellectual property as it relates to business and its everyday dealings.

Learners will recognise that a business operates within a diverse legal framework. Aspects such as anti-competitive practices through monopolies, mergers and the use of intellectual property rights are key, as are domestic consumer provisions and associated provisions within the EU.

Learners need to understand the penalties applicable for failure to comply with these areas of law that follow from the basic rules of contract and tort.

The best business practice is to avoid such liability. Learners need to understand potential liability and the expense involved in such liability needs to be appreciated.

Outcomes and assessment criteria

Outcomes	Assessment criteria
	To achieve each outcome a student must demonstrate the ability to:
LO1 Be able to apply the main principles affecting the **legal relationship between business organisations and their consumers**	1.1 apply the legal rules on implied terms relating to the sale of goods and supply of services
	1.2 apply the statutory provisions on the transfer of property and possession
	1.3 evaluate the statutory provisions on buyer's and seller's remedies
	1.4 apply product liability statutory provisions
LO2 Be able to apply the legal rules on **consumer credit agreements and agency**	2.1 differentiate between types of credit agreements
	2.2 apply rules, termination rights and default notices in a given scenario
	2.3 differentiate between the different types of agent
	2.4 evaluate the rights and duties of an agent
LO3 Understand the legal rules relating to **monopolies, mergers and anticompetitive practices**	3.1 outline monopolies and anti-competitive practice legislation in the UK
	3.2 explain the role of the Competition Commission within the context of monopolies and anti-competitive practices and the UK Office of Fair Trading
	3.3 define dominant positions within the EU common market
	3.4 consider the application of EU exemptions to potentially anti-competitive practices

Outcomes	Assessment criteria
	To achieve each outcome a student must demonstrate the ability to:
LO4 Know the key provisions relating to **intellectual property rights**	4.1 identify differing forms of intellectual property
	4.2 outline the principles relating to the protection of inventions through patent rights and their infringement in a given business scenario
	4.3 describe the principles relating to copyright protection and their infringement in a given business scenario
	4.4 compare and contrast the protection of trade marks and business names.

Content	Covered in chapter
1 **The legal relationship between business organisations and their consumers**	
Sale of goods: statutory implied terms, transfer of property and possession, seller's remedies against the buyer, consumer's remedies against the seller	7
Supply of services: statutory implied terms, seller's remedies, consumer's remedies	7
Product liability: defective goods, consumer remedies against the producer of defective goods	7
2 **Consumer credit agreements and agency**	
Forms of consumer credit agreements: restricted use of credit, unrestricted use of credit, debtor-creditor supplier agreements, debtor-creditor agreements, relevant legislation	8
Other agreements: exempt agreements, small agreements, multiple agreements, linked transactions, cancellable agreements	8
Consumer credit licensing: general requirements, the issue of licences, termination of consumer credit agreements; early repayment, right to terminate, termination statements; enforcement of consumer credit agreements; creditors' remedies, default notices, relevant legislation	8
Agency: definition, types of agent, authority of agent, rights and duties of agent and principal, agent's liability to third party, termination of agency, relevant legislation	1
3 **Monopolies, mergers and anti-competitive practices**	
Monopolies and competition in the UK: Competition Act, Fair Trading Act, scale monopolies, complex monopolies, restrictive trade practices, Director General of Fair Trading	9
Competition Commission: role of the Commission, appeals tribunal	9
Dominant positions within the EU: treaty provisions, the abuse of a dominant position and enforcement	9

Content	Covered in chapter
Exemptions: treaty articles and definitions, individual and block exemptions	9
4 Intellectual property rights	
Protection of inventions: registration of patents, designs, trademarks and copyright, role of the Patent Office (UK), European Union Patent Office	11
Patents: patent legislation, patent rights, inventions, patents and employees	11
Copyright: copyright legislation, ownership of copyright, duration of copyright, using copyright materials	11
Trademarks and business names: defining trademarks, applying to register a trademark, registering business names	11
Infringement of intellectual property rights: unauthorised use of intellectual property, patent hearings, copyright tribunal, passing off	11

Delivery

Much of the material in this unit can be delivered actively through the use of case studies and learner-centred learning both as a small group and individual exercises. The use of case studies can be used as both a means of encouraging individual and group learning in addition to providing a vehicle for assessment.

Small group, tutor-led, workshops can be used to develop the learners' understanding of individual outcomes and their conclusions may be used to develop their knowledge base.

Alternative methods of delivery include online materials which may be centre-devised using centre-specific resources such as the posting of hand-outs, assignments and the use of other non-centre devised electronic sources and materials.

Learners should be encouraged to undertake self-directed study and present their findings during seminars and workshops. This may be particularly effective due to the number of government Internet sites particularly in relation to intellectual property and competition.

Wherever possible, a link should be made between academic underpinning knowledge and its practical application through decided cases and the application of that knowledge to given classroom tasks which may be discussion-based, question and answer sessions or through tasks which may be used within the context of learner assessment.

Typical class sessions will begin with an explanation of the relevant legal rules appropriate to the outcome under study. This factual introduction may be followed by a learner-led discussion on how the relevant legal rules were applied within decided cases. In some instances the learner may be given a pre-prepared number of cases to read in advance of classes and then contribute during the session in a manner appropriate to set classroom tasks. Learners may also be given self-directed study handouts through which they present a seminar or lead a discussion on stated outcomes.

The unit may be delivered as a stand-alone unit, although there may be opportunities for mapping outcomes through the integration of assessed outcomes made up from other units.

Assessment

The assessment strategy should aim to encourage use of primary and secondary legal legislation and the application of suitable common law principles to the outcomes.

Aspects of the unit may be further explored through case studies which link consumer protection and the function of those responsible for ensuring fair trading in a manner which highlights the effectiveness of alternative courses of action other than the consumer suing the supplier through the civil courts.

In addition the sections on monopolies and intellectual property may be explored through assessment vehicles, the aim being to determine how companies can potentially create a dominant position through the use of intellectual property rights which lead to anti-competitive practices.

The assessment of this unit can be through individual and group assignments. These may be in the form of submitted reports, written memoranda, business letters and presentations. The presentations may be formal and include electronic presentations using software such as Microsoft PowerPoint. Alternatively, presentations may be in the form of a moot or discussion, or learner-led seminar on an outcome during which the learner, either individually or in a group, orally conveys assessment material to the group.

Evidence may be produced by the learner at outcome level only, although there exist opportunities for the design of assignments that cover different outcomes. Resources such as class materials or handouts may include case study material and which may be used in conjunction with assessments made under time-constrained conditions.

Alternative assessment methods may include peer assessment during presentations, seminars, multiple choice questions and in class open-book timed assessments.

Links

This unit has particular links to *Unit 5: Aspects of Contract and Negligence for Business, Unit 25: English Legal System, Unit 27: Further Aspects of Contract and Tort, Unit 28: European Law, Unit 35: European Business, Unit 36: Employment Law* and *Unit 37: Company Law.*

Resources

Learners will require access to a library which contains key texts and materials suitable to studying business law.

Additional resources include Iolis, an interactive CD-Rom for law students available from the University of Warwick, and Seneca, a legal information service also on CD. (See websites.)

Suggested reading

Sufficient library resources should be available to enable learners to achieve this unit. Texts that are particularly relevant are:

Textbooks

- Steiner, J. *Textbook on EC Law* (7th ed, Blackstone, October 2000)
- Smith and Keenan. *Advanced Business Law* (Prentice Hall, January 2000)
- Crystal, Phillips and Davis. *Insolvency Law Handbook* (Butterworth, June 2003)

- Coleman, M. and Grenfell, M. *The Competition Act 1998: Law and Practice* (Oxford University, June 1999)
- Ottley, M. *Briefcase on Company Law* (Cavendish, April 2002)
- Cranston, Scott and Black. *Consumers and the Law* (Law in Context) (Butterworth, August 2000)
- Colston, C. *Principles of Intellectual Property Law* (Cavendish, September 1999)
- Davis, J. *Butterworth Core Text: Intellectual Property Law* (Butterworth, September 2003)
- Groves, P. *Sourcebook on Intellectual Property Law* (Cavendish, May 1997)
- Brown, I. *et al. Commercial Law* (Butterworth, January 2000)
- Judge, S. *Business Law* (Palgrave, November 1998)

Journals/newspapers

- *The Times*
- *New Law Journal*
- *Law Society Gazette*

Websites

www.europa.eu.int	European Union online
www.jurist.law.cam.ac.uk	Legal information for educational purposes
www.lawtel.co.uk	Lawtel online legal information service
www.lexis-nexis.com	Lexis-Nexis online legal and business information service
www.timesonline.co.uk	Website of *The Times* newspaper
www.patent.gov.uk	The UK Patent Office
www.companies-house.gov.uk	Companies House
www.european-patent-office.org	The European Patent Office
www.competition-commission.org.uk	Competition Comission
www.senecaweb.co.uk	Seneca website
www.law.warwick.ac.uk/lcc/iolis	Iolis website

Table of Cases and Index

BPP
LEARNING MEDIA

NOTES

Index

Review Form – Business Essentials – Commercial and Company Law (07/10)

BPP Learning Media always appreciates feedback from the students who use our books. We would be very grateful if you would take the time to complete this feedback form, and return it to the address below.

Name: _____   Address: _____

_____

_____

How have you used this Course Book?
(Tick one box only)

☐ Home study (book only)

☐ On a course: college _____

☐ Other _____

Why did you decide to purchase this Course Book? *(Tick one box only)*

☐ Have used BPP Learning Media books in the past

☐ Recommendation by friend/colleague

☐ Recommendation by a lecturer at college

☐ Saw advertising

☐ Other _____

During the past six months do you recall seeing/receiving any of the following?
(Tick as many boxes as are relevant)

☐ Our advertisement

☐ Our brochure with a letter through the post

Your ratings, comments and suggestions would be appreciated on the following areas

	Very useful	Useful	Not useful
Introductory pages	☐	☐	☐
Topic coverage	☐	☐	☐
Summary diagrams	☐	☐	☐
Chapter roundups	☐	☐	☐
Quick quizzes	☐	☐	☐
Activities	☐	☐	☐
Discussion points	☐	☐	☐

	Excellent	Good	Adequate	Poor
Overall opinion of this Course Book	☐	☐	☐	☐

Do you intend to continue using BPP Learning Media Business Essentials Course books? ☐ Yes ☐ No

Please note any further comments and suggestions/errors on the reverse of this page.

The BPP author of this edition can be e-mailed at: pippariley@bpp.com

Please return this form to: Pippa Riley, BPP Learning Media L:td, FREEPOST, London, W12 8BR

Review Form (continued)

Please note any further comments and suggestions/errors below